A Phenomenology of the Alien

I0130460

A Phenomenology of the Alien: Encounters with the Weird and Inscrutable Other considers both literal and figurative experiences of the alien from a psychological, psychoanalytic, and philosophical perspective.

Throughout the book, the authors wrestle with the unexplained, ineffable, unspeakable, sublime, uncanny, abject, and Miéville's abcanny. This collection provides phenomenologies of encounters with the inscrutably alien from lights in the sky, dark corners of Weird fictional landscapes, architecture, technology, or the clinical symptom. The chapters examine fictional and nonfictional encounters with what exceeds the capacity to "make sense," taking a new approach to the topic of alterity and inviting the reader to examine how these encounters reflect our contemporary condition culturally, individually, clinically, theologically, and philosophically.

Bridging cultural, psychoanalytic, literary, clinical, media, and religious studies, the novel approaches in this volume will be of interest to students and scholars alike.

Aaron B. Daniels, PhD, is an associate teaching professor, mindfulness fellow, and leader of the Psychological Humanities Research Group at Northeastern University in Boston, Massachusetts.

The Psychology and the Other Book Series

Series editor: David M. Goodman
Associate editors: Matthew Clemente, Brian W. Becker, Donna M. Orange and Eric R. Severson

The Psychology and the Other book series highlights creative work at the intersections between psychology and the vast array of disciplines relevant to the human psyche. The interdisciplinary focus of this series brings psychology into conversation with continental philosophy, psychoanalysis, religious studies, anthropology, sociology, and social/critical theory. The cross-fertilization of theory and practice, encompassing such a range of perspectives, encourages the exploration of alternative paradigms and newly articulated vocabularies that speak to human identity, freedom, and suffering. Thus, we are encouraged to reimagine our encounters with difference, our notions of the "other," and what constitutes therapeutic modalities.

The study and practices of mental health practitioners, psychoanalysts, and scholars in the humanities will be sharpened, enhanced, and illuminated by these vibrant conversations, representing pluralistic methods of inquiry, including those typically identified as psychoanalytic, humanistic, qualitative, phenomenological, or existential.

Recent titles in the series include:

Meaningless Suffering
Traumatic Marginalisation and Ethical Responsibility
Edited by David Goodman and M. Mookie C. Manalili

Hosting Earth
Facing the Climate Emergency
Edited by Richard Kearney, Peter Klapes and Urwa Hameed

A Phenomenology of the Alien
Encounters with the Weird and Inscrutable Other
Edited by Aaron B. Daniels

For a full list of titles in the series, please visit the Routledge website at: www.routledge.com/Psychology-and-the-Other/book-series/PSYOTH

A Phenomenology of the Alien

Encounters with the Weird and
Inscrutable Other

Edited by Aaron B. Daniels

Routledge
Taylor & Francis Group
LONDON AND NEW YORK

Designed cover image: David Wall / Getty Images

First published 2025
by Routledge
4 Park Square, Milton Park, Abingdon, Oxon OX14 4RN

and by Routledge
605 Third Avenue, New York, NY 10158

Routledge is an imprint of the Taylor & Francis Group, an informa business

British Library Cataloguing-in-Publication Data
A catalogue record for this book is available from the British Library

ISBN: 978-1-032-85629-2 (hbk)
ISBN: 978-1-032-85627-8 (pbk)
ISBN: 978-1-003-51910-2 (ebk)

DOI: 10.4324/9781003519102

Typeset in Times New Roman
by Apex CoVantage, LLC

Contents

Contributors

Anna Bugajska, Associate Professor at the Ignatianum University in Cracow, is the Head of the Language and Culture Studies Department. She is a member of the Utopian Studies Society–Europe and sits on the Scientific Committee of the City and Philosophy Association. Her research focuses on the interdisciplinary aspects of technological development.

Dorothy Chang recently received her PhD in the history of Christianity from Fordham University. Her dissertation is titled *A Divine and Supernatural Light: Scientific Theories and Theological Metaphors of Light in Jonathan Edwards*. She specializes in late medieval and early modern theology, as well as the history of science. She is also broadly interested in ecumenical dialogue between Greek East and the Latin West, and her research interests include Byzantine theology, critical theory, history of science, and political theology. Dorothy received an MA from Columbia University in the philosophy of religion and a BA from Rutgers University in religious studies.

Aaron B. Daniels is Associate Teaching Professor in the Psychology Department at Northeastern University and is also a mindfulness fellow in the Spiritual Life Center. He is the faculty leader of the NU Psychological Humanities Research Group. His PhD is from Pacifica Graduate Institute. His MA is from Duquesne University. His books include *Imaginal Reality*, Volumes 1 and 2 (both in 2011), and *Jungian Crime Scene Analysis: An Imaginal Investigation* (2014), and he wrote four chapters in and edited *Dante and the Other: A Phenomenology of Love* (2021). His current research centers on the "inscrutably alien" and spiritual direction, a field in which he completed certification in 2022.

Jason Marc Harris teaches creative writing, folklore, and literature at Texas A&M University in College Station, Texas. He is the author of *Folklore and the Fantastic in Nineteenth-Century British Fiction* and the Weird fiction novella *Master of Rods and Strings*. Jason has contributed creative fiction and critical articles in journals such as *The Journal of Popular Culture, Marvels and Tales, New Directions in Folklore, Studies in Hogg and His World, The Saturday Evening Post*, and *Western Folklore*. More info on his work can be found here:

https://jasonmarcharris.com/. Recently, he guest-edited *Humanities* for a special issue, "Seen and Unseen: The Folklore of Secrecy" (www.mdpi.com/journal/humanities/special_issues/5B24EV0BD4).

Emily McAvan is an Australian literary critic and theorist whose work addresses the intersection between religion, literature, and the environment. She is the author of several books, most recently *Divinity, Hospitality, and the Posthuman: The Material Sacred* (2024), and is a research fellow at Deakin University, Australia.

Scott R. Scribner grew up in New England. He studied astronomy and cultural anthropology at Harvard University's Mount Hermon Liberal Studies Program; physics and the sociology of technology at Rensselaer Polytechnic Institute, where he was a student member of NASA's Mars Survey Vehicle Development Group; philosophy, cognition, and experimental psychology at the University of New Hampshire; and clinical psychology and religion at Fuller Graduate School of Psychology, where he did fieldwork on UFO religions. During a distinguished career in software engineering, he continued to contribute to several UFO books and conferences. His doctoral research examined how traumatic fears, language, subjective perceptions, and media images interact to reflect adaptive and iterative personal and social processes leading to alien abduction narratives (AANs). His social transmission model (STM) illustrates, for example, how alien abduction stories select and synthesize elements from multiple channels—including visual media and dreams—before a prominent AAN is formalized. Scott lives in Long Beach, California.

Michael Waldon, LCSW, is a therapist and clinical social worker providing remote and in-person psychotherapy services to clients based in New York and California. He is a graduate of the Smith College School for Social Work and the Stephen Mitchell Relational Study Center, specializing in relational psychodynamic and somatic approaches to the treatment of trauma. He is currently based in the San Francisco Bay Area and is on the supervising faculty at the Psychotherapy Institute. For more information, visit his website: www.michaelwaldon.com.

Gregory J. Wheeler grew up in Yakima, Washington, where he was introduced to the Kenneth Arnold "flying saucer" story at an early age. He studied astronomy and psychology at the University of Washington. While pursuing degrees in clinical psychology and religion at Fuller Graduate School of Psychology, he became interested in the historical and philosophical relationships between cosmological models and theological beliefs. In addition to fieldwork on UFO religions, he wrote a UFO column for *Continuum Magazine* and has contributed to several UFO books and conferences. Following 25 years in private practice in Southern California, he joined the Indian Health Service on the Wind River Shoshone/Arapahoe Reservation in Lander, Wyoming. Dr. Wheeler developed the concept of first contact science (FCS) as a scientific standard for exploring the psychological and cultural impacts of expanding cosmological understanding on beliefs about and evidence for extraterrestrial life. Dr. Wheeler lives in Monterey Park, California.

Acknowledgments

In addressing the inscrutably alien, the tension of this volume—between the unspeakable and the ineffable—is one of the longest arcs of my scholarship—and perhaps life. It encompasses my work on esotericism, criminal profiling, and Dante. Nevertheless, the more specific eldritch seeds of this volume were first sewn as I began teaching personality psychology classes and attempted, tongue in cheek, to use the writings of H. P. Lovecraft to illustrate some core concepts about different approaches to the unknown, unknowable, and unconscious. Many students from Seattle Central Community College, Saint Martin's University, New England College, Curry College, Mount Ida College, and Emerson College proved game. They advanced, challenged, and shaped this discourse—not least of which through their suggestions of often terribly campy horror films.

Along the way, a host of comic book store owners and workers, convention creators, strongly opiniated fans of all things alien and unspeakable, and Miskatonic University alumni pawned cryptically drawn maps of this territory to me. Particular credit should go to William J. Kiesel of Ouroboros Press; Duglas Kilbride; Willow of . . . a lot of places and in between; Aron Tarbuck of the Dreaming; Ann S. Koi of Catalyst Studios; the Lovecraft Film Festival of Portland, Oregon; the late Alan D. Eames, creator of the Vermont Lovecraft Festival; Tristan Gallagher of Coast City Comics and the Fun Box Emporium and Michelle Souliere of the Green Hand Bookstore, both of Portland, Maine; and many more.

To the Baltimore crew, who must remain nameless, a deep bow of thanks.

Eventually, I realized that other scholars were indeed doing more than writing about monsters and the unknown but were, like me, using them as teaching tools. Thus, I owe a deep debt of gratitude to my colleagues Rob "Zombie" Smid, Melissa "Queen of the Night" Anyiwo, Julian "Tritone" Bryson, Brian "Who's the Real Monster!?" Duchaney, and Karen "Under the Bed" Hussar, who bravely shone a flashlight into dark rooms full of monsters with me in our team-taught courses.

Intrepid student Kathleen Giffels began the review of literature with me, creating binders I still use.

Once established at Northeastern University, I have found legions of eager and brilliant students wanting to contribute to this sort of interdisciplinary inquiry.

Emma Baronowski bravely and quite ably undertook the editorial administration for the collection and first editing phases of this volume, offering strong guidance and withering looks. Sammie Keenan gamely took on the mantle to see it to completion with aplomb and admirable determination. For this volume, a remarkable team of students listed with each chapter provided copyediting, including Naomi Anbar, Hayley Dording, Kaitlyn Guay, Rose-Maelle Florestal, Gracie Vogel, Amelia Maybrun, McKenna Dahlen, and Sarah Breckner. Thank you also to Mary Nickita for research.

The essays in this collection came from the first Alien Salon I created for the Psychology and the Other conference at Boston College, held virtually in 2021. In the thick of the pandemic, these exceptional authors chose to share their passion, scholarship, and hunger for discussions with like-minded colleagues. Far from the cacophony such a collection could become, their voices play and segue with an elegance wrought purely of their genius. Thank you to one and all, and many thanks for your patience with the lengthy process. Thanks also to David Goodman, the conference creator, chair, and series editor, for welcoming these initiatives.

Many thanks to Brian Evenson for permission to quote extensively from his brilliantly unsettling short story "Windeye."

I would be remiss if I did not thank Thomas Ligotti for his generosity in communication. And I am very grateful to my friend William Franke for his insightful and erudite foreword bridging several themes of this volume.

To the writers, scholars, directors, collectors, artists, and musicians cited throughout this work, thank you for doing exactly what you do, and thank you for being so marvelously Weird.

Finally, I offer my deepest gratitude and love to my wife, Laura, who has continued to journey with me, endlessly drawing me from the unspeakable to the ineffable.

Aaron B. Daniels
Northeastern University
Boston, Massachusetts
October 2024

Foreword

Nietzsche and Nihilism: Opening to the Dimension of the Other

This foreword received editorial review by Sarah Breckner, Mckenna Dahlen, and Sammie Keenan as part of the Psychological Humanities at Northeastern University Workgroup.

An absolute respect for the other and for otherness is a core value of Western culture. It finds probably its most rigorous philosophical formulation in the ethical thinking of Emmanuel Levinas (1906–1995). This thinking centers on the infinite obligation to the Other. As Levinas (1974) apprehends it—or is rather apprehended by it—there is an ethical imperative to which we are called in the presence of the Other, as expressed poignantly in *le visage de l'Autre* (the face of the Other). The other person present before us, facing us, demands our utmost solicitude and respect. This ethical obligation is prior to all thought or reflection of the self on itself or on anything else, because we are always already in relation to the Other before we even begin to think or reflect. Hence, ethics replaces metaphysics as "first philosophy," reversing Aristotle, in Levinas's epoch-making revolution of thought. Levinasian ethics orients us to the Other or alien even before we come to consciousness of self or world, before we can take stock of "what is" or of "how we know."

This ethical imperative vis-à-vis fellow human beings grows especially from Judeo-Christian roots and the reverence for a wholly other, transcendent God. Each individual person, being made in the divine image, is seen as wholly other and, therefore, as worthy of unconditional respect. The *otherness* of the other person places an infinite ethical obligation on me. However, such unconditional reverence for whoever or whatever is other also runs the risk of turning into a kind of idolatry. This Levinasian, and arguably Judeo-Christian, reverence for the Other and for everything other can become a mythification and can be seen as offensively sanctimonious. A precedent for such an objection can be found, somewhat surprisingly, in Friedrich Nietzsche (1844–1900) and his critique of the agenda of the "ascetic priests" in *The Genealogy of Morals* (1887) well over a century ago. In the guise of defending the weak and powerless—purportedly the victims—the priests undermine aristocratic values of superior strength as naturally good and call it evil in their moral system. Through this subterfuge, they induce individuals to condemn themselves and their own natural egoism. Moral individuals are praised for championing the weak, the victims, rather than affirming themselves. Superior strength, dominant power, is made reprehensible ethically. Nietzsche saw this as a deceptive scheme through which the priests underhandedly exert their own will to power.

These positions toward which Nietzsche directs his criticism are far from an artifact of the past. Today, certain "woke" ideologues embody, in some rather striking and paradoxical ways, the sort of perverse turning against oneself in Western culture that Nietzsche aimed to expose and denounce in something approaching prophetic tones of voice. He denounced *avant la lettre* the cultural politics of favoring whatever or whoever can be labeled as "other" to—and as a victim of—the dominant race, gender, and class. Nietzsche would have rudely rejected the consequent condemnation of strong and dominant races and genders considered to be guilty, at least historically, of imposing White supremacy and patriarchy.

Nietzsche, a defender of aristocratic values, would surely have directed his savage attack against the systematic, even forced, valorizing of "diversity, equality, and inclusion" as a principle of social ethics. He could easily have proved that these "values" have an especially Judeo-Christian genealogical descent. Nietzsche saw this rejection or inversion of natural egoism as a disaster for civilization and for the entire species; it entails a denaturing of healthy animal instinct. Self-preservation, not genuflecting to the Other, is the law of the jungle and the inescapable imperative of life. Our denial of this vital impulse and instinct was leading humanity, in Nietzsche's view, to self-annihilation. This denial of one's own vital instincts, and therewith the canceling of oneself, is what Nietzsche means, in the first instance, by "nihilism." It is grotesquely manifest today in the "cancel culture" movements that are launched from a dizzying array of camps within the bosom of Western society (Daub, 2022/2024). For Nietzsche, all genuine value is rooted in the *Wille zur Macht* (will to power), and the forced denial of oneself and one's natural power on moral grounds of deference to the other he saw as pure perversion.

The struggle to survive, for Nietzsche, is what keeps the species fit and sound and, in our case, even sane. When we entirely moralize life, as is the fashion in the academy and in liberal, "enlightened" society today, it sickens and dies: we enclose ourselves in a cocoon, reasoning only in terms of how we think things should be, or would like them to be, and refuse to confront the hard facts and necessities of how things actually are. Philosophers since Nietzsche's death have sought to abridge, reinterpret, and selectively read passages as sarcastic or sincere; but any reading of Nietzsche that ignores this first sense of self-denial as nihilism misses a powerful underlying thrust of his thinking.

Nevertheless, there is yet another, prima facie opposite sense in which the kind of self-enclosure just mentioned leads to what Nietzsche warns us against as nihilism. Nihilism can come from too little as well as from too much regard for the other or alien. The natural state keeps us constantly face-to-face with alterity in different forms, and the denaturing that Nietzsche loathes is also a loss of openness to and confrontation with genuine alterity. In the case of too little regard for alterity, the other in question is not the other person or the other social identity on a horizontal plane but rather something other to all our possible conceiving, something that utterly escapes our comprehension. This self-transcendence or self-overcoming (*Selbstüberwindung*) of the human is necessary to the atheist as much as to religion. The loss of the ability to fathom something that is radically and irretrievably other than human is the predicament suffered as the death of God—the ultimate Other—which Nietzsche tremblingly announces, not in a triumphant but, rather, in an ominously tragic spirit.

Nietzsche's *der tolle Mensch* (the madman), who makes this announcement of the death of God, has entirely lost his bearings as a consequence of his terrible realization. Standing in for humanity, this madman is reeling with the sense of guilt and apprehension over the fact that we have killed God. We no longer respect any kind of absolute alterity; instead, we have idolized a petty "diversity," understood in our own identitarian terms. Thus, we have made ourselves, and various variants of ourselves, the be-all and end-all of existence. This, too, is unnatural. It is not only an overreaching of ourselves and our current state of being but also an overreaching of nature and of reality—the order of things itself—to impose ourselves and our own order as absolute. This is no longer a natural and necessary expression of the will-to-power; it is an absurd, self-deluding extension beyond the natural limits of a power or faculty abstracted from its proper use and domain. In his "Parable of the Madman" from *The Gay Science* (1882–1887/1974), Nietzsche has his protagonist light a lantern in the day and declare, "I seek God! I seek God!" (para. 125, p. 181). The townsfolk mock him, since they do not take ideas about God seriously. Here is the madman's announcement:

> The madman jumped into their midst and pierced them with his eyes. "Whither is God?" he cried; "I will tell you. We have killed him—you and I. All of us are his murderers. But how did we do this? How could we drink up the sea? Who gave us the sponge to wipe away the entire horizon? What were we doing when we unchained this earth from its sun? Whither is it moving now? Whither are we moving? Away from all suns? Are we not plunging continually? Backward, sideward, forward, in all directions? Is there still any up or down? Are we not straying, as through an infinite nothing? Do we not feel the breath of empty space? Has it not become colder? Is not night continually closing in on us? Do we not need to light lanterns in the morning? Do we hear nothing as yet of the noise of the gravediggers who are burying God? Do we smell nothing as yet of the divine decomposition? Gods, too, decompose. God is dead. God remains dead. And we have killed him."
>
> (para. 125, p. 181)

The madman further confronts his audience with the aftermath of this *deicide*, this murder of divinity:

> How shall we comfort ourselves, the murderers of all murderers? What was holiest and mightiest of all that the world has yet owned has bled to death under our knives: who will wipe this blood off us? What water is there for us to clean ourselves? What festivals of atonement, what sacred games shall we have to invent? Is not the greatness of this deed too great for us? Must we ourselves not become gods simply to appear worthy of it? There has never been a greater deed; and whoever is born after us—for the sake of this deed he will belong to a higher history than all history hitherto.
>
> (para. 125, p. 181)

Finally, the madman, shattered from his realization and bewildered by his audience's astonished indifference, relents in his onslaught. Throwing his Diogenesian lantern to the ground, he declares:

> I have come too early. . . . [M]y time is not yet. This tremendous event is still on its way, still wandering; it has not yet reached the ears of men. Lightning and thunder require time; the light of the stars requires time; deeds, though done, still require time to be seen and heard. This deed is still more distant from them than most distant stars—and yet they have done it themselves.
>
> (para. 125, p. 182)

At this point, Nietzsche's madman seeks refuge and attempts a *requiem aeternam deo* (eternal rest to God) within some churches. "Led out and called to account, he is said always to have replied nothing but: 'What after all are these churches now if they are not the tombs and sepulchers of God?'" (para. 125, p. 182).

Here Nietzsche describes the death of God as a disaster in the literal sense of a *des-aster* (unstarring), a loss of orientation to any higher reality. On the other hand, however, and again following Nietzsche, it is the death of God that opens the space of human creativity that alone can throw up a bulwark against nihilism. According to Italian philosopher Emanuele Severino (1929–2020), "[t]he announcement by Nietzsche that God is dead signifies precisely that the world has realized not only that it has no need of an immutable transcendent being but that such a being would render human creativity impossible" ("L'annuncio di Nietzsche che Dio è morto significa appunto che il mondo si è accorto non solo di non aver bisogno di un ente immutabile trascendente, ma che tale ente renderebbe impossibile la creatività dell'uomo") (Severino, 1972/1995, p. 258, English translation by W. Franke, the current author).

This is the line of thought I have pursued in "The Death of God as Source of the Creativity of Humans" (Franke, 2024). Human creativity can be jump-started by the death of God and the shock of having to create values for ourselves. However, it would be another distortion of Nietzsche to cast him as simply celebrating this unlimited human potential. His experience of the death of God remains a shattering encounter with the Other or with absolute otherness. Nietzsche recognizes the necessity of such an encounter for the creativity he exalts in his *Übermensch* (Overman). It is a transhuman or ultrahuman creativity. Nietzsche is thus a discoverer of this possible dimension of experience beyond the human, "all too human," as crystallized in his 1878 book of aphorisms bearing that title (1996). The tension between these contradictory "perspectives"—one diminishing otherness and the other exalting it—will bring madness on him by 1889, as he seems to have divined already before 1882, the date of publication of the first edition of *The Gay Science* (1882–1887/1974), containing this famous "Parable of the Madman."

In effect, as presented earlier, Nietzsche offers us two contrasting ways of approaching nihilism. It can, in the first place, signify the loss of animal instinctiveness and a movement against natural life caused by human self-consciousness and hyperconsciousness that alienates us from our concrete being as animals surviving on the earth and turns us against our own vital instincts. But nihilism can also mean the loss of foundations due to the collapse of religious faith brought about by what Nietzsche calls the death of God. These realizations of nihilism are different, and their divergence shows up most starkly in the responses they provoke in those who adapt Nietzsche to their philosophies. The death of God can be conceived of as paving the way to full human realization and supposedly fully overcoming alienation, as Hegel and Marx hoped and projected; or it can lead to an inconsolable torn-openness in which one lives out of a never-to-be-filled lack in relation to an unattainable otherness. The latter has been the tack taken generally by French postmodern thinkers such as Jacques Derrida (1930–2004), Gilles Deleuze (1925–1995), Michel Foucault (1926–1984), and Jacques Lacan (1901–1981) with their insistence on the difference of an absolute otherness that cannot be appropriated. These French philosophers have placed themselves expressly in the following of this alternative, posthuman Nietzsche.

Nietzsche, accordingly, remains the origin and fundamental point of reference for numerous expressions of postmodernism: he opened the horizon of a structural relation with unencompassable alterity, an alienness that can never be appropriated and that empties our world of reality. We are accordingly left in the kind of nihilism that is often attributed to postmodernity. What is the remedy to realizing our subjection to this nihilism? Either adhering more closely to natural life and instinct or, else, opening to the "beyond"—beyond all concrete existence and all definable, graspable reality. I outline something like these contrasting directions as corresponding to Hegel and Nietzsche, respectively, in "The Deaths of God in Hegel and Nietzsche and the Crisis of Values in Secular Modernity and Post-Secular Postmodernity" (Franke, 2007b).

We find modeled in these diverging ways of taking up the legacy of Nietzsche the contrasting types of response that can be found also in relation to aliens: either doubling down on human nature as pointed out by the encounter with aliens and the awareness of the need to preserve some kind of essential humanity or, else, the challenge to be utterly transformed and "othered"—"transhumanized," as Dante puts it in *Paradiso* (I:72). Either response can be embraced as a result of the encounter with the absolutely Other, whether this otherness is conceived of as divinity or simply as the alien. These alternative movements consist in either the allergic reaction of rejecting or a compulsive receptivity in offering hospitality to the alien. In either case, Nietzsche's mistrust and loathing of nihilism is symptomatic of the discomfort concerning aliens that is certainly widespread among us: the two reactions embody an instinctive fear of or fascination with the alien, respectively.

The absolute Other of medieval mysticism, and more generally of apophatic thought and discourse across the ages, remains remote and absolutely unknowable as such. For a reconstruction of this millenary tradition of thought from a range of religious authors, poets, mystics, esotericists, and philosophers, I defer to the two volumes of my collection *On What Cannot Be Said*: *Apophatic Discourses in Philosophy, Religion, Literature, and the Arts*, (Franke, 2007a). These encounters with the absolute Other need to be brought more tangibly into the sphere of our experience if they are to be intelligible to us. Dante does this in *Comedy* through his poetic discourse, with its sensorial imaginary for the other worlds of Christian eschatology. God is par excellence the Other who remains beyond and above all attempts to describe and express the divine essence. Hence, Dante's poetics outline, analogically, a stretching toward a kind of negative theology. His imaginings make sensorially concrete the theological dimension that transcends literal representation.

Another, not unrelated and, in any case, likewise intriguing mode of this mediation is found in the cultural discourse on aliens and, indeed, in the whole wild west of imagination concerning aliens that has been invented in science fiction and fantasy literature and in film exploring the Weird.[1] This corpus of culture makes at least concretely imaginable the appearance and even the invasion of the unknown Other into our ordinary space of the Same. The alien cannot be dealt with through any of our tried and tested categories and methods. We are at a loss in the face of the absolutely new and alien.

Rather like Aaron B. Daniels in his introduction to the volume in hand, Slavoj Žižek takes horror films as the ultimate confrontation with the strange and unassimilable that defeats our ability to comprehend it. Žižek recognizes this by treating horror films, in effect, as a kind of negative theology, pointing us toward the "vertiginous void" (as Daniels puts it) of the unknown. "I think horror films are the negative theology of today. I don't think we can understand the logic of negative theology without appreciating good horror movies" (Žižek, 2010, p. 180).

Negative theology is operative in forms of popular culture such as Weird film and literature about eldritch aliens and points to the deeper sense of alterity that is truly beyond us and all our means of domesticating it. These types of media explore the greater challenge posed by encounters with aliens or with the great, cosmic unknown. Nietzsche's thinking of the death of God opens to just such an abyss and does so with a high degree of fear and trembling, not to say outright terror, in facing it. Such is the reaction registered by Nietzsche's madman.

Nietzsche's negative theological take on the death of God also opens a pathway toward post-structuralist theories of alterity and the Other, even of *Altarity*, as Mark Taylor (1987) wittily imagines, bringing out the ambiguously religious aspect of this relation to alterity. From this perspective, aliens can be seen as a site of transcendence still within our thoroughly secularized modern culture. Becoming fully receptive to the alien is what turns our typically secular modernity into a post-secular postmodernity.

What sorts of conceptual innovations, then, are called forth by this unprecedented encounter? Are there methods of suspending our own conceptual apparatus so as to allow what does not fit into it to make an appearance? Or are there self-cancelling concepts that could enable some kind of access to what we are, in principle, unable to conceptualize? The words and notions used to communicate an experience of the alien would have to be, in some sense, self-alienated or self-alienating.

There are numerous attempts in psychoanalysis and phenomenology to cope with varied experiences of the alien in conceptually innovative ways. Julia Kristeva developed the notion of the *abject* for dealing with a certain kind of experience of repulsion or horror in *Powers of Horror: An Essay on the Abject* (1980/1982). Kristeva's abject, like the discarded placenta, is what we feel the need to separate ourselves from in order to survive as autonomous. What disgusts us in the manner of the abject is a reminiscence of this primal repression by which the "I" emerges from the maternal matrix and establishes itself over against the "not-I."

Crucial for Kristeva and for innumerable other theorists is the notion of the "uncanny" that Sigmund Freud's famous 1919 essay "Das Unheimliche" (SE XVII) put into circulation (1953). An unsuspected, unconscious, alien side of our own psyche emerges in experiences designated as *unheimlich* (uncanny). This expression literally suggests that what is closest to home—*heim* in German means "home"—can be experienced as alien and strange.

For Martin Heidegger, we are ordinarily and all-too-obliviously immersed in an inauthentic experience of the world in terms of the conventions we are familiar with and that interpret what anyone is supposed to feel and perceive. Only the mood of existential *angst* and being confronted with something uncanny can jolt us out of such a benumbed state of imperturbability into actually experiencing things for ourselves. Heidegger's *das Unheimliche* (uncanny) indicates that, emerging from its usual absorption into *das Man* (the they), a more authentic being-in-the-world, as being-thrown-into-nothingness, makes itself felt.

In introducing this volume, Aaron B. Daniels adopts British theorist China Miéville's notion of the "abcanny" to bring out a kind of alterity that is not straightforward negation but more of an apophatic negation—though this designation, too, is eventually negated by Daniels. This is a negation that distances and positions what it relates to rather than simply suppressing it. Such is the force of *ab-* in this neologism instead of the *un-*, as in the existing word "uncanny" for something strangely familiar. The *ab-* is actually a powerful affirmation or setting into relief by a marking of difference from simple negation. The earliest use of the *ab-* that

I know of in something like this sense is Charles Sanders Peirce's (1839–1914) coinage "abduction" used to designate the generation of new hypotheses that can be derived neither by *de*duction nor by *in*duction.

Miéville finds the abcanny especially in what he calls the Weird: "The Weird is the assertion of that [which] we did not know, never knew, could not know, that [which] has always been and will always be unknowable" (Miéville, 2012, p. 380). The more "radical otherness" or "counterpoising alterity" in question here is, according to Daniels, "not mere opposition," because it "slips beyond the containment of the modified term" (Daniels, p. 61). Miéville thus radicalizes the uncanny with the abcanny, emphasizing the "implacable alterity" of a "hallucinatory/nihilistic novum" (Daniels, p. 59).

The *abcanny* is "the unrepresentable and unknowable, the evasive of meaning" (Miéville, 2012, p. 381). Miéville highlights "the abcanny's beyond-meaning-ness" (p. 382). Abcanny monsters can be used to mean, but they "meta-unmean." There is an essential antimeaningness at the core of the abcanny (p. 382), and as such, the abcanny is unknowable. Of course, even being meaningless is a way of meaning. Nevertheless, the abcanny foregrounds "the deterioration of the capacity to make meaning" (Daniels, p. 48). "Are audiences drawn to mysteries, mysticism, Weird fiction, and even puzzles because it awakens, for however briefly, an encounter with the unknowable?" (Daniels, p. 50).

Daniels reasons that "[a]lthough Miéville may be pointing to similar ineffable/ unspeakable edges as some postmodern thinkers, he is more boldly asserting the inevitability, the unavoidability, the comprehensiveness, and the ubiquity of the abcanny" (p. 62). In Daniels's analysis,

> every person is dogged by the Weirdness of life and simultaneously adopts vast structures of meaning—personality, relationships, political affiliations, epistemologies, economic systems, religious faiths, brand loyalty, and so much more—as tenacious yet ineffectual defenses against the indicting abcanny.
>
> (p. 63)

As mentioned previously, Daniels ends up abjuring the apophatic:

> An abcanny-informed theology cannot be simply apophatic. A suspicion of language and constructs as reifying what cannot be held in such boxes can only go so far. The abcanny demands a commitment to movement if one is not to fall into the idolatrous comfort of any convention. The yearning of the heart, the stretching toward hope, the belief in love.
>
> (p. 82)

However, as I use it, the *apophatic* already stands for this elusive state that Daniels is describing as "abcanny." I do not see any functional difference between the two terms, since both operate equivalently in order to dance away from any fixed formulation. I welcome the constant innovation in terminology as a signal that these are all necessarily unstable concepts. I think that the very same inadequacy is inscribed into "abcanny" as into "apophatic": both terms need to abjure themselves. Of course, they signal different routes and way stations along this path of conceptual self-subversion, so the multiplicity of different angles and nuance that "abcanny" introduces I willingly embrace.

As Daniels describes the operation of the abcanny, "[w]e are thrown into a meaning-devouring world" (p. 63). In one of his striking images referring to psychopathology, he writes: "[T]his symptom-complex is a clutching to a meaning that the abcanny has already so thoroughly worm-eaten as to render the meaning toxic" (p. 76). This is indeed nihilism, a relentless reduction to nothing. Is it to be passed beyond, as Nietzsche hoped, and as negative theology certainly intends? The negative is not an end in itself but a stage to be passed through toward liberation. Is Weird literature proposing it, instead, as a fatality that we can always only struggle against in an ongoing war against the universe?

Saying that reality is incomprehensible and means nothing, a point on which China Miéville and Thomas Ligotti agree (Daniels, p. 68), is, after all, a way of "comprehending" it. The same can be said of the unknowing propounded by negative theology. The idea that all attempts to make meaning then show up as evasions and denials or refusals to recognize the universe's "fundamental antipathy to human existence" (Daniels, p. 68) expresses an emotional reaction or an attitude, but one that is not necessary. We wind up again saying how things are instead of having the radical openness to letting be and participating in making things what they will be. In this regard, Heidegger was not in arrears of the science fiction writers; he was analyzing existence as structurally open to the future rather than casting a captivating emotional spell, as cinema and comparable forms of entertainment are apt to do.

Daniels emphasizes that the abcanny is based on the impermanence of everything. This makes it a perfect embodiment of nihilism as construed by Emanuele Severino in our time's most thorough and penetrating philosophical analysis of "the essence of nihilism." As long as we see beings not in their eternity but in terms of their originating and being extinguished, their being born and dying, we are in a chronically nihilistic mode. Such nihilism is of a piece with metaphysics and modernity. However, it is not our only option. Severino offers an alternative. It consists in refusing to let beings be separated from their being. This being of things is their truth, and this truth is eternal:

If the truth of being is the appearing of the being (the entity) and of the being of the entity, and thus is the appearing of the eternity of every entity (from the most shadowy and nuanced to the richest and most concrete, from the most ideal to the most real, imagined and lived, human and divine), and if the appearing of the truth of being is not then an activity that issues from and returns to the nothing, or that begins and ceases to appear, but is the place that is always already open and in which every event comes to manifest itself and every word is announced. The millennia of history and the totality of time extend themselves within this eternal place in which the essence of man consists. The eternal appearing of the truth of being is open to overtaking by the event.

Se la verità dell'essere è l'apparire dell'inseparabilità dell'ente e dell'essere dell'ente, e dunque è l'apparire dell'eternità di ogni ente (dal più umbratile e sfumato al più ricco e concreto, dal più ideale al più reale, immaginato e vissuto, umano e divino), e se l'apparire della verità dell'essere è l'ente la cui essenza è l'apertura della verità di ogni ente, l'apparire della verità dell'essere non è allora un'attività che esca e ritorni nel nulla, o che cominci e finisca di apparire, ma è il luogo già da sempre aperto in cui giunge a manifestarsi ogni evento e si annuncia ogni parola. I millenni della storia e la totalità del tempo si distendono all'interno di questo luogo eterno, in cui consiste l 'essenza dell'uomo. L'eterno apparire della verità dell'essere è aperto al sopraggiungere dell'accadimento.

(Severino, 1972/1995, p. 275, translation by the current author)

In these terms, Severino proposes what he sees as the alternative to the nihilism of the modern world. Encountering aliens is not his concern, but he would see such encounters as symptomatic of a fundamental alienation of our entire civilization from itself and from the eternity of everything that is. We imagine aliens who disappear when one draws close and tries to verify perception of them because this is what happens to everything in our apprehension of it. We have condemned ourselves to an alienated nihilism by refusing to recognize the eternity of beings that was realized at the dawn of philosophical thought in Greece with Parmenides.

Another leading Italian philosopher, Massimo Cacciari, observes that today the essential debate in philosophy is between Heidegger and Severino. Heidegger interprets beings as temporal and their being as time, while Severino interprets their being, following Parmenides, as eternal. Severino defines Heidegger's—and modern technological society's—position as nihilistic. Severino's understanding of the being of beings as eternal echoes some crucial intuitions expressed in Nietzsche's theory of *die ewige Wiederkehr des Gleiche* (the eternal return of the same) (see both 1882–1887/1974, 1883–1892). Of course, Nietzsche is usually taken as an unrepentantly worldly philosopher and the nemesis of everything purportedly eternal and ideal. He, nevertheless, projects this unending dimension of existence in the form of eternal repetition. Eternal repetition is fundamental to human self-fashioning in the all-surpassing mode that Nietzsche envisages for his superman. This suggests how Nietzsche opens the way to postmodern and post-secular rethinking of the religious or divine and even of eternity.

In this volume, Emily McAvan uses the idea of the "divinalien" to explore post-structuralist differences in Levinas, as well as in Lacan, Irigaray, Derrida, and others. She emphasizes the psychological dimension whereby the encounter with the alien is always also an encounter with the unknown strata of one's own psyche. The divinalien is not intelligible like the human stranger in need of hospitality and placing an ethical demand on us through the face of the Other, as Levinas insists. In the Bible, this Other could be the God of Mount Moriah demanding the sacrifice by Abraham of his son Isaac. This carries beyond anything that is ethically intelligible, as Kierkegaard's *Fear and Trembling* (1843/1986) so compellingly argues. God, in effect, demands of Abraham an ethically appalling murder of his son Isaac, as well as the religious sacrifice of Abraham's own dearest and nearest. Yet still, looking at the science fiction corpus, McAvan emphasizes the psychological dimension whereby the encounter with the alien is always also an encounter with the unknown recesses of one's own psyche.

We recall that Nietzsche places the human being back among the animals by recognizing the thoroughly natural being of humans. Nietzsche develops a philosophy of "indistinction" in thinking of humanity in relation to other species, notably animals—a notion examined ably by Calarco (2014). The same principle of indistinction would certainly apply just as well to the relation with other extraterrestrial beings. Nietzsche identifies being with the will to power. The lack of the will to be in, and to be maximally in, one's greatest possible realization or "power" is, for him, nihilism. This is the problem with God and the reason God must die: God drains the world of its vitality and power. At least modern humanist sensibilities feel this.

Heidegger extends Nietzsche's thinking of nihilism through to the technological revolution of the twentieth century. Technology is the manner in which nihilism is manifest in the world today. Things are deprived of their intrinsic being and become *just* things subject to manipulation as "resources" for purposes not their own. In the words of Severino, "techne [τέχνη] realizes itself as the effective production and distribution of beings. The nothingness and annihilation of the being is thus also understood here as a fact and reality incontrovertibly manifest" ["la τέχνη si realizzi come effettiva produzione e distruzione degli enti. La nientità e nientificazione dell'ente è così anche qui intesa come fatto e realtà incontrovertibilmente manifesti]" (1972/1995, p. 259, translation by the current author).

For Severino, the true source of nihilism is thinking of beings as coming into existence in the world and then ceasing to exist. This is the horizon of thought since Greek metaphysics and throughout Western culture, down to our present technological civilization. We do not think of or conceive the eternity of beings because that would lead us out of the world, and the world has been the theater of our thinking—man and world—ever since Greek metaphysics. Our thinking of aliens, too, surely places them within our world or universe, even though the radical challenge of the alien is that it should upset this notion of the world, leading us outside any framework that is familiar to us.

Of course, this dimension of not just the otherworldly but the other-than-the-world is not what most popular culture concerning aliens emphasizes. The battles for destruction of one race or the other, as enshrined in George Lucas's *Star Wars* (1977) and the like, are all conceived within the horizon of a universe of beings which come to exist and can or will perish. This usual conception misses the eternal dimension of being. For Severino, only the latter type of thinking can save us from nihilism. And perhaps only our encounter with aliens, in our imaginations or psyches, if not in outer space, can provoke the disruption apt to catalyze such thinking.

Perhaps trying to think of the eternal rather than our more familiar, time-conditioned things and existence would be the most radical exercise necessary to prepare and habilitate us to go meet the alien. Perhaps we need to think of the eternal in order to fall out of the hypnosis of our world as the inescapable frame—and cage—of all our thought so as to become able to participate with other, non-human, nonhistorical beings in a truly new dimension of consciousness. For Severino, thinking within the parameters of "the world" is the essence of our nihilistic culture, which arches in its reign from Greek metaphysics to modern consumer society. Such is the essence of nihilism, which Nietzsche, especially as post-structuralist thinkers understood him, elevated to the crucial issue of our civilization and its destiny.

The popular culture surrounding aliens, as expressed in fiction and film, as well as in comics and other forms evoked in this volume's essays, describes a continuum. It develops from fighting them off in order to save humanity from alien invasion and conquest, as in the *Star Wars* model, to finding the alien already within us as a revelation of the condition of our very own existence in its perpetual dissolution. However, this discovery is perhaps itself already an expression of our nihilism. Severino's thinking might lead us to think of the encounter with aliens as pointing us beyond our seemingly fated nihilism to an embrace of the truth of being that we have abandoned throughout the arc of our cultural and intellectual history, ever since the metaphysical mindset prevailed in Greece, and all the more in our technology-dominated culture today. These are the codes of our own self-alienation that could be broken out of in order to undo and exit from nihilism. This conversion of mind would enable us to hail the advent of the incomprehensibly alien as our savior—as saving us from ourselves, from our all too reductive sameness with ourselves.

William Franke

Note

1 There is a long-standing and also a burgeoning literature on the alien, around which Aaron B. Daniels has organized alien salons as sections of the Psychology and the Other conferences sponsored by Boston College.

References

Calarco, M. (2014). Being toward meat. *Dialectical Anthropology*, 38(4), 415–429.
Daub, A. (2024). *The cancel culture panic: How an American obsession went global.* Stanford University Press (Originally *Cancel Culture Transfer: Wie eine moralische Panik die Welt erfasst.* Suhrkamp, 2022).
Franke, W. (Ed.). (2007a). *On what cannot be said: Apophatic discourses in philosophy, religion, literature, and the arts* (Vols. 1 & 2). University of Notre Dame Press.
Franke, W. (2007b). The deaths of God in Hegel and Nietzsche and the crisis of values in secular modernity and post-secular postmodernity. *Religion and the Arts*, 11(2), 214–241.
Franke, W. (2024). The death of God as source of the creativity of humans. *Philosophies*, 9(3), 55.

Freud, S., Strachey, J., Freud, A., & Rothgeb, C. L. (1953). *The standard edition of the complete psychological works of Sigmund Freud*. Hogarth Press and the Institute of Psycho-Analysis.

Kierkegaard, S. (1986). *Fear and trembling*. Penguin Classics (Original work published 1843).

Kristeva, J. (1982). *Powers of horror: An essay on abjection*. Columbia University Press (Original work published 1980).

Levinas, E. (1974). *Autrement qu'être ou au-delà de l'essence*. Martinus Nijhoff.

Lucas, G. (Director & Writer), Kurtz, G. (Producer). (1977). *Star Wars* [Film]. Lucasfilm Ltd.

Miéville, C. (2012). On monsters; or, nine or more (monstrous) not cannies. *Journal of the Fantastic in the Arts, 23*(3), 374–392. Citation 380 [Cf. Daniels, p. 61)].

Nietzsche, F. (1883–1892). *Also sprach Zarathustra: Ein Buch für Alle und Keinen*. E. W. Fritsch.

Nietzsche, F. (1887). *Zur Genealogie der Moral: Eine Streitschrift*. C. G. Naumann.

Nietzsche, F. (1974). *The gay science* (W. Kaufmann, Trans.). Vintage (Original work published 1882–1887).

Nietzsche, F. (1996). *Human, all too human: A book for free spirits* (R. J. Hollingdale, Trans.). Cambridge University Press (Original work published 1878 as *Menschliches, Allzumenschliches: Ein Buch für freie Geister*).

Severino, E. (1995). *Essenza del nichilismo* (2nd ed.). Adelphi (Original work published 1972).

Taylor, M. C. (1987). *Altarity*. University of Chicago Press.

Žižek, S. (2010). A meditation on Michelangelo's Christ on the cross. In J. Milbank, S. Žižek & C. Davis (Eds.), *Paul's new moment: Continental philosophy and the future of Christian theology* (pp. 169–182). Brazos Press.

Chapter 1

Introduction

The Abcanny: Encounters With the Inscrutably Alien

Aaron B. Daniels

This chapter received substantive editorial guidance from Emma Baranowski, Mckenna Dahlen, and Sammie Keenan as part of the Northeastern University Psychological Humanities Workgroup.

The best way I know how to enter the topic of the inscrutably alien and move toward a case for China Miéville's coining of the term *abcanny* is to begin in a darkening movie theater. At least, that's where my journey toward these frontiers began. In inviting its audience into this liminal storytelling space, this chapter is at risk of resonating with—among other sources—the poetry of Jim Morrison accompanied posthumously by the rest of the Doors on the album *An American Prayer* (1978), beginning with "*Is everybody in?/Is everybody in?/Is everybody in?/The ceremony is about to begin,*" but especially in the cut "The Movie," which opens with the line "The movie will begin in five moments/The mindless voice announced." These and many other cinematic, poetic, and literary examples from the last 100-plus years utilize the movie theater to create a frame narrative that invites the audience into that interstitial space and the curious experiential tension of cinematic spectacle. Cinema did not invent the tug and pull of absorption and shifting self-awareness. Storytellers have winked and made asides to their audiences for millennia; even Shakespeare frequently invited his audience into, and occasionally out of, his plays with practices that now seem quite "meta."

Nevertheless, as seductive as the idea of the ritual opening in a darkening theater may be, the theater-based ritual of cinema is in flux, if not dying. But I'm not sure how to tell this story with a cell phone's screen. For many of us born into the twentieth century, a cinema's ability to entice and pull us into other realities entailed a very particular type of magic. Since the late nineteenth century, in the darkness, we become just a little alienated from ourselves, only to watch parts of us play out on the screen. In my passivity, I am both me and a little not-me. In encountering the characters and landscapes on the screen, I project various aspects of me that are also not-me but carry the potential to inform who I am becoming. With the conceit bought for the price of the ticket, the audience distends into the darkness.

DOI: 10.4324/9781003519102-1

If this chapter's narrative needed to remain ostensibly nonfictional, there would be many other places to begin. I could just as easily take readers to another liminal space, a therapist's office, offering snapshots of people on the couch beginning to come to terms with their bafflement at their condition. Or I could tell a story of culture shock and alienation with subjects in a radically foreign land—which could be just around the corner from their familiar world. Even describing an unexpected love might allow for the startling relativization of self and other, the revolutionary potential of the encounter with alterity. Those intersections could also give way to more unsettling landscapes of disgust, prejudice, hate, psychosis, and trauma, among others.

But that's not where my story begins; and fiction and nonfiction are not going to behave appropriately in this chapter.

We are in an aging "movie palace" whose plaster Churrigueresque décor decays around us. With the house lights now fully down, the ceiling reveals its pinprick stars. The velvet curtains ascend with squeaks and groans, exposing a massive screen looming before us.

I am 3 years old.

My father, a classical music radio announcer, has brought the family because he is reliably informed that the film's soundtrack abounds with orchestral master-pieces, old and new. My early-teenage brother, a future pilot, will find the detailed depictions of near futuristic technology absorbing. My mother? I'm not entirely clear what brings my mother, other than to spend time with "her boys," since this film is a far cry from her preferred British cozy mysteries.

The first image of the film is darkness accompanied by the almost-intuited rumble of a deep pedal tone from symphonic double basses. The blackness sweeps down to reveal the luminous crescent of a planet—is it Earth? A sun emerges over its horizon. A trumpet describes open intervals. Then a symphonic exclamation! Tympani undergird the gravitas. Only today do I wonder if that initial blackness is the first appearance of the monolith.

The film is, of course, Kubrick's 1968 masterpiece *2001: A Space Odyssey* on a mid-1970s re-release tour. I have written elsewhere (Daniels, 2021) about Stanley Kubrick's (1928–1999) portrayal of the silent vacuum of space in contrast to Dante's effulgent heavens in *Paradiso*. In that essay, I also noted that the repeating encounters with the monolith are strangely significant in that those approaching it could not make any discernable sense of it. Its bold presence is undeniable; but what does it mean? Its meaning is its stark refusal to offer meaning, which forces the encounter to become one of meaning-making—that is, imagination—driving us to farther horizons.

By the end, Kubrick's 1968 film indelibly imprinted on me, overwhelming my developing mind with its sharp lines, the silence of its space, the inexplicability of it all. In my boundary-blurring experience, even the stars on the theater's ceiling blended into the film's spacescapes. The film did not impact the rest of my family in the same way. The film's portrayal of early hominins in the first "Dawn of Man" section insults my father's Spiritist creationism—to the extent that I'm not sure if he did much with the rest of the imagery or story. My brother will go on to a successful airline career, but not flying a PanAm Orion III "Space Clipper" as portrayed by Kubrick. (By the year 2001 that happened off the screen, PanAm had ceased operations for 10 years, and "commercial" flights to space would be another 20 years in coming.) My mother has continued to love a cozy mystery. And me? I have—usually unwittingly—spent the intervening decades returning in countless ways back to that indecipherable monolith, into the journey of meaning-making and imagination that the unknowable begets.

2001 (1968) and Star Wars (1977)

As noted by filmmaker Christopher Nolan in a 2018 interview with the *Los Angeles Times'* Whipp, the mid-1970s re-release of *2001* (Kubrick, 1968) sought to play off the blockbuster success of Lucas's *Star Wars: A New Hope* (1977). I am unsure which film I saw first, but Lucas's space opera and its mythic images also stuck with me, only rather more overtly than Kubrick's 1968 work did.

With *Star Wars* (1977), Lucas gives the audience cannily familiar images, even though they are, as the first words on the screen promise, from "[a] long time ago, in a galaxy far, far away . . ." (After all, "Once upon a time . . ." was already taken.) Within the first three minutes of the film, Lucas establishes a palpable dread at the insurmountable dark power of Darth Vader. Most of his characters scarcely need to speak or act for the audience to recognize them as protagonists or antagonists: open-faced, white-clad heroes versus masked and armored or black-clad villains. By the end of the film, the mystery of the Jedi haunts anyone pulled into the narrative. And weaving together all this iconic storytelling is John Williams's soon-to-be signature soundtrack style. You don't have to be a committed fan or a film scholar to know that *Star Wars* is, in large part, Lucas's love letter to Jungian mythologist Joseph Campbell (1904–1987) and filmmaker Akira Kurosawa (1910–1998). In homage, Lucas offers bold images, worthy of propaganda films.

From the release of *Star Wars* (Lucas, 1977) until present, children—and adults—have played out moments from the ever-growing inventory of films and series. These characters and their storylines, now easily in the hundreds or thousands, invite imitation, repetition, innovation—and parody. At their best, these stories evoke and invoke archetypal themes which practically beg for re-enactment. An orthodox Jungian might even state that we cannot help but re-enact these themes. In fact, the *Star Wars* films and series unapologetically repeat and re-enact their own themes, catchphrases, conflicts, character types, architectural features, and on and on. Lucas describes these recurrences with the idea that the imagery and stories should "rhyme" (Shenk, 2001, 3:16). This intentional mythic resonance thus makes it so that the imagery and storylines of the *Star Wars* universe echoed back long before 1977 and echo through to today.

Amply supplementing this overabundance of imagery, from its release, *Star Wars* (Lucas, 1977) was merchandised within an inch of its life, with action figures, playsets, spacecraft, and collectibles targeting a preteen audience. On the screen, the children watching encountered a film that was excitingly loud and big. Lucas's space is full of rumbling engine noises, the shriek of swooping craft, the sound of blasters and explosions, the hum and sizzle of lightsabers—all of which beg audiences to imitate them as best as they can. Off the screen, children could not avoid seeing tie-ins to the film at fast-food restaurants, on television, and in their friends' toy boxes. Thus, given this onslaught of media saturation, one can even ignore the archetypal forces at work to understand how children with action figures—who would become adults with "figurines"—came to imitate the films. But fans did and continue to do more than imitate; they create new stories. This imitation and innovation are easy since most of the protagonists are apparently human, and even Lucas's robots and aliens are mostly anthropomorphic in their forms and stories—like the vast majority of characters in the competing *Star Trek* universe. Although some droids and Jabba the Hutt may defy a bipedal standard, the exceptions tend to support the rule. Lucas offers mythic characters and creatures in that "galaxy far, far away" that are recast presentations of themes and types we all know deeply. One need not strain to produce interpretations and meaning for a *Star Wars* story. The real struggle for film critics and scholars when approaching any *Star Wars* film or series lies in which of a host of applicable interpretative stances to take and how to gauge the quality of any one product within the franchise's massive output. A surfeit of imagery and meaning overflows any *Star Wars* media from a firm grounding in storytelling and cinematic tropes—many of which Lucas helped popularize or even establish.

In sharp contrast, I cannot recall one instance of my young Gen X peers ever wanting to re-enact a scene from *2001: A Space Odyssey* (Kubrick, 1968). One can maybe imagine delightfully odd children saying to one another, "Okay, Billy, you be the monolith," or "Ooh! Ooh! You be HAL, and I'm going to ask you to open the pod bay doors!" When the music of Strauss or Ligeti stops, Kubrick's space is famously silent, with no "pew-pew-pew" of lasers. Kubrick's actors offer mostly flattened affect, further deepening the film's ambiguity. An internet search informs the curious that there were, in fact, tie-in toys of a sort for *2001*, but nowhere near the scale that Lucas's media empire revolutionized. Yet I am not alone in having Kubrick's film infect my psyche at a young age. Christopher Nolan responds to Whipp (2018, "I understand you showed"), asking him, with some incredulity, to explain showing the film to his toddlers:

> I did. I think they're able to absorb it on the most important level at a young age. That's what happened to me. I saw it when I was 7 years old, and that's the level I think it works the best—pure cinematic spectacle. I was extremely baffled by it, but excited by it. . . . And if you look at "2001" and you think about it, you can't parse it anyway as an adult. The experience is the thing. You don't know what the hell is going on. You just let the experience wash over you and maybe talk about it later.

Nolan admits that his *Interstellar* (2014) "is very much, as people would say, in dialogue" (Whipp, 2018, "Growing up") with Kubrick's (1968) enigmatic masterpiece.

Devoted fans of *2001* (Kubrick, 1968), however, may raise an objection to Nolan—and to me—embracing this perplexing imagery as fundamentally inscrutable. Arthur

C. Clarke (1917–2008), Kubrick's (1968) screenplay collaborator, goes on to elaborately explain the monoliths, HAL's malfunction, and even the final psychedelic sequence of *2001*, "Jupiter and Beyond the Infinite." After all, through Clarke's subsequent novels *2010: Odyssey Two* (1982), *2061: Odyssey Three* (1987), and *3001: The Final Odyssey* (1997), he describes the relationship between humans and the aliens that sent the monoliths. Therefore, those who persist in devoted bafflement with *2001* (Kubrick, 1968) must remain in willful and perhaps nostalgic ignorance of Clarke's elaborations. With these explications of the backstory, the imagery may have been initially mysterious, but viewers can now take up the explanations with as much ease as interpreting Lucas's parade of putative archetypes, can't they? The cryptic images in "Jupiter and Beyond the Infinite" are merely a series of artfully portrayed clues—floating breadcrumbs for the audience to decipher the underlying story. There is no real, fundamental mystical mystery or terrifying encounter with the epistemologically unknowable, ineffable, or unspeakable. Is there?

Questions for a Phenomenology of the Unknown

How one frames and addresses questions regarding mysteries-versus-explanations defines the crux of my investigation in this chapter. To honor the experience of confronting frontiers of what we do know and can know, I would like to move toward a phenomenology of the encounter with the unknown. Through a schematic of levels of mystery, examples from film and literature, key authors of Weird fiction, and Miéville's idea of the abcanny in comparison to the uncanny and the abject, I aim to navigate readers toward the vertiginous voids of the unknown and the unknowable.

That is not to say that I am attempting to pursue any type of thorough nihilism, although I do want the question of nihilism to not be buried under unexamined assumptions of any sort of "self-evident" ground of being. Nor am I attempting to undermine the often-epic fabrics of meanings offered by psychotheocosmologies, such as Freudian, Jungian, Lacanian, object relations, Kristevian, and a host of other psychodynamic theories. These theories give powerful explanations of what our ongoing encounters with the unknown can mean—including the affects that drive them. But as I will discuss, these theories also, ultimately, strive to define what lies behind the unknown. Thus, I hope to present the prospect of Greater Mysteries as a trans-archetypal force or ultimate frontier that could render most other archetypes or meaning structures as more provisional than they may at first appear.

Ultimately, this journey orients and leads itself to horizons of meaning-making, asking if the inscrutably alien is merely an exceptional fringe encounter for those prone to fevered imaginations or if these confrontations with what Miéville calls the abcanny are constitutive of the human kind of being. Along the way, I will consider what this journey has to say about the practice of psychotherapy, offering an invitation to new ways of considering that curious manifestation of the unknown: the psychiatric symptom.

As this discourse builds, readers will become increasingly aware of a series of questions in various levels of orbit around this examination.

Hermeneutics—interpretation—and epistemologies—ways of knowing—are at stake in every human act. We are constantly making various types of meaning that provisionally explain and constitute our experiences. Yet so that we can get on with our days, we are, simultaneously, covering over the asking of fundamental questions most of the time. What can we and can't we know? How would we know that we really know or don't know something? What does it mean to later know something we previously didn't? What does it mean to learn that we didn't know something we thought we did? As abstract or obstruse as these sorts of questions may seem, in this current era of "post-truth," "fake news," "deep fakes," and "fake science" (Roscoe, 2023)—much of it now generated by or with non-humans—it may be only our dim apprehension of the nihilistic potential of these questions that keeps us from asking them. Thus, the discussion must continue to return to the experience itself: what is the phenomenology of encountering the unknown?

If I succeed, to any extent, in my effort to describe the qualities of an approach to what is unknown and possibly unknowable, then, beyond offering descriptive themes, this chapter is much more likely to generate further questions in a rhizomic sort of way.

- Does an explanatory truth that later emerges undo the validity of the previous unknowing? That is, if I were merely ignorant, does that type of dispellable unknowing bring with it the same experience as an unfolding encounter with what I will come to see as the ultimately unknowable?
- Is there even such a thing as the "ultimately unknowable"? Am I merely not using the right kind of knowing?
- Did a popular and long-held explanation that covered over what I later came to realize is an unknowable carry the same valence as the "truth"?
- Can I meaningfully reject a meaning that others take up to be adequate or even "true"?
- What does it mean to be mistaken?
- Can one be willfully ignorant in any meaningful way?
- What value is there in the searching for a satisfactory explanation, even as that searching leaves me firmly in a place of deeper unknowing? If this search leads to some satisfactory explanation, has this eventual revelation shaped the journey toward it? Does truth exert a gravitational pull?
- If I am transformed in the searching, can I meaningfully declare that I have found the answer since "I" have been changed in the process? What if my memories and realities change in the journey toward my goal of knowing and understanding?

Should this inquiry allow for these and other questions to inform this journey toward the abcanny, it will not be able to avoid addressing the ideas of the unconscious, the uncanny, the sublime, and the abject. These experiences of alterity haunt this discussion. But to build on my previous two contrasting cinematic examples, perhaps it is best to dive next more fully into one landscape of encountering the unknown—"mystery"—to help expand the vantage of these abysses.

Unfolding Layers of Mystery

If this investigation adequately describes the approach to the unknown, it is, in some sense, interrogating "mystery." The term can appear religiously or esoterically but is far more common as a broad genre of fiction. It falls to other essays and volumes to examine in any depth the relationship between detective or mystery fiction and encounters with the unknown, but a few considerations growing from my previous writings can help take the exploration closer to the inquiry into the inscrutably alien by setting aside less-unfathomable forms of mystery.

In the course of my examination of the use of imagination by—nonfictional—criminal profilers (Daniels, 2014), I consider what some key types of fictional detectives might tell us about the eras and worldviews from which they emerged, and thus what the popularity of "criminal profiling" in media since *The Silence of the Lambs* (Demme, 1991) might tell us about our world today. I describe the epistemological shift from the triumph of logic in classic detective fiction, to the in-over-their-heads struggles of noir detectives, to the psychic contagion at play with today's fictional criminal profilers. Regarding epistemological frontiers, the grittier detective fiction becomes, the more likely the reader is to encounter "the unspeakable"—as compellingly and often-stomach-churningly portrayed in Nordic noir works. But how often does one encounter the ultimately inscrutable in a murder mystery? Unless the discussion expands to welcome the "occult detective" of urban fantasy, one of the closest approaches non-supernatural detective fiction has to that epistemic frontier is when the investigator knows the truth but cannot prove it or pursue prosecution. Frustrating, to be sure. Morally injurious, often. But not likely an encounter with the truly ineffable, sublime, or inscrutable. This commitment to material certainty is so deeply rooted that most murder mysteries would appear to be a complete denial of the inscrutability of death. Possibly, only the madness of a serial killer might welcome some linguistic whisps of nihilism, pitch-black mystery, or apotheotic hyperviolence. But in the face of these assaults, the arc of the detective's story will strive to render impotent any potential dark power these villains once claimed.

Shifting to another narrative landscape that often leads to pressing mysteries, in the two volumes of *Imaginal Reality* (Daniels, 2011a, 2011b), I catalog a range of art, film, literature, and music that present the trope of two seemingly incommensurate worlds that collide and, ultimately, reach some sort of transcendent synthesis—although often by way of destruction. Here, audiences enter multiverses, parallel worlds, nations at war with each other, global schisms, veiled and unmappable streets within a city, and hidden ghostly or fairy realms on the edge of our knowable worlds. Various gender polarities may also help drive these stories. Frequently, the intrusion of one world into another appears as a great mystery, heralded by mounting portentous and uncanny experiences.

These incursions of another world may appear scientific, psychological, spiritual, ecological, or various blends of all four.

Readers can take up these tales of conflicting worlds as a classic dialectic. One world—thesis—is often an everyday, waking world of knowable objects and predictable outcomes. The other world—antithesis—may be an irrational, nightside, seductive, potentially hostile world. The arc of the story is the synthesis. Neil Gaiman offers readers many now-classics of this dialectic process, such as *Neverwhere* (1996), *Stardust* (1999), and *Coraline* (2002). When the dialectic centers on one protagonist's journey, these are—sometimes overtly but always structurally—stories of the character's initiation into the Greater Mysteries of transformation. That opens the potential for Campbell's (1949) hero's journey, further discussed later, in which the heroes-to-be must leave the everyday world to enter an otherworld in which they win a great victory, only to return to where they began, but transformed from the experience and offering some gift to the community. In these cases, the "unknown" is a catalyst for transformation—a confrontation that leads to a further unknown, that is, what one will become.

Thus, thinking of fictional works of worlds colliding, science fiction adventures, detectives trying to put the pieces together, dark descents into horror, as well as mysterious journeys of transformation and initiation, such as psychotherapy, I describe three levels of mysteries: riddles and puzzles, natural Mysteries of life, and ultimate Mysteries.

Riddles and Puzzles

The most basic type of small "m" mysteries are riddles and puzzles to be solved. Here the cast of characters returns to those logician-detectives who reassure readers that they live in a world that is ultimately rational and knowable. The whodunit and the howdunit offer readers a journey in which the facts emerge and fall into place and the story resolves. Here, too, are those scientistic gospels within science fiction in which intrepid protagonists overcome a challenge when they discover the explanatory presence of some exotic particle, as often happens in the *Star Trek* cosmology, or jury-rig a solution out of bailing wire, bubble gum, and some radioactive isotopes, drawing on their existing scientific acumen and moxie (a.k.a. "MacGyvering"), or devotedly apply the scientific method and declare, as memorably observed by Matt Damon's character Dr. Mark Watney in *The Martian* (Scott, 2015), "In the face of overwhelming odds I'm left with only one option. I am going to have to science the shit out of this."

Though existing within this knowable context, a story that sits firmly within the solving of riddles and puzzles may still allow for farther horizons of the unknown. Nevertheless, adding complexity to a story may only be a ploy to encourage audiences to keep streaming or reading. For instance, a science fiction series could leave the audience with unanswered questions about the origins of some alien race or phenomenon. Those questions may, after all, allow for second and third seasons. Maybe readers are flummoxed by having to sort out recursive timelines that repeatedly rewrite the plot they thought they knew. If done engagingly, it keeps audiences guessing—and watching or reading—to be sure. But if, by the end, there really is an answer to be found that explains everything—or most of it, anyway—then the story has remained in this first level of puzzles and riddles. This is the known unknown—solve for "x"—that promises to render all mysteries into known knowns.

As genre mysteries give way to suspense, which gives way to horror, readers may still find themselves lingering at the level of puzzles. Without question, horror and its extended family can open moral vistas onto twisted ethical landscapes, philosophical abysses, crippling existential anxieties, and cosmic madness. But if one initially thought some super- or sub-natural incursion might be afoot yet the dilemma resolves through evidence-gathering and deduction? Then the reader returns to that ultimate logician-detective, Sherlock Holmes—in this case, likely in the form of *The Hound of the Baskervilles* (Doyle, 1902), where greed and phosphorous paint are all the explanation necessary for the spectral appearance of an alleged hellhound. To illustrate this collapse of any Greater Mystery to mere puzzles, Miéville cites a different hound in his conversation with Jeff VanderMeer (2008/2011). Miéville credits author Toby Litt with calling this logical revelation the "Scooby Doo Impasse" (p. 58). For those who—somehow—have escaped the franchise beginning in 1969 of the animated exploits of this talking dog and his human companions riding in their groovy van, the Mystery Machine, and solving . . . well . . . "mysteries": the resolution to nearly every story was the removal of an oddly effective mask from some seeming phantom, ghost, monster, etc. to reveal a character introduced in act 1 of the episode, typically with the now-exposed villain uttering, "And I would have gotten away with it, too, if it weren't for those meddling kids." All thrills and chills, all suspicion of the supernatural, all details and questions are neatly wrapped up with a reassuringly rational bow and a Scooby Snack™.

This encounter with puzzles brings with it a range of emotions. We may experience the delightful drive of curiosity. That interest could give way to determination. We might fume in vexation at our ignorance or anger at a problem impacting the disadvantaged that others have ignored. Solving the puzzle can bring pride, relief, resolute commitment to further investigation—all of which reassure and strengthen the character of the protagonist. We might have hoped that we were truly piercing into some deeper Mystery and experience disappointment at the shabbiness of the explicability.

Nevertheless, firmly resting in the rational does not mean deeper mysteries were expelled, as many a supernatural storyline gleefully plays with as the far-too-often bespectacled rationalists of the group find themselves stunned, shaken, or thoroughly undone by the irrefutable "proof" of the supernatural. Even without these irruptions of the irrational, should the story hint at the level of wonder, awe, angst, or horror, these puzzle-solving quests have likely opened up further vistas into the second or third level of Mysteries. Depending on the authors' skills and insight, a range of arcs can grace a story that can deepen a plot into the second level of

Life Mysteries. Should genuine character development, moral and ethical struggles, cultural issues that go beyond mere efforts to catch audience demographics, or mythic themes that allow archetypes to escape stereotypes appear, the audience may well be pulled out of the comfort of rationality to deeper reasons for why we live, love, endure, hope, and grow—or merely survive, hate, suffer, despair, and degrade. If these story elements are more than window dressing, then the story has escaped from the tyranny of the knowable, even if the story was seemingly about solving a puzzle.

With their foundation in a materialist, positivist, and narrowly defined empiricism, cognitive behavioral and neurobiological modalities for the treatment of mental illness operate within this first level of puzzle mysteries. From their perspective, cognitive distortions, unwanted behavioral patterns, and chemical imbalances are identifiable and eventually correctable. Thus, anyone resorting to an appeal to the unconscious or questions about meaning-making is in danger of needless obfuscation and occultism. For the cognitive behavioral therapist, psychopharmacologist, or biotechnologist, those other unwarranted and unscientific approaches simply muddy the waters and distract both practitioner and patient from identifying clear treatment goals and taking action. From this perspective, a "mystery" is just a problem that hasn't had adequate research and a cogent treatment plan.

To be clear, I do not intend to impugn these approaches to mental health treatment unto themselves. Many patients benefit from learning better self-care in the form of, say, sleep hygiene or diaphragmatic breathing—easily conveyed in a conversation, an instructional video, or a handout. And today, artificial intelligence can offer one mental health screenings, chat therapy, or dieting tips. Excelsior! Sarcasm aside, psychoeducation provides explanations and exercises that may reduce or eliminate discrete distressing symptoms.

Yet in the apparent relief from the problem, what can go unnoticed is that the explanation was purely causal: "You struggled with sleep because you had poor sleep hygiene. Your sleep has improved because you applied many of the best practices to get a good night's sleep." In terms of meaning, this is no explanation at all. Which need not necessarily be all that distressing, if the relief from the previous problem is genuine. After all, a misdirected seeking for meaning or explanation can actually be part of a pathology. Some forms of anxiety can provide an apt example. Many forms of anxiety can well be described as "pointless autonomic arousal." That is, the autonomic nervous system has gone into the "fight, flight, or freeze" arousal pattern with no apparent identifiable threat. Were there a specific threat, it would be "fear," not "anxiety." This lack of an identifiable fear-inducing stimulus tends to lead sufferers to displace their dread onto the future or occasionally the past, scrambling for some explanation for the body rushing to "battle stations." Thus, since there isn't truly a point to that type of anxiety, one can—and perhaps ought to, initially—address the symptoms without much insight beyond "I really ought to depotentiate this autonomic arousal!" This serves as an example for how one can have perfectly effective treatment for relatively discrete symptom patterns—"syndromes"—and not only never address but also conspicuously avoid any sense of "why." The vacuum of meaning this sort of instrumental reasoning begets may only dimly appear later in a different sort of anxiety: angst.

Natural Mysteries of Life

Plato (*Apology*, 38a 5–6) attributes the saying "The unexamined life is not worth living" to Socrates during his trial. Typically taken as making a case for philosophy, it is simultaneously an indictment of uncritical living. But is the rational materialism I presented in the previous section truly uncritical? To a greater extent, I indeed implied that it is not adequately critical. But I should show caution here: one can adopt any psychotheocosmology at the shallowest of levels. Imitation, repetition, credulity, and absorption in the necessary rituals of fealty to any life philosophy—any relatively effective epistemology—can insulate one from having to actually take up the responsibility for one's life and meaning-making that has always already been ours. This second level of Mystery involves a pivot away from the typically unacknowledged convictions and certitude of the previous level and into an acceptance that life is rather messier than an actuarial table.

Long before ancient Greek, Chinese, or even South Asian thinkers began head-scratching over the big questions, the power and ubiquity of myths demonstrated that humans need stories—often Big Stories. This second level of Mysteries is often cited within Mystery Cults and ancient religions—as well as those esoteric, neo-pagan, and new religious movements that claim these archaic provenances. These Mysteries merit a capital "M" for their role within rites of passage, initiatory ceremonies, and occasional use as outer revelations of Greater Divine Mysteries. These Mysteries are fundamental lessons about change, loss, transformation, relationships, love, harmony and dynamic balance, sacrifice, death and rebirth, and sometimes how all that intertwine with sex, the seasons, the sea, the earth, and the stars. That is to say, these natural Mysteries are about life.

This level is, however, absurdly broad. Stories in which the character "learns an important lesson" are a far cry from, say, "unravelling the epistemic web that blinds one to one's complicity in the exploitation of those whom one claims to be helping." Nevertheless, at this second level, meaning is no longer fixed. Meaning was taken for granted in the first level. On this second level, meaning-making is at stake, in whatever sort of storyline it entails.

Science adventurers in the previous puzzle-mystery level may complete their missions and finish an episode with some philosophical speculation while staring through a porthole at the stars, but only those more literary or ambitious authors allow for this second type of Mystery's more wisdom-based truths to shape their protagonists' quests. The most positive encounters with these Life Mysteries engender wonder and awe, perhaps humility, and maybe respect for Nature, the Universe, or some other Capitalizable Reality. But to truly belong at this second level, these moments must change the characters who experience them. More contentious encounters show up in various versions of the "Man (or Science) vs. Nature" trope in which the vanity or hubris of humans smacks into the tenacity of natural forces.

In the face of such encounters, one either adapts—transforms—or dies. This configuration finds memorable summation in *Jurassic Park* (Spielberg, 1993), when Jeff Goldblum's Dr. Ian Malcolm observes, "Life—uh—finds a way."

Considering the hero's journey, first popularized by the aforementioned Joseph Campbell in his *The Hero with a Thousand Faces* (1949), raises interesting questions about levels of mystery. Today, many films, TV series, novels, and graphic novels integrate elements of Campbell's monomyth. Thanks in no small part to Lucas and hordes of fantasy novel authors, the monomyth has become overplayed. Mercifully, decades of criticism have led to alternative mythic arcs that describe different sorts of protagonists' epic journeys. Feminist revisionist mythology, for instance, has offered rich entrée into previously erased landscapes. But utilizing any sort of hero's or heroine's journey as a story structure does not necessarily guarantee real depth. As noted previously, archetypal potentials can be cheapened into stereotypes, rife with cliché and formula, and devoid of any real invitation into the sort of depths this second level of Mystery ought to bring. Even having a protagonist utter some seemingly heart-rending realization like "I thought I knew what I wanted, but I just don't know anymore" does not mean that there's been any real epistemological Mystery afoot. Instead, within these synthetic stories that defend against real uncertainties, the audience finds themselves back at the first level of puzzles, practically picking from an à la carte menu of choices as to which version of "betrayal," "digging deep," "romantic entanglement," or "villain is actually a representation of the hero's self-doubt" they will see. In the face of this dishearteningly predictable landscape, it is no surprise that a host of writers now create postmodern, self-aware snark about heroic story arcs that may eventually reach escape velocity and pull the story into new and unexpected directions. If the postmodern convictions truly prevail, then the story may well jump the snark and skip from the first level of puzzles to the third level of Mystery's epistemological frontiers. Regardless, though many creators acknowledge that this second level of Mystery is critical for a story to have real life, they engage it with widely varying skill and insight.

In the realm of detective fiction, a character-driven whodunit or howdunit might allow for the sort of soul-searching, transformations, and ethical impasses this second level of Mystery demands. The whydunit, which sometimes drives criminal profiling stories, is even more likely to bring up interior landscapes. Looking into unconscious motivations can open a story into more hauntological themes—the revenant of the past finally heard, indicting a whole way of being, for instance. In the world of detective series, one may have to read half a dozen or more of the series before the detectives—stand-ins for all of us trying to make sense of our lives—finally come to grips with how the real Mystery has always been their own lives. Conversations with priests, psychotherapists, ex-spouses, kids, retired or hospitalized colleagues, or maybe even the villain provide key moments of reflection for our haggard heroes.

Horror has no shortage of life tenaciously pushing back against human conceit. Here, one encounters werewolves as snarling representatives of "Nature, red in tooth and claw" (Tennyson, *In Memorium, A. H. H.*, 1850, Canto LVI). Here, too, are genetic mutations, especially zombies, and post-apocalyptic landscapes, all as products of the hubristic pursuits of science. These Mysteries are practically a defining pillar of folk horror, as in *The Wicker Man* (Hardy, 1973) or *Midsommar* (Aster, 2019). The protagonists in folk horror stories are out of touch with the realities of nature. This may be due to the characters' urbanity, puritanical abstemiousness, or denial of their heritage. Regardless, it will all end in fire, tears, death, and maybe madness.

M. Night Shyamalan's output raises some intriguing questions within the first two levels of mysteries. If, as in *Signs* (2002), it looks like it might be aliens, audiences are briefly unsure if it is aliens, but in the end, it really *is* aliens? Then we are merely on the first level of puzzles and riddles, however cunningly conveyed. If, conversely, deeper lessons about life, loss, regret, denial, trauma, and acceptance hide behind the puzzle, as in *The Sixth Sense* (1999), then the first level reveals truths of the second Life Mysteries level. This scaffolding of mysteries can prove particularly effective, keeping the audience from being disappointed when they finally piece together the puzzle clues leading to the big reveal, because the real big reveal is about character.

Because this second level of Mystery often presents the resurgence of a fanged, spectral, tentacled, or shambling avatar of what has been denied, repressed, written out of the narrative, unseen, or otherwise undone, Miéville (2012) marks this configuration as the "unknown known," which brings with it the distinct experience of the uncanny. As discussed in what follows, the uncanny often easily slips into the language of "conscious vs. unconscious" because these are stories of the return of the repressed. Starting in the eighteenth century, this is the territory described by the Gothic response to advancing modernity and its smog- and blood-choked blossoming into the Industrial Revolution and hypercolonialism. Ghosts, revenants, genealogy, atavism, archeology, buried secrets, and unwelcome guests from the (un)forgotten past tell stories that indict and undo the "truths" of the present. Thus, Miéville appropriates Jacques Derrida's (1930–2004) "hauntology" to characterize this way in which the present moment founders in a sea of ghosts. Derrida's *hauntology* is a pun on "ontology." That is, he intends hauntology itself to problematize being—ontology. Derrida first introduced hauntology in *Specters of Marx* (1993/1994), and his sense may be a bit broader than Miéville's. Derrida implies how our sense of present reality is shot through with misremembrance, temporal displacement, nostalgia for futures that have never been, and the perpetual dislocation of presence through endless tattered skeins of traces. Nevertheless, ever-mindful of the tension between his Marxist political sensibilities and the danger of turning his fiction into mere allegories, Miéville does not eschew the Derridean resonances but shows them in his fictions through story and character, rather than expounding them through rhetoric.

Psychotherapeutically, we now find ourselves on the couch. Psychodynamic theorists dominate this territory of uncomfortable but unavoidable truths we ignore at our own peril. Sigmund Freud (1856–1939) and his psychoanalytic descendants warn us that living the defended life of the isolated ego cuts us off from the impulses dwelling in the unconscious in the form of the id. The more estranged or in denial we are, the more vicious the revenge of the unconscious becomes. This is also the shadow described in Carl Jung's (1875–1961) analytical psychology. Although the dragon's shadow-filled cave may contain the alchemical gold necessary for our growth, we may not survive the encounter with it if we have made too long of a habit of villainizing that dragon. The archetypal turning of the wheel of seasons and life cycles where ancient myths play out and we ignore them at our own peril—as in folk horror—also carries powerful Jungian resonances.

Oedipus, Freud's ur-type for all psyches, shows, among other important lessons, how one can have puzzle-level knowledge of Life Mysteries and still hubristically fall prey to their riptide. After all, Oedipus solves the Riddle of the Sphynx. In all its versions, the riddle is always about change and development. But Oedipus remains tragically—willfully?—ignorant of how those lessons might apply to him until the moment that his unwillingness to see concretizes into his self-blinding.

The unwanted past, not fully forgotten, but not allowed to piece itself together in its full import, is the nuanced version of what has become the chestnut of "repressed memories." Were memories fully erased, reminders would not elicit discomfort. Were the trauma truly repressible, we would not suffer further distortions of our speech, relationships, and other memories. What passes for complete "repression" is actually a fragmentation and distortion of the self, memories, relationships, and more. It is this twisted, defended self that suffers in a haunted world, dogged by uncanny experiences.

Clinically, this is also the territory of Yalom's (e.g., 1980, 1989) existential psychotherapy. In this intellectually accessible presentation of existentialism, one deals—or doesn't—with the "givens": things change; people die; I specifically will die; I can't appropriately know people like I know things; I am responsible for and to the moment in which I find myself, regardless of whether I take up this responsibility well or like it; and so forth. As with the resistance to the unconscious in psychodynamic thought, living in denial of the existential givens distorts one's experiences, lived world, self-concept, and relationships.

As true as these existential givens or psychodynamic lessons may be for the individual, one inevitably sees family systems, communities, and whole cultures—with their accompanying epistemologies—living in opposition to these psychodynamic or existential realizations. Conversely, even the broadest of societal issues are deeply personal for all parties. Thus, psychotherapy or psychoanalysis can be a startlingly radical act, challenging the too-convenient partitions we draw between the personal and the social. Granted, psychotherapy can also potentially be an impotent act of personalizing what is fundamentally social or vice versa. For some, the insights achieved in the consulting room can facilitate rebellion against repression and oppression. The realizations can aid in acknowledging one's own wounds incurred in the mechanisms of vast systems of control and domination. So too, perhaps, therapy can make one acutely aware of one's complicity in the suppression of unflattering truths about the cost of a society's status quo. Nevertheless, if the balance and connection between the personal and the societal does not find voice in the session, the patient can easily fall too far to one side or the other of the equation. In truth, however, this is not simply a two-sided equation. Though the realization is ancient and fundamental for some cultures, the last 50 years have seen a growing sense that the "environmental" also belongs on that list of overly convenient categorical divisions that deserve revision and merit attention in depth-oriented psychotherapy.

When therapy dares to broach systemic sexism, racism, hetero- and cis-normativity, classism, environmental degradation, and other deeply embedded and successfully shrouded injustices, the same uncanniness can pervade the work as when one wrestles with personal ghosts. Patients from marginalized communities or with identities for which language doesn't offer an easy purchase find themselves unsettled as they attempt to grasp what would seem to be right in front of them but is simultaneously invisible. That is, one seems to have never had access to some secret code that allows others to blithely operate without concern or fear of reprisal for simply being. Or one experiences that unsettling split in oneself between two worlds which are not only entirely incommensurate but also not even composed of the same substances. The uncanny clouds one's vision with a strange miasma as one asks, "Am I just crazy?" "Why doesn't anyone else seem to get it?" "Am I missing something?" and struggles to not drown in waves of self-doubt, rage, panic, incredulity, and so much more.

Race wove itself into many early streams of horror fiction and film. Race was, however, typically applied with vicious othering that allowed unconscious fantasies to play out their tortured scripts. Only recently have writers actively and consciously begun to imagine race and horror. The horror landscape has changed with Jordan Peele's *Get Out* (2017) and with *Lovecraft Country* (Green, 2020), in which Peele also had a hand. *Lovecraft Country*, based on Ruff's (2016) novel of the same name, is notable for a particularly poignant flipping of perspective. The interwoven stories take the racist panic that fueled much of horror author H. P. Lovecraft's (1890–1937) early twentieth-century output and show the commensurate landscape of racism in Jim Crow–era America that creates a quintessentially Weird landscape.

Setting aside the evangel of increasing self-awareness, this second level of Life Mystery can be clinically misdirected beyond misbalancing the individual, societal, and environmental considerations. Another psychotherapeutic danger at this second level of Life Mysteries that can pull it back to a muddled version of the first puzzle level comes in using a formulaic approach to a "theory of cure." A theory of cure is what one thinks makes the patient "better." Both the patient and the therapist bring conscious and unconscious theories of cure with them into the consulting room. Treatment may involve some lengthy discussions and negotiations about what patients overtly describe as their sense of how therapy works. Treatment may also involve patients realizing that they have covertly or implicitly been holding out for some particular event (e.g., "closure," "catharsis," a "recovered memory") that, in actuality, may never happen or may not really provide any direct relief or resolution to their struggles. For that matter, a formulaic "theory of pathology" can be equally at issue in treatment. A theory of pathology addresses the question of "what's wrong." This involves a sense of the fundamental cause of the suffering and likely entails some sense of what sort of theory of cure, if any, will be necessary to address it. Yet the therapist and patient can conspire together to pin the patient's suffering onto an overly adroit explanation that distracts away from the current responsibility for change that lies with the patient.

A formulaic approach to theory of cure or pathology betrays real Mysteries when the therapist has a prefabricated approach to apply to all patients. In this case, "treatment" becomes a preordained ritual orchestrated to achieve a fixed solution. Though they may use the language of individuality, growth, wellness, and health, these therapeutic abuses are anything but. Notably, the clinical professions seem to have feared the reality of the unknown and engaged in rampant mass projection of their fears and failures onto the marginalized. Today, there can be no doubt that the history of psychiatry and clinical psychology portrays an exercise in reinforcing White, middle-class, heteronormative, cisgender male supremacy. The soul-crushingly inequitable application of more severe diagnoses and more drastic treatment measures to those not fitting the profession's normative biases bears witness to this history. And the legacy of this history continues to haunt the profession.

Leaving aside the mass cultural bigotry embodied in doing treatment *to* rather than *with* someone, formulaic treatment can hide behind any overly facile sorting of clients into types. Even if there is a menu of possible resolutions rather than only one, therapists still violate the complexity and specificity of the patient if they impose their expectation onto—into—the patient. To be clear, this is a long-standing form of gaslighting that passes for "psychotherapy." That is not to say that the patient will not be changed or believe themselves to have been "helped" or even "cured." The process of this kind of prescribed (pseudo)depth therapy initiates patients into a particular cult of self-definition, world definition, relationships definition, and problem definition, simultaneously providing patients with the necessary *pharmakon*—poison and cure—to "grow" and "work through" their defined suffering, however long that takes.

Though they may pose as deeper life lessons, the imposition of these facile explanations into the patient's complex narrative turns their pathos into bathos— cheap and tawdry digestible therapeutic pablum. Here, the therapist's impositions render the complexity of the patient's specific suffering and lifeworld into mere complications that do not yield a greater unfolding whole but, instead, a reduced— but defined—fragment. It is simply a larger equation to be solved on that first level of puzzles and riddles.

Miéville (2012) warns of this type of "essentialism" in his critiques of Freud and Kristeva. The reader senses that Miéville does not specifically object to the possibility that one may indeed have Freudian, Kristevian, or perhaps Kleinian unconscious conflicts enacted in, for instance, horror. Indeed, classically psychoanalytic incestuous themes show up frequently in brooding Gothic horror.

Various monstrous permutations of the *vagina dentata* appear throughout many versions of horror fiction, giving Kristevians plenty of abject material on which to chew. And Kleinian splits, doubles, and doppelgangers can be archly uncanny in any landscape. Utilizing a feminist expression of such currents, Clover (1992) transformed horror scholarship as she broached the slasher subgenre of horror films and introduced the "final girl" to the argot of criticism. Creed (1996/2015) extends this discourse with the addition of Kristeva's abjection.

Miéville (2012) readily admits that many monsters are understandable through these lenses. But the very act of explication may well dodge the power of the uncanny and be more of a defense against its invitation into a different way of living and knowing. Moreover, although a wide range of configurations may bring the uncanny with them, they are, in Miéville's formulation, ultimately not the unknowable. Miéville not only refutes that the unknown known of the uncanny can be so specifically and universally attributed but also questions whether these species of hauntological uncanniness explain our human condition. Miéville refuses to allow the truly unknowable to be reduced to facile, individually focused unconscious mechanisms. By narrowing the scope of the "uncanny" itself to be a hauntological confrontation with the unknown known, and thus only one species of encounter with the unknown, Miéville moves to assert the abcanny to characterize the encounter with the truly unknowable.

Ultimate Mysteries

Each of us makes our way through our days utilizing a reassuringly effective set of maps. Thus schematized, uncertainties become simple questions: agree or disagree; left or right; stop or go; steak, chicken, or veggie burger; and so on. So long as the maps are seemingly comprehensive and don't have too many gaps between them, the vast majority of individuals are blithely content to operate as though the maps are the territory to such an extent that they do not believe there are such things as "maps." I do not intend to necessarily dive into the map/territory discourse started by Korzybski (1933), beyond noting that these long-standing discussions do not often discuss the uncanny experience of when the map and the territory inevitably and unsettlingly diverge . . . unless you are reading Jorge Luis Borges (1899–1986).

For many, important life transitions mean changing maps. My self-map may change, my map of the world and how it works may alter, and my ability to conclusively map others may tatter. From living a contentedly mapped life in the puzzle level of mystery, map-changing can serve to invite one into the second level of Life Mysteries. After all, one of those life lessons is that "things change." Yet this second level still sits within schematics, no matter how wise or humble. That is, most archetypes are still rather jealous gods—entrapping in their complete worldviews and need for devotion.

What of those portions of the map that famously admit, "Here there be monsters"? More importantly, how might we come to know that the territory we currently occupy is, in fact, not mapped? Most radically, is any territory actually, adequately mapped or mappable? What are those experiences which bring us face-to-face with those most unsettling of encounters?

With ultimate Mysteries, one encounters total epistemological frontiers. Here lies the unknown that is—at least for now—unknowable. In detective fiction and the art of two worlds colliding, one can have all three levels of mysteries—one often giving way to another. But few stories sit comfortably with these final unknowables as the ultimate arc. A McGuffin—some sought after relic, cursed book, destination, or answer—may pose as an unknowable unknown, but McGuffins operate to advance plots and character development, not challenge their audiences with unfathomable frontiers.

The Romantics, in fear that the consummation of the Enlightenment's rationality in the Industrial Revolution would render the world a trivial and petty place, introduced the sublime as a foil to a worldview of mechanization, rationality, progress, and commodification. The sublime was distinct in that it offered a type of powerful aesthetic experience that was startling, unsettling, and served to deeply relativize the individual, the human, and civilization, to the extent that it was often no longer beautiful in any traditional sense. For the Romantics, nature provided the most striking examples: epic landscapes, roiling seas, natural disasters. One might think that the power of a tornado, for instance, should place the sublime firmly in the previous level's Natural Mysteries, and if one can compartmentalize a tornado in a box on a shelf labeled "examples of the sublime that I should respect and often avoid," then it may well be. (I've read many well-crafted student essays that assert that thrillers and horror films serve as a ritual to encapsulate the terrifying and unspeakable into the screen like a strange demonic binding.) Nevertheless, direct relationship to the sublime does not simply make one wiser. It deeply destabilizes one specifically in this moment—it may even undo time and space in the convenient ways with which one has taken them up.

Mark Freeman, in his *Toward the Psychological Humanities: A modest manifesto for the future of psychology* (2023), enshrines "openness to mystery" as the first attribute of his vision of a psychology rooted not in the natural sciences, in isolation from the rest of the academy and life, but in its rich origins in inquiry, philosophy, the arts, theology, poetics, and more—that is, the humanities writ large. To state it more clearly, our very humanity rests not in our certainties. Perhaps we are least human when we are most certain. Freeman advances with this first tenet that psychology will only truly serve its subject of the human when it admits that humans are fundamentally, ontologically in relationship to Mystery.

This deepest level of Mystery occupies the rest of this chapter. Beginning by interrogating examples from film and fiction, the examination moves to Freud's uncanny, Kristeva's abject, Heidegger's uncanny, and finally, Miéville's abcanny. From there, Lovecraft and Ligotti will offer insight into how one portrays and responds to the Weird's revelation of the abcanny. Finally, the chapter concludes with thoughts on how the abcanny can influence a range of disciplines and practices, returning to the crumbling theater for one last scene.

Some Fictional Examples

If this chapter is to truly start to limn the edges of the encounter with the unknowable, I need to interrogate sources that unapologetically confront their audiences with the truly alien. To dive more deeply into these fathomless waters, I present some examples of fiction that offer a means by which to think through some key descriptors of an encounter with the inscrutably alien. Starting with Russian cinema from the early 1970s and tracking Weird horror themes since then, this list is not exhaustive. Instead, these are some key examples that can facilitate discussion and clarification of what role the inscrutably alien can play in speculative fiction. These various examples build toward Garland's *Annihilation* (2018), which integrates many of the central themes.

Solaris *(1972) and* Stalker *(1979)*

Russian director Andrei Tarkovsky released *Solaris* in 1972. It was his third feature film. Artful, understated, and brooding, the film has many enigmas embedded in it. Tarkovsky presents a distant world called Solaris that is itself, seemingly, the alien. A space station occupied by scientists orbits Solaris. The planet would appear to be fully sentient and deeply telepathic yet, unto itself, incomprehensible and inscrutable to the humans. Initially, Solaris sends "guests"—creations from the station's occupants' memories—into the midst of the station's crew. The guests are initially unaware of their ex nihilo creation by Solaris as fully formed humans. The protagonist is a psychologist sent to make some sense of the station's descent into an expressionist filmscape. By the end, the psychologist appears on a sort of memory island on the surface of Solaris's swirling seas. Tarkovsky embeds themes of grief, loss, angst, longing, nostalgia, regret, and even questioning the reality of one's own existence. The ostensibly human characters encounter what is certainly unknown—and may well be unknowable to the human kind of consciousness—and spiral into strange existential reveries.

To apply the levels of mysteries, Tarkovsky's (1972) characters encounter the unknown—the third level of Ultimate Mysteries—and find themselves thrust into the second level of Life Mysteries with deeply existential themes. Although the scientists—the psychologist included—desperately try to turn the whole experience into a puzzle mystery, they themselves prevent this reduction from successfully happening in the very specificity of their human experiences. The space station is a sort of ego figure trying to puzzle its way through the incomprehensible that bubbles up from below in the form of hauntological figures from the past.

But is Solaris truly incomprehensible? The viewer wonders if the planet is not simply trying to communicate. Or perhaps the planet is, by human standards, more malignant and wants to entrap the human consciousnesses in its uncanny simulations of human life. One could reduce this all down to Solaris being a substitute for the unconscious, but that may miss a more startling frontier than merely one's own unknown knowns. Tarkovsky (1972) offers the audience enough possibilities that

Solaris might best merit the label "not-yet-known" with the possibility of becoming known. Nevertheless, the kind of encounter humans have with this planet-being deeply unsettles humans in their existential condition.

Revisiting themes from *Solaris* (Tarkovsky, 1972), with the 1979 release of *Stalker*, Tarkovsky allows the unknown to become more fundamentally unknowable. A proscribed Zone has emerged within a bleak, colorless Soviet landscape. Nature overgrows the Zone and colors it in rich, deep greens. The titular stalker is a tracker, a guide, and something of a shaman. Stalkers smuggle people into this Zone, which is startlingly Other. Visitors must follow strange paths determined not by rational logic—the path to a desired point is never a direct line in the Zone. But here, Tarkovsky presents no alien planet, no identifiable supernatural phenomena, and no science fiction scenario to explain this inscrutable Zone. Nevertheless, the stalker and his two charges find their innermost selves exposed in this encounter with: is it the real? If this is the real, then it is in the context of an outside world that has become startlingly unreal, colorless, and lifeless.

With *Stalker* (1979), Tarkovsky offers a deep meditation on what remains stubbornly inscrutable. Once the stalker and his companions come to the center of the Zone—the Room—there is no numinous, glowing, inexplicable supernatural phenomena. Though it has an ambiguous reputation of granting what one desires, the Room is only another chamber, its floor covered in several inches of water. The three characters choose not to enter, each for their own reasons. Each is unsettled, perhaps transformed, but the narrative to describe the encounter is ragged, slippery, and word-shy. They cannot stay in the Zone. They return to a world that they know not only cannot make sense of the Zone but also scarcely has anyone left in it who can travel to it. The true Ultimate Mysteries appear as a deep phenomenology—a confrontation with what constitutes every instant of life yet from which we have become inextricably alienated. But the second level of Life Mysteries is such a tangled maze of speculation, ideologies, and fears that nearly everyone is thrust back farther into the deadness of the first level of a colorless but explicable world. Here, Tarkovsky makes a case that retroactively casts a different light on *Solaris* (1972). In *Stalker* (1979), the personal unconscious cannot be the ultimate explanation. The Zone and its Room may be turned into angst-ridden Rorschach tests, but their reality exceeds these projections.

Alien (1979)

Released on the same day as Tarkovsky's *Stalker*—May 25, 1979—Ridely Scott's *Alien* presents oddly similar themes in a radically different film. Into a hyper-commercialized twenty-second-century galaxy in which multi-world corporations engage in (neo)neocolonialism, all wonder and shininess in space travel are long-lost in the grimy banality of interstellar wage slavery. Manipulated by their corporate overlords, a crew becomes the victims of what would seem to be the ultimate predator, capable of turning its victims into mere hatcheries for the next generation of nightmare creatures.

Scott's (1979) original film left many questions unanswered and, combined with the utter terror in the face of the titular alien, brings audiences to the threshold of the abject. There is plenty of body horror and, with only a cat and Sigourney Weaver's character, Ripley, surviving, the unspeakable horror of death's visceral immediacy is palpable for the viewer. In a sense, the colorless world outside of *Stalker*'s (Tarkovsky, 1979) Zone matches the gritty functionality of the spaceship *Nostromo* that Scott (1979) offers his audience. Scott gives capitalism as the fundamental motivation for any human actions, with "science" as a secondary means of achieving acquisitive ends. Tarkovsky (1979) offers a wonderless, simple, materialistic world. But where the Zone's wonder and the everyday numinous weave throughout Tarkovsky's work, Scott's (1979) alien is the darkest of shadows cast everywhere by pointless existence. The alien is inexplicable in that it is not a predator in the sense of a lion, python, or shark. Those creatures kill to eat. The alien is more like a virus writ large—it kills to replicate. Although it is somewhere between bipedal and quadrupedal, H. R. Giger's design of the alien—called a "xenomorph" within the larger *Alien* mythos—deliberately unsettles audience's categories for even the most frightening of terrestrial creatures. The alien could be an avatar of death, putting it in the darkest corners of the second level of Mystery. So too does the body horror—violating all boundaries and integrities—place it into the abject at the ichorous edges of the second level of Mystery. But does the alien, in its inexplicability, undo meaning? To the extent that it does, it hints at a pitch-black Ultimate Mystery—the unknowable as unspeakable, quite possibly Miéville's abcanny.

In a 2000 interview with Bould, Miéville cites *Alien* (Scott, 1979) and *Alien3* (Fincher, 1992) as among his favorite films. Miéville (Bould, 2000) admits that, as he ages, he increasingly dislikes the rest of the films in the series—by the time of the interview, there were already four. The other films focus heavily on larger plots, machinations, and explanations. In a sense, they attempt to turn what Miéville takes up as hints of the abcanny into merely scary unknown knowns that rapidly become grizzly known knowns. In 2000, Miéville was 8 years away from publicly coining "abcanny" (Miéville, 2008), and 12 years from elaborating on the concept (Miéville, 2012). Nevertheless, as early as his interview with Bould (2000), Miéville was thinking about what encounters truly defy meaning.

The Thing *(1982)*

In an era when slasher films and their sequels dominated horror films, John Carpenter chose a different path with *The Thing* (1982). An alien life-form makes its way through an Antarctic base by absorbing and imitating the inhabitants. Soon, no one knows who to trust, and the film ends with the two survivors—potentially themselves extensions of the alien—seemingly agreeing to freeze to death to contain the phenomenon.

Like *Alien* (Scott, 1979) before it, *The Thing* (Carpenter, 1982) gives its audience plenty of body horror with writhing masses that present glimpses of familiar body parts in disturbingly uncanny fashion. One can easily get to Kristeva's abject, in which something pre-egoic is threatening to undo basic identity and bodily integrity, and Butler makes just that case in a 2000 essay. The infection-like vectoring of the alien life-form does not offer audiences an easy target for their fear. Thus, anxiety abounds in the film, floating to every dark corner, reticent character, or unexplained sound. The audience assumes that characters know if they are actually the alien and not an originally human life-form, but that is never conclusively established. Thus, viewers begin by asking, "Who is human?" "How do we know?" "How do they know?" And as the plot unfolds, if the audience has successfully identified with the doomed crew, one cannot help but ask, "Am I human?" and "How would I know?" To the extent that one is left not merely unsettled by an upwelling of identity-blurring disgust as in Kristeva's abjection but can no longer comfortably say what one knows or doesn't, then the abcanny has successfully made its (un)presence (un)known. Carpenter offers audiences a massive spacecraft buried under ice to anchor some science fiction sensibilities but then has a character deduce that the layering of the ice implies that the craft has been there for over 100,000 years. Even the familiar trope of the crashed alien craft becomes vertiginously unsettling as the scale of time relativizes human history.

In the Mouth of Madness (1994)

As noted by Topolsky (2012), Carpenter conceptualizes In the Mouth of Madness (1994) as the final installment in his Apocalypse Trilogy, following The Thing (1982) and Prince of Darkness (1987). Interpreting a creature feature like The Thing (1982), as in the preceding text, to raise fundamental questions about epistemology and existence might seem a stretch unto itself, until one views Mouth of Madness's (1994) far more overt pursuit of those themes. Sam Neill offers the audience John Trent, a noir-style detective with rationalist convictions. He is a chain-smoking insurance investigator, initially unimpressed with the writings of the Weird fiction author he is sent to find in order to secure the manuscript for his final novel. But from the first images of the film, the viewer knows that things have gone terribly wrong. To open the film, Trent is in a Hollywood cliché of an insane asylum—one that, by the end of the film, he escapes, only to wander into an abandoned cinema showing the very film we, the audience, are just completing viewing. Between these frame narrative anchors, Trent tells his tale. As he does so, he slips back and forth between reading horror fiction and being in the story, dreaming and waking, the present and the future, speaking to the author and being written by the author, and more. At one point, Trent literally tears through a wall made of pages of the sought-after and unsettlingly unavoidable McGuffin text to find himself on the edge of an abyss which paradoxically becomes his means of escape. Even the film's title is an intertextual homage to Lovecraft's novella At the Mountains of Madness, originally written in 1931, serialized in 1936, and frequently added to collections since then (e.g., Lovecraft, 2008). Carpenter (1994) offers the sort of levels of reality-blurring for which Christopher Nolan has become famous; but in Carpenter's hands, he adds an extra fictive layer, as all of it has an element of tongue-in-cheek. Carpenter makes the self-awareness of so much of horror by the 1990s into a postmodern campiness. The audience can do little but hysterically laugh along with Trent as he watches his descent into madness play out before him as the film concludes. This is, indeed, the ultimate, apotheotic, autophagic apocalypse of horror text eating itself.

Carpenter's (1994) McGuffin text must itself blur between a sought-after manuscript, an already-released book, a film adaptation, and the film the audience watches. Within the film's storyline, reading the novel drives its readers murderously mad since the text seems to come to narrate the life of the reader while reading. Carpenter portrays some psychically infected readers with double irises, as though the very exposure to the intertextuality of the book creates an untenable double consciousness, with madness as the inevitable result. Unquestionably, Carpenter has made meaning at stake. Where are the characters to stand? Where is the audience to stand? With a wink, Carpenter offers his audience the necessary campiness to reassure them that it is all in good fun. This isn't an art film, after all, is it? One does not leave a horror film questioning the nature of reality and narrative, does one? This was not a philosophy lecture. But then this archcampiness so easily adopted by the audience allows the film to slip past the audience's filters as the ultimate psychic contagion. What is the audience left to believe? What *is* left to believe? Has the audience actually left the theater? Has the audience left the film?

Whether Carpenter (1994) succeeds in taking his audience to the true edge of meaning, and thus blows through the second level of Mysteries to the third, depends greatly on the specific viewer. Nevertheless, the film updates a classic trope of Weird fiction: madness. In the original iterations of the Weird, madness is the natural by-product of even the briefest insinuation of how things truly are in the cosmos. As discussed in later text, Lovecraft has a deeply misanthropic, cosmic pessimism. Humans are small, recently evolved blips in a scale of time which hosts epic, eons-spanning beings whose very existence indicts humans' logic, consciousness, being, significance, and sanity. Carpenter brings in elements of the postmodern text-within-a-text-within-a-text story structure to bridge Weird madness to postmodern disorientation, and, with the addition of camp self-awareness, offers his audience a chance to laugh while it happens. Whether or not the Weird horror trope of madness has any intersection with Foucault's (1961/2006) multiple types of madness—such as the madness to label others as "mad" and the madness inherent in all humans—remains for other authors to examine.

Contact *(1997)*

Arguably the most benign entry on this list, Zemeckis's *Contact* (1997) offers no grotesquerie or overly ambiguous artful sequences. Instead, Zemeckis presents dialogue that holds the audience's hands as it walks them through the ethical and scientific landscape it explores. Based on Carl Sagan's 1985 novel, Zemeckis (1997) presents aliens who transmit encoded instructions for building a device which will allow them to welcome an explorer from Earth. When Jodi Foster's character, Dr.

Ellie Arroway, eventually goes through the device, those observing see an elaborate lightshow with some gravitational anomalies, but little else. Arroway's capsule appears to have never gone anywhere. Yet Arroway describes—and the audience has seen—an elaborate series of provocative images as Arroway slips through multiple wormholes, seeing alien worlds and a cosmic event that leaves her ecstatic. Finally, like Solaris (Tarkovsky, 1972) creating guests, the aliens (Zemeckis, 1997) appear to draw from Arroway's memories and offer her a familiar beach, but with a starscape from their corner of the galaxy. The aliens use a recreation of Arroway's long-dead father as an intermediary between their highly advanced intelligence and humans' limitations. They explain that this contact is only a first step and that she will have to return to Earth with most of her questions unanswered. Moreover, her various recording devices yield only static back on Earth. Nevertheless, as two government officials note, it is 18 hours' worth of static.

By offering audiences Arroway's journey through wormholes and ecstasy at glowing cosmic visions, Zemeckis (1997) presents a far less enigmatic version of Kubrick's (1968) "Jupiter and Beyond the Infinite" sequence. Zemeckis (1997) updates the first-contact enigma to be more of a plucky science story. Yet one aspect of the film pulls the narrative away from a mere puzzle-level mystery to be solved. Beyond the 18 hours of nothing, Arroway has only her powerful memories of the encounter. Matthew McConaughey has played a charming Christian philosopher, Palmer Joss, throughout the film. A close friend of Arroway, Joss has tried to challenge her to not exclude all religious or theological considerations in the buildup to the alien encounter. Now, with only her memories and emotional transformation to guide her, Arroway finds herself admitting that she must appeal to others' faith that she did indeed have this experience. Joss finds himself offering her exactly that faith as they reunite. Arroway is not "undone" by the experience. She is not driven to Weird madness. But Zemeckis and Sagan (1985) introduce a type of deeply transformative wonder as a fundamental motivating force for the pursuit of science. As such, *Contact* stretches beyond a simple science adventure, placing it in the second level of Mystery, gazing with wide eyes toward the third.

Under the Skin *(2013)*

In Glazer's 2013 film, an alien, played by Scarlett Johansson, travels about Glasgow and the Scottish Highlands, abducting lonely Scottish men. Taking them to an abandoned house, she lures them into a black abyss, where they are eventually flayed and processed into goo. The story unto itself is a new take on an old Hollywood story: an alien/zombie/vampire takes on the comely form of an Earth woman and draws men to their doom. But Glazer and Johansson bring something far bleaker to the story. Johansson's delivery is so flat and alien that even her first fully nude scene on film is notably unsexy. By the end of the film, the audience sees that the alien has been mostly wearing a skin suit and that underneath is a black, featureless form.

Glazer (2013) refuses to give the audience easy narrative explanations, with any dialogue serving as something more like "human noises" and the alien's imitations thereof. Along the way, the alien has become increasingly confused by her—its?—encounters. Has she developed empathy? The audience is given little reason to think so. Perhaps something more like discontinuities in her narrative have made it increasingly difficult for her to seamlessly pursue what is clearly her mission to harvest humans. By the end, a logger attempts to rape the alien and, seeing what is "under the skin," burns her alive.

Glazer (2013) offers a pervasively uncanny vision. This is uncanniness that has as much to do with the uncanny valley as with any psychodynamic explanation. An audience could simply take up the themes and events Glazer portrays as horrifying realizations; but what Glazer and Johansson accomplish unsettles the audience significantly more profoundly. Since seduction and violence are pervasive themes, it is surprising that a traditional Freudian interpretation does not inhere smoothly to the film. That humans are turned into something like a consumable product and that the alien wears a skin suit, perhaps one could move to Kristeva's abject. Conceivably, that sort of ego-unsettling encounter with the disgusting comes closer to accounting for the film's tone. But the overall effect—and affect—of the film as it defies empathy, undoes expectations, and leaves the audience in bleak bewilderment is closer to the meaning-eating resonances of the abcanny.

Arrival (2016)

Like *Contact* (Zemeckis, 1997) before it, *Arrival* (Villeneuve, 2016) offers viewers a scientist-protagonist whose own story intertwines with the process of communing with the alien. With *Arrival*, Amy Adams gives the audience linguist Dr. Louise Banks, whose own story cannot be understood aright until the audience has undergone the same transformation she and the world must undergo. Although the audience first sees Banks mourning the loss of her daughter, by the end of the film, viewers come to realize the daughter's life and death at age 12 are in the future to the action of the film. Coming to understand the deep structure of the aliens' language rewrites the communicant's temporality in a startling application of the Sapir–Whorf hypothesis's linguistic relativity. This profound transformation is the aliens' gift to humanity, one that humanity could only receive if they allowed themselves to collaborate between nations and share the various pieces of the alien message offered from each of their 12 spacecraft.

In one sense, Villeneuve (2016) has created a variant of the hero's journey. The hero must venture to a magical land and come back with a boon for humanity. Moreover, the hero is transformed in this journey. Yet Banks's transformation is so profound, fundamentally altering her ontology, that one questions whether one can meaningfully say it is she who has come back from the alien encounter or some new Banks. The dark version of this tale is something like a failed hero's journey, in which the protagonist returns deeply corrupted into something fundamentally other than how they began the journey. (Often, that storyline must continue with a new protagonist attempting to not repeat the same mistake and either save the previous failed hero or defeat them.) But Villeneuve's version avoids this deep transformation being an unspeakable corruption by involving a profound sacrifice necessary for true transformation. (In the film's knotted timeline, the love interest with whom she finishes the film will become the father of their child, who will be born with an incurable disease, which Banks already knew because of her time-altering linguistic epiphany, leading to the father leaving Banks not only for not having shared her foreknowledge but also for having chosen to bring a child into the world to die.)

How profound the audience believes Banks's (Villeneuve, 2016) transformation is depends in part on how radically Other they allow the aliens and their transtemporal consciousness to be. The aliens are massive, seven-limbed, cephalopod-like creatures that must live in a distinctly different atmosphere and write in a sort of recursive circular script looking something like Zen ink drawings. Their ships resemble massive, smoothed river rocks. Villeneuve goes to great lengths to convey how fundamentally incomprehensible they are. Thus, one cannot take this story up as a mere first-level puzzle, in which humans apply rationality and computing power to solve the problem. Banks exhausts those efforts relatively early in the story. We learn that, even before first meeting the aliens, she has already begun to have dreams and memories of that daughter she has not yet had. Thus, she has become entangled on the second level of Life Mysteries from the very start—although the audience does not yet know this. The aliens' fundamental inscrutability remains. That is, humans, as we know them, cannot, in fact, understand these aliens. Humans must necessarily make nothing short of an ontological transformation—evolution?—allowing the language to existentially reconstitute them in order to comprehend the language. It would thus seem that, although benign in its own way, it is in allowing the encounter to be fully with the abcanny that the human is undone, remade, and becomes other to what it once was.

In 2011, Miéville published another award-winning novel, *Embassytown*. In this novel, Miéville presents aliens who use multiple mouths, rituals, and other exotic extremities to communicate and create their language. Humans have used genetically engineered twins to simulate the simultaneous streams of sounds to communicate with these aliens. But when humans send a non-identical pair of interlocutors and furthermore begin introducing various levels of abstractions, metaphors, and untruths into their speech, all hell breaks loose in the alien culture.

Arrival (Villeneuve, 2016) is based on Ted Chiang's 1998 short story "Story of Your Life" (1998/2002), the original story for the film preceding Miéville's *Embassytown* (2011) by roughly 13 years. Nevertheless, the idea that language and its deep structures contain fundamental fibers of reality had adequately established itself to become an intriguing focus of speculative fiction—where intriguing philosophical and, in this case, philological ideas go to grow.

Annihilation (2018) and the Synthesis of the Weird

One of the intriguing attributes of most authors of the Weird—whatever era or version of it they may promulgate—is their scrupulous attention to a theory of horror, and specifically of the Weird. This scholarly commitment goes back at least to Lovecraft and his correspondences with contemporary authors. This theoretical commitment continues today with Miéville and Ligotti presenting their ideas about how the Weird works in fictional and nonfictional forms. But it is Jeff VanderMeer who has, perhaps, made some of the greatest contributions over the past decades to advance the writing and thinking about the Weird through his critical essays, his collections of other authors' works, and his own singular vision presented in such startling creations as his *Area X: The Southern Reach Trilogy* (2014). In 2019, Ersoy published an article about VanderMeer's *Southern Reach* (2014), focusing on the first book, *Annihilation*. In the essay, Ersoy (2019) makes the case that the work is archly abcanny for a range of reasons rooted in VanderMeer's very clear commitment to give literary voice to important themes not only of the Weird but also of the current tenuous human condition. The assertion is not surprising, given that VanderMeer (2008/2011) and Miéville have had ongoing conversations going back at least to 2008, when Miéville was first formulating his ideas of the abcanny.

Thus, when Alex Garland began working on a film treatment of a manuscript of the first book of the *Southern Reach* (VanderMeer, 2014), *Annihilation*, he drew upon the tone and setting of VanderMeer's text, but also a clear sense of the Weird shambling about in VanderMeer's work. Garland's film *Annihilation* (2018) presents Lena, an army veteran and cellular biologist, played by Natalie Portman. A meteor has struck the Florida coastline and created an expanding zone called the Shimmer. Viewers first meet Lena being interviewed after her return from the Shimmer. Like *In the Mouth of Madness* (Carpenter, 1994), the audience for *Annihilation* (Garland, 2018) know, from the start, that things have gone very wrong. We learn that Lena's husband, Kane, was on a previous mission into the Shimmer and was the only one to return, after a year. Kane has no memory of the last year and soon needs intensive medical care. Lena joins a new expedition into the Shimmer. The mission, predictably, deteriorates quickly. People morph into plants, animals take on new unsettling and dangerous characteristics, and eventually, the human expedition has been reduced to only Lena, who enters the lighthouse, which has been the center of the phenomena. In the cave-like foundation of the lighthouse, Lena encounters an amorphous shimmering which offers a vast array of psychedelic fractal undulations. Absorbing a drop of Lena's blood, part of the shimmering coalesces into a quicksilver approximation of her that becomes increasingly doppelganger-like. The audience soon becomes unsure who is the original Lena. One of the Lenas tricks the other into seemingly self-annihilating with a phosphorous grenade. The remaining Lena leaves the Shimmer—which may have begun to dissipate. A Lena reunites with a Kane who now doubts if he is the original Kane. He asks if she is Lena, and although she does not answer, both of their irises shimmer as they embrace.

Because VanderMeer and Garland (2018) are so keenly theoretically aware of the Weird, the film blends many important themes from the history of Weird cinema and literature. Yet they manage to innovate and disturb in new ways. With the rest of this section, some comparisons between Garland's film and the previous examples can help situate our themes. But first, an unexpected connection to a modernist novel.

Garland's *Annihilation* (2018) made "the lighthouse" its goal throughout. In an unexpected Virginia Wolf connection, by the end of the story, Lena—whether original or doppelganger—can indeed state, in concert with Wolf's protagonist in *To the Lighthouse* (1927/1981), "I have had my vision" (p. 209). Indeed, Wolf's middle "Time Passes" section of the novel, in which the house, objects, landscape, and lighthouse experience the passage of time without any human presence, casts a fleeting gaze to the Weird which *Annihilation* (Garland, 2018) stares into as one comes to wonder if the landscape itself, perhaps even the lived world, has become the alien.

Garland (2018) offers that "vision" as a visually grand and unsettling psyche-delic sequence, like *2001*'s (Kubrick, 1968) "Jupiter and Beyond the Infinite." Except Garland's (2018) new birth is not Kubrick's (1968) Star Child but an am-biguous life-form that is itself unclear on its own status. Like in *Solaris* (Tarko-vsky, 1972), in *Annihilation* (Garland, 2018) humans are duplicated, created, and morphed, yet the creation is far less specific and bounded. Forms of life blend one into the next—plant or animal, intelligent or mimicking, dead or alive. Characters come back from these confrontations undone by the overwhelmingly abcanny, yet in a decidedly understated, almost-Sartrean form.

In its own unsettling way, the film *Annihilation* (Garland, 2018) could be profit-ably shown with *Stalker* (Tarkovsky, 1979). Both stories have a proscribed territory in which inexplicable phenomena occur with little to no comprehension outside of it of the rules by which this territory operates. Both stories involve expeditions with circuitous and ambiguous trajectories toward the center. Both stories have characters deeply unsettled and transformed in their encounters. But where one can take up Tarkovsky's work as the sad fate of a world deeply alienated from the numinous offered in every moment, Garland's (2018) film shows the apocalyptic, dark-numinous—"bad-numinous" in Miéville's (2008) terms—consequences of this estrangement's extended tenure. One can imagine the consequences of Tarko-vsky's (1979) scenario to be humans shuffling meekly through a bleak, colorless world, having forgotten how even to access life and wonder. In VanderMeer and Garland's (2018) vision, it seems unlikely that what will survive will actually be human anymore.

Although the whole landscape of *Annihilation* (Garland, 2018) offers ample op-portunity to undo the human characters who can "refract" in the Shimmer's alien force, specific unsettling predators do emerge. A skull-headed bear that can mimic the cries of team members creates a particularly tense and terrifying sequence. The humans transform—refract—between forms of life, including a revelation from a recovered video that a human's innards have been turned to a writhing, slither-ing mass. Thus, the kind of abject body horror that goes beyond slasher gore and begins to unsettle fundamental boundaries binds *Annihilation* and *Alien* (Scott, 1979). Garland's (2018) Weird resonances continue as the Shimmer can alter and, at the lighthouse, create doppelgangers that can leave the proscribed zone. Thus, Garland leaves the audience unclear on who was or now is still human, drawing upon themes at the center of Carpenter's *The Thing* (1982).

Garland's (2018) protagonist is taken beyond madness, as in *In the Mouth of Madness* (Carpenter, 1994), but rather than laughing hysterically, Garland's (2018) Lena endures, regardless of her ontological status. Although both films share a framing narrative of an interview of protagonists who have endured extreme situations, *Annihilation* is free from any campiness, has not a bit of kitsch, and could not even be accused of being cool. There is no breaking of the fourth wall, no overt intertextuality, no winking. The film is played straight, is deadly serious, and as such, is devastating.

It seems cruel to compare the unsettling darkness of *Annihilation* (Garland, 2018) to *Contact* (Zemeckis, 1997), since *Contact* is, ultimately, an optimistic film that attempts to reclaim themes of hope, wonder, and faith. Nevertheless, both films present an intrepid female scientist who has past struggles and losses which drive and color her quest. Both culminate with vibrant imagery which proves deeply transformative. And both films conclude by leaving the audiences to wonder what comes next now that the reality of the alien presence is undeniable yet has made contact in such unexpected ways.

Glazer's (2013) *Under the Skin* seems decidedly intimate in scope compared to Garland's (2018) vision. Glazer (2013) offers a small-scale incursion of aliens interested in something like harvesting a few forlorn Scotsmen, compared to Garland's (2018) planetary and ontological reformatting of Earth, life, and existence itself. Yet both films bring the viewer to the edge of inscrutability. The audience of both films finds questions about "why?" become twisted in the storylines in large part due to the delivery and ambiguity of boundaries. Portman often plays Lena as flat and interpersonally disengaged, which leaves the audience unclear on her motives or status. This uncertainty in the face of flattened affect parallels Glazer's (2013) and Johansson's artistic choices. Both films offer an amorphous, glistening alien figure as part of the climactic reveal, and both films make the revelation unsettlingly ambiguous.

Finally, the transformation of the protagonist in *Arrival* (Villeneuve, 2016) in which a fundamental aspect of the existential condition must alter resonates with Garland's (2018) blurring and eventual collapse of all edges of animate, inanimate, life, death, subject, and object. But where Villeneuve's (2016) vision ends with bittersweetness—a sacrifice for the sake of a new humanity—Garland's (2018) final message is likely the heralding of the end of humanity.

Some Further Examples

The Weird evolved over the course of the twentieth century and, in the twenty-first century, is now as likely to be found in campily self-conscious, postmodern productions, like Goddard and Whedon's *Cabin in the Woods* (2011), as it is to be in arthouse releases, like *Uzumaki* (Higochinsky, 2000). It is worth noting that *quirky* is not necessarily the same thing as Weird. For that matter, *weird* is not the same as Weird. Weird demands, however subtle, some elements of taking characters and audiences to the edges. That can, of course, happen with the uncanny, the abject, and as this chapter has been making the case, the abcanny. The deterioration of the capacity to make meaning is the key for the abcanny and brings with it the power of the Weird as it does so.

To this list we could easily add *District 9* (2009), in which Blomkamp presents powerful intercultural images of how alterity is a fluid boundary that can easily slip past our skin. Blomkamp offers the audience the alien as a refugee in South Africa and adds the further twist of having the Afrikaner human protagonist begin to turn into the alien.

Sorokin's *The Ice Trilogy* (2011) raises intriguing questions about interpretation. The reader, with a basic understanding of Russian history and current affairs, is left with a distinct impression that, were one to know more about such matters, perhaps from the inside, this story would reveal its secrets. Yet Sorokin has taken Russian history, Soviet ideology, and post-Soviet nationalism and added such inscrutable elements that the reader comes to see history and culture as truly capable of undoing the meanings we would think to inherit from them.

Aronovsky's π (1998) could also be added to this list. The ineffable, the irrational, the apotheotic pursuit of one's art, mental illness blurring with Weird madness, revelation, mysticism, math, the stock market, and Orthodox Judaism all swirl together in Aronovsky's first feature film. It would be kind to call the film's conclusion "ambiguous" when it is far easier to see it as quite bleak. Capitalist, religious, and mathematical forces have all taken the protagonist to a place where the implication of a great universal meaning has, in fact, annihilated any chance for the character to make his own meanings. Only the most symbolic interpretations could turn the protagonist's ultimate self-trepanation into anything other than a virtual suicide.

Nolan's *Interstellar* (2014) has already entered the discussion, as its imagery and themes belong in discussions of not only *2001: A Space Odyssey* (Kubrick, 1968) but also the legacy of science fiction that culminates in an epiphanic restructuring of self, narrative, and the universe. In a sense, films like *Interstellar* (Nolan, 2014), *Contact* (Zemeckis, 1997), and *Arrival* (Villeneuve, 2016) could be considered in a metamodern light, as they don't simply twist and undo our perceptions of reality in the postmodern sense but take this deconstruction as a means to new hope, wonder, and radical transformation.

Stranger Things (Duffer & Duffer, 2016–present) is garnering increasing scholarship. See, for example, Langley's (2023) collection of essays. However, the series' pastiche of horror tropes and conscientious nostalgia creates a haze through which it can be easy to lose sight of the references' origins. Having a monster called the "Mind Flayer"—albeit a reference originally from Dungeons & Dragons—clearly plays with classic Weird fiction themes of madness. The alternately playful and deadly serious tones of the series place it more in the lineage of *In the Mouth of Madness* (Carpenter, 1994). Like the camp self-awareness in Carpenter's work, *Stranger Things* (Duffer & Duffer, 2016–present) lets the nostalgia provide a smokescreen behind which the abcanny continues to threaten to indict the era portrayed, the portrayals from that era, and eventually, our own times.

Admittedly, in trying to nuance an understanding of what an approach to the abcanny means, I need to be careful not to automatically equate the state of un-knowing with an encounter with the unknowable. Many speculative fiction works play, with varying degrees of facility, with delaying "the big reveal." In most of those cases, breadcrumbs were, perhaps, left along the way which only show them-selves as such in hindsight. Nevertheless, is some of the joy of the pursuit, at least for some readers, in being placed firmly in relationship to the unknown and, thus, at least for a moment, the unknowable? Are audiences drawn to mysteries, mysti-cism, Weird fiction, and even puzzles because it awakens, for however briefly, an encounter with the unknowable? In its simplest form, I experience this as I pick up a fresh, unopened book that promises to take me on a journey I don't yet know. Nevertheless, various hauntological configurations of the unknown known and its uncanniness have been woven throughout this chapter so far that are not truly the abcanny. In order to best finally place the abcanny beyond the proper frontiers, Freud's uncanny, Kristeva's abject, and Heidegger's uncanny deserve more precise definition. But before those comparisons, a word on female protagonists in many of these examples.

A Feminist Post-Credit Scene

As the credits roll on this film reel of mostly cinematic examples, I cannot resist the convention of a post-credit scene, now past *de rigueur* and firmly cliché in superhero films. While reviewing a later draft of this chapter with me, my editorial assistant for the first stages of this volume, Emma Baranowski, smirked and said, "You know, a majority of your examples have women protagonists or prominent characters, usually in peril, written and directed by men." I laughed. She laughed. And then we wondered what to do with that.

To give some context, this sample is not unusual. The majority of films over the history of cinema have been written and directed by men. Though the repre-sentation of women in the industry has increased, most writers and directors are still men.

When discussing Jung's structure of psyche with my students, I sometimes glibly ask if men can actually write about women or if we are merely viewing a series of anima projections. That's a cheap shot to be sure, but when it comes to the encounter with the ineffable, unspeakable, or sublime as a distinctly hostile en-counter, are we perhaps describing a particular phallocentric resistance to the void? Does the Oedipal conflict, so deeply embedded in a striving, grasping, violent, conquering, possessive culture, render an encounter with the unknown inherently, as Miéville says, "bad-numinous"?

Moreover, with the number of women-in-peril in these examples, is the Weird asking to have a fresh take on Clover's (1992) "last girl"? The preceding examples do not follow one narrative arc for the female characters. Some of the women barely survive, others are overcome by madness, yet some survive fundamentally transformed. A discourse on gender and the abcanny will form a critical piece of a scholarship of the abcanny. For now, the question will need to remain, and the discussion will move on to theoretical formulations of the Weird encounter.

Freud and the Uncanny

In his 1919 essay "The Uncanny" (SE XVII), Freud tackles the not-at-homeness, or un-homely, intended in the German word *unheimliche*. Freud's argument is nuanced and complex, with intriguing examples throughout. Yet ultimately Freud summarizes his stance with regard to the uncanny:

> We can understand why linguistic usage has extended das Heimliche [home-like] into its opposite, das Unheimliche; for this uncanny is in reality nothing new or alien, but something which is familiar and old-established in the mind and which has become alienated from it only through the process of repression.

> (Freud et al., 1953, SE XVII, p. 241)

Thus, as Miéville (2012) concurs, Freud's *uncanny* is the *unknown known*. The uncanny is simultaneously familiar and seemingly alien—it is the alienation of the familiar, rendered such by the twisting of the ego through the defenses that impotently try to disavow, disown, and repress. The only product is a haunted lived world.

In explaining the mechanics, the psychodynamics of the uncanny, Freud is not automatically populating the unconscious with specific contents. Nevertheless, his dream interpretations, case studies, lectures, and writings do establish a vocabulary and an inventory of typical unconscious contents beyond which Freud is loath to admit. Yet within Freud's writings, an intriguing prospect of something beyond the tripartite structure of id, ego, and superego appears. Inspired by a letter from Roman Rolland (1866–1944), Freud allows for the possibility of the "oceanic feeling" in his 1927 work *Future of an Illusion* and his 1929 publication *Civilization and Its Discontents* (SE XXI). The oceanic feeling bears mentioning since it allows for a pre-egoic possibility that is potentially wonder-filled and linked to the numinous and mystical. But what Jung will spend copious scholarly and personal work to explore, Freud ultimately links to a resonance with the undifferentiated consciousness of the infant. For Freud, this is likely not as dismissive as one might think, and many Freudian apologists have seized upon the oceanic feeling as offering the possibility that Freud's anti-theism and dour attitude to religion need not be a whole-sheet dismissal of mystical experiences.

On the darker side of the equation, Freud can be read to explain most of the madness-anxiety found in Weird fiction and present in examples of the abcanny to be a deteriorative anxiety in the face of being drowned in the unconscious. That is to say, psychosis.

Kristeva and the Abject

At the time of its publication, and for many subsequent years, Kristeva's theory of the abject was arguably the single most important contribution to the study of horror—both fictional and ostensibly nonfictional. With *The Powers of Horror: An Essay on Abjection* (1980/1982), Kristeva crafted a structural explanation for a type of ontological disgust at that which indicts our very existence. No mere memento mori, the abject does not promise eventual annihilation; it undermines the ground upon which we stand:

> A wound with blood and pus, or the sickly, acrid smell of sweat, of decay, does not signify death. In the presence of signified death—a flat encephalograph, for instance—I would understand, react, or accept. No, as in true theater, without makeup or masks, refuse and corpses show me what I permanently thrust aside in order to live. These body fluids, this defilement, this shit are what life withstands, hardly and with difficulty, on the part of death. There, I am at the border of my condition as a living being.
>
> (p. 3)

Kristeva hints that this may indeed be an encounter with Lacan's *real*—an inaccessible reality that our self, in its imaginary and symbolic orders, can never access. But Kristeva is also, in concert with preceding object relations theorists, simply moving the timeline back from Freud's Oedipal conflict to basic differentiation from the mother in the earliest and most visceral of senses. Thus, what Freud may hint at with his references to the oceanic feeling may be experienced by Kristeva as far more threatening.

In multiple sources, Miéville (e.g., 2012, and interview with Tranter, 2012) goes to great lengths to distinguish the abcanny from the abject. He does not deny the power of the abject but clarifies:

> I actually want quite carefully to distinguish the "ab-" in "abcanny" from the "abject," at least in the Kristevan sense. Which is counterintuitive given how flabby, gloopy, disgusting so much of the Weird is—so abject in that very broadly descriptive sense, certainly. But I'm skeptical about Kristeva's model as a heuristic so wouldn't want my abcanny to be read as particularly Kristevan. . . . [T]he abcanny represents . . . that which shriekingly declaims that it has *never been known*, is beyond any notions of repression, could not have been known to be repressed in the first place.
>
> (pp. 424–425)

Thus, in Miéville's estimation, the abcanny will need to occupy a radically different position relative to the self than what Kristeva proposes with the abject. Nevertheless, for many psychoanalytically and/or postmodern-minded theorists, Kristeva's abject offered an essential step toward the frontier that Miéville claims to point beyond.

Heidegger and the Uncanny

Martin Heidegger's (1889–1976) major work, *Being and Time* (1927/1996), is dense and requires significant study simply to conceive of an interpretation. In the world of existentialism, and in Heidegger's specific existential phenomenology, it is a seminal work that draws upon specific currents of philosophy stretching into ancient Greek, early Christian, and the first threads of what would come to be called early existentialism and even postmodernism. Yet Heidegger the person, and certainly Heidegger in public remarks and writings, creates ethical misgivings for those who hope to utilize his writings. Heidegger's membership in the Nazi Party cannot be excused as merely vocationally expedient. Heidegger remained a member of the Nazi Party throughout the Second World War. He expressed sentiments sympathetic to German nationalism and, most damningly, never uttered the unqualified apology for which so many hoped. Therefore, like Lovecraft and his horror-fueling racism, one cannot read Heidegger uncritically—if one chooses to read him at all.

Reading pre-Socratic philosophy, Augustine of Hippo (354–430), Wilhelm Dilthey (1833–1911), Friedrich Nietzsche (1844–1900), Edmund Husserl (1859–1938), Gabriel Marcel (1889–1973), Edith Stein (1891–1942), and others could allow one to not only patch together Heidegger's theses in *Being and Time* (1927/1996) but also encounter thoughts that extend well beyond Heidegger's achievements and, likely, capacity. Nevertheless, *Being and Time* is the first work to synthesize those currents.

Heidegger (1927/1996) asserts that the very question of being has been lost to Western philosophy since Aristotle. Most people participate in a blithe, self-blinding conspiracy of falling into *Das Man* (the them/they), not only losing that there is a question of being but also believing they are a thing amongst things. Because this understanding is inherently inauthentic, one is dogged by *angst* (existential dread/anxiety). Should one yield to the call contained in this angst, one is confronted by the nothingness—the not-thing-ness—of what was previously taken to be a coherent world of self-evident and self-existing things. Heidegger explains:

> The caller is unfamiliar to the everyday they-self, it is something like an *alien* voice. What could be more alien to the they, lost in the manifold "world" of its heedlessness, than the self-individualized to itself in uncanniness thrown into nothingness? "It" calls, and yet gives the heedfully curious ears nothing to hear that could be passed along and publicly spoken about.
>
> (p. 277)

Uncanniness is a sign that the individual is no longer adequately absorbed into the them. One might think about how, driven by a question no one seems to be able to answer for him, Neo's world begins to unravel during the first part of *The Matrix* (Wachowskis, 1999). Uncanniness is not the joy Heidegger promises in those fullest moments of authenticity, but it is a signpost that one has failed to stay absorbed in the hubbub and nonsense of what passes for the everyday world. Uncanniness is a product of angst, as Heidegger states, "In *Angst* one has an '*uncanny*' feeling" (p. 188).

Thus, plenty of horror and psychological thrillers offer one opportunities to apply this type of Heideggerian interpretation. Aliens replace human with aliens, or robots, or humans replace their wives with robots in a range of science fiction–inflected horror, from *The Stepford Wives* (Forbes, 1975) to *Invasion of the Body Snatchers* (Kaufman, 1978) to *The World's End* (Wright, 2013). The folk horror community that holds a secret and grows silent in the presence of a stranger can also enact these themes. But awakening to a world that is, unto itself, meaningless, and that one's life is the taking up of the responsibility of meaning-making? That is a tall order for the extended metaphors of horror or science fiction. But setting aside those films making claim to realism where existential morals may well be afoot, these themes show up more commonly in comedic mind-benders, like *Groundhog Day* (Ramis, 1993), *The Truman Show* (Weir, 1998), or *Being John Malkovich* (Jonze, 1999).

Heidegger (1927/1996) seems to promise that this angst and uncanniness are transient. One will never fully be free of them, as one can never always be authentic. But uncanniness is not inherent to authenticity. Conversely, in reading Miéville's various accounts of the abcanny, the reader gets the idea that the insubstantiality of every aspect of our world and being, the not-thing-ness, the ever-present processes of undoing, cares little for the individual's relative authenticity or inauthenticity. For Miéville, the uncanny and the abcanny are inherent to our lived world. He finishes his first essay introducing the term *abcanny*, stating, "If we live in a haunted world—and we do—we live in a Weird one" (2008, p. 128).

China Miéville's Abcanny: Beyond the Uncanny and Abject

China Miéville's assertion of the abcanny is not exclusively or merely a literary suggestion or a philosophical experiment. To understand the horizons to which he intends to point, the broader context of his career and work will prove illuminating.

Miéville's first novel, *King Rat*, published in 1998, is an urban fantasy set in the flux between everyday London and a hidden world beneath the surface. As Tranter (2012) notes, Miéville outlines in *King Rat* many of the themes he will pursue in future novels. His locations are often underground and alternative "scenes" that serve as gateways to other worlds and ways of being. He blurs human and animal and emphasizes the power of the interstitial and hybrid. He valorizes the *great work*—whether in science and/or art—that transforms practitioners and their worlds. And he gives voice to the downtrodden attempting to rise up but who are betrayed or subverted by those who claim to lead on their behalf.

Miéville's breakthrough came with his second novel, *Perdido Street Station* (2000), which received numerous nominations and awards. Here he whole-sheet-creates a new world: Bas-Lag, a world he revisits with the two equally awarded subsequent novels, *The Scar* (2002) and *Iron Council* (2004). In Bas-Lag, Miéville offers alchemical pollution, dream-consuming eldritch moths, exploitative political structures, multicultural and intercultural blurring with beings that appear to be various human/animal amalgams but are their own distinct species, as well as humans obscurely punished with hybridization to machines, animal parts, and other human appendages. And through it all, against an ambient susurration of violation and exploitation, characters try to carve out room for themselves to love, create, grow, and strive against massive oppressive power structures. This culminates in a great people's uprising in *Iron Council* (2004) that, poignantly, is frozen in amber.

Miéville is a Marxist in theory and practice. His 2001 PhD from the London School of Economics is in international law, and his dissertation became his 2004 work *Between Equal Rights: A Marxist Theory of International Law*. Two of his latest works are also nonfictional political works: *October: The Story of the Russian Revolution* (2017) and *A Spectre, Haunting: On the Communist Manifesto* (2022). Thus, when Miéville writes or discusses literature, he is never not discussing politics, power, and freedom, though he typically leaves the readers of his fictions to make the connections.

Readers could be forgiven for considering Miéville to belong to a broadly postmodern turn of philosophy, politics, and art. However, this would be a misdating of the provenance of Miéville's influences. In a 2010 interview with Venezia, Miéville notes:

> There has been a tendency over the last probably decade and a half, maybe longer, which is a sort of flattening out of the sharp edges of theory within certain kind of arenas, and one of the effects is that certain types of concerns have become default associated with particular theoretical paradigms. So if you come across a text which is anyway interested in interstitiality, or marginality, or subalternity, there's a notion that *ipso facto* this can be thought of as a "postmodern" text.
>
> (p. 5)

Miéville is no stranger to postmodern theory. The interstitial, marginal, and subaltern that he mentions are all prominent themes in his work, as he frequently presents what is between, on the edges, or entirely beyond various configurations of power, narrative, and space. Nevertheless, postmodern perspectives do not form the foundation of his thought. A leading example of this can be found in his *The City & the City* (2009). The novel takes place within two cities which exist completely intertwined. Citizens of one city must learn to "unsee" the people and features of the other city. This perceptual contortionism proceeds at pace until a corpse is found which cannot be satisfactorily placed in one city or the other. One can certainly go to Derrida and *différance*, or perhaps Deleuze and Guattari's schizophrenia. But Miéville, along with Deleuze and Guattari, shares a common inspiration in Franz Kafka (1883–1924).

Thus, more accurately, one can note that Miéville and a range of post-structural and postmodern philosophers share the same important influences. There is no

question that Miéville is reacting against modernity both philosophically and lit-
erarily, as the conclusion to his 2008 essay indicates: "Hauntology and Weird are
two iterations of the same problematic—that of crisis-blasted modernity showing
its contradictory face, utterly new *and* traced with remnants, chaotic and nihilistic *and* stained with human rebukes" (p. 128). But Miéville is a Marxist with
strong sympathies to Surrealism and Dada, among other late nineteenth- and early
twentieth-century artistic and philosophical movements. This shows, in both the
plot and dialogue of his 2016 alternative history novella *The Last Days of New
Paris*, in which an "S-Bomb"—a surrealism bomb—creates dreamlike manifestations over Paris in response to the artless literalism of the occupying Nazis.

In his 2008 essay, even Miéville's title, "M. R. James and the Quantum Vampire: Weird; Hauntological: Versus and/or and and/or or?" slides off the edge of the
page, defying boundaries. With this article, Miéville sets the stage for the abcanny,
though he only sketches the term itself. Instead, he uses the Weird to stand in for the
landscape in which the hauntological uncanny begins to tatter and a further "implacable alterity" (p. 112) looms. In part, the essay emerges in response to various
arguments about his and VanderMeer's writings as a New Weird. Miéville dodges
the debates and chooses to focus on setting forth a broader theory of the Weird
beyond the unsettling uncanniness of a returned-repressed. The hauntological may
be a "radicalized uncanny" (p. 112), but the Weird is "a hallucinatory/nihilistic
novum" (p. 113). Finally, he states, "The Weird is if anything ab-, not un-, canny"
(p. 113).

Navigating ghosts and Victorian themes, Miéville (2008) is weaving a story
about modernity and its haunting while setting forth a more radical possibility.
Though subtly remaining in the realm of literary criticism, Miéville even notes
how materialism and "the horror of matter" (p. 120) are critical to the Weird. Cit-
ing an image from the films of Jean Painlevé (1902–1989), Miéville describes and
includes a picture of an octopus wrapping around a skull. Miéville also provides
his drawing of what he calls a "skulltopus" and an even more playful image of
himself as a pirate-like action figure with a toy octopus. Devoted followers will
note that a *Nautilus English Books* blog from 2012 has an image of Miéville with
the skulltopus tattoo stretching from his right shoulder down past his elbow. Giving
the imagery even more room to extend its tentacles, Miéville's 2010 novel *Kraken*
returns to the urban fantastic and places the titular giant cephalopod as more than
mere McGuffin but an inky metaphor-devouring/creating abcanny force.

Though no stranger to the world of comic books—he has written several—
Miéville (2008) is strangely silent about the fact that his skull-and-octopus symbol
bears a striking resemblance to the symbol for the fictional villainous organization
HYDRA in the Marvel universe. A creator of video game content, graphic novelist,
and podcast host, David Gallaher (personal communication, 2023) notes that the
skull-and-tentacles symbol for HYDRA first shows up as a creation of Jack Kirby
and Stan Lee in the mid-1960s drawing from antisemitic Nazi imagery. Nevertheless, HYDRA's elitist world-dominating philosophy and Nazi resonances have
nothing to do with Miéville's leftist and surrealist agenda with the symbol. This

is, perhaps, why all his portrayals of the skulltopus are fluid, lacking the rigid, gear-like symmetry of the HYDRA symbol. One might speculate that the use of the symbol by HYDRA betrays an unconscious apprehension of the nihilistic grounds of their world-dominating plots. One cannot, after all, capture, tame, or structure the abcanny.

Finally, in a 2012 presentation to the *International Association for the Fantastic in the Arts*, Miéville hyperbolically—and humorously—presented a host of "Not Cannies" that dance with the Weird and the Sublime and attempt to bring back the eldritch strangeness of the ubiquitous and impinging frontiers we encounter every moment and in every direction. Miéville establishes his intention when he describes that "[t]he Weird is the assertion of that we did not know, never knew, could not know, that [which] has always been and will always be unknowable" (p. 380). This is "radical otherness, a counterposing alterity" (p. 380) and "baleful not-canny . . . sublime backwash" (p. 381). From this foundation, he builds the case for "abness"—that which is not mere opposition but slips beyond the containment of the modified term.

At last, Miéville (2012) brazenly and playfully points to the abcanny as "the unrepresentable and unknowable, the evasive of meaning" (p. 381). He again reinforces how the slipperiness and unclearness of the abcanny cannot be contained in what he characterizes as the essentialist assertions of Freud, Kristeva, or even Lacan. As noted earlier, Miéville does not deny that those various layers of explanatory meaning may come along with monsters that appear within Weird literature. But ultimately, "[t]hese monsters mean, while they meta un-mean" (p. 382).

Giddily, Miéville (2012) storms through literature and film looking for the ways in which every aspect of human existence is undermined and undone by great devouring undefinable monstrousness. After his frenzied cataloging, there is nowhere left to stand. One can almost imagine a Zen Buddhist recitation of how every certainty is undone in a sort of Weird gloss on "Form is emptiness; emptiness is form." Miéville offers:

- "Subcanny": From watery depths, we know and fear what we know lurks there. A form of the unknown known.
- "Katacanny": From the trembling earth, undermining our certainties.
- "Postcanny": The insurgent discarded that we no longer understand. Garbage.
- "Surcanny": From above, but no longer emancipating heavens.
- "Precanny": The vastly ancient.
- "Juxtacanny": The random, the surreal, Dada.
- "Recanny or Paracanny": The beside—for example, doppelganger.
- "Supercanny": The autophagous hyperrational.

But all these are meant to direct the audience to the abcanny. Miéville is deconstructing more than the supremacy of the ego. The abcanny is "beyond-meaning-ness" (p. 382). Were this postmodern deconstruction, Miéville would show how the component parts of some image or idea monstrously contradicts itself. The closest he comes is with the autophagia of the "supercanny"—surely the realm of much postmodern thought. Although Miéville may be pointing to similar ineffable/unspeakable edges as some postmodern thinkers, he is more boldly asserting the inevitability, the unavoidability, the comprehensiveness, and the ubiquity of the abcanny.

Outside of works directly concerned with Miéville's writings (e.g., Pike, 2019), "abcanny" has slowly begun to show up in literary criticism but has not yet made its way into philosophical or psychological discourse. As described earlier, Ersoy (2019) applies it to VanderMeer's work. March-Russell (2017), interpreting the work of Lucy Wood and her landscape of Cornwall, allows the abcanny to embrace place and class in a way that seizes upon Marxist resonances in the term. Witzel (2018) notes that "the climate crisis thwarts conceptualization" (p. 561) and thus brings an abcanny lens to two pieces of Weird fiction in which 'the flood" brought on by global climate change serves to undo the putative meanings of the characters.

Two More Weird Figures

Throughout this chapter, I have referred to the Weird mostly as a literary sensibility—if that is the right word. But I have also implied that the Weird is a sort of existential given. That is, every person is dogged by the Weirdness of life and simultaneously adopts vast structures of meaning—personality, relationships, political affiliations, epistemologies, economic systems, religious faiths, brand loyalty, and so much more—as tenacious yet ineffectual defenses against the indicting abcanny. From this perspective, we are not merely thrown into a neutrally meaningless world; we are thrown into a meaning-devouring world. Whether meaning-making is a worthy undertaking in the face of the abcanny depends on how devotedly nihilistic the advocate of the Weird is.

In addition to Miéville and VanderMeer, addressed earlier, two more authors of the Weird span the twentieth century and address the fundamental question of the Weird in their own ways: H. P. Lovecraft and Thomas Ligotti. As one considers their stances on meaning, one cannot avoid the realization that Lovecraft continued to write, collaborate, and edit nearly until his death. And Ligotti continues to write, correspond, encourage other authors, and collaborate. That is, even an author as pointedly nihilistic as Ligotti faces the emptiness of meaning and chooses to create. After discussing these authors and injecting the abcanny into other discourses, this chapter will conclude by considering what type of audacity is necessary to create in the Weird.

Do We Still Need H. P. Lovecraft?

As implied earlier, though Lovecraft is a key figure in synthesizing the currents that will become the Weird, his pervasive racist themes make it impossible to address his work in any uncritical manner. Paradoxically, this race panic renders his fiction a startlingly effective panorama of the terror-filled imaginal landscape of the bigot. As Miéville notes of Lovecraft, "[e]veryone knows that what gets his monster-loving blood pumping is race-hatred, antisemitism and an ecstatic terror of miscegenation" (2012, p. 382).

Lovecraft's protagonists teeter on the edge of Weird madness. Their world tilts before their very eyes, revealing unspeakable vistas of horror. Lovecraft is almost phenomenological in his scrupulous portrayal of the lived world of the rationalist desperately clinging to the always, already-pustulant, decaying "truths" of modernity. The preceding century and the dawn of the twentieth presented Lovecraft with ample indictments to progress, rationality, colonialism, White supremacy, and other articles of faith of an ardent disciple of Western European ascendancy and dominance. Charles Darwin (1809–1882) not only classed humans among other animals but also dizzyingly expanded the scale of time. Fredrich Nietzsche informed his readers that, having killed God, European cultural progress was built on a conflagration of nihilism. Sigmund Freud declared that we are not even in charge of our own selves. Edwin Hubble (1889–1953) made our Milky Way merely one galaxy among countless others. Albert Einstein (1879–1955) blurred time and space, matter and energy, and relativized the very capacity to ground oneself in anything. And sadly, most germane to Lovecraft's fears, during his lifetime, waves of immigrants from countries across the globe came to America in numbers not matched until the late twentieth century.

Thus, although no one ought to turn to Lovecraft as a role model—quite the opposite—one might argue that, since racism and delusions of endless progress at the hands of an ethically neutral "science" still abound today, his panicked rhetoric may still need to be heard:

> The most merciful thing in the world, I think, is the inability of the human mind to correlate all its contents. We live on a placid island of ignorance in the midst of black seas of infinity, and it was not meant that we should voyage far. The sciences, each straining in its own direction, have hitherto harmed us little; but some day the piecing together of dissociated knowledge will open up such terrifying vistas of reality, and of our frightful position therein, that we shall either go mad from the revelation or flee from the deadly light into the peace and safety of a new dark age.
>
> (*The Call of Cthulhu*, 1928/2008, p. 355)

This is among the most quoted passages from Lovecraft from his most-cited story. It is notable that, in spite of its popularity, *The Call of Cthulhu* has not received a large-scale cinematic adaptation. The unspeakable can be tenaciously unfilmable. The most successful version to date is a 2005 silent featurette by Leman. The film describes that it is filmed in "mythoscope"—playing on the "Mythos," the term used for the shared settings, invented mythology, and storylines Lovecraft and affiliated authors use. In black and white, with a silent film soundtrack rife with scratches, the film looks as though it was created in the 1920s—the era of the original story's publication. With the film's tongue firmly in cheek, Leman plays it camp. This sliding between camp and kitsch is the attitude that many fans of the Mythos necessarily hold in order to be able to enjoy the ongoing industry spawned by Lovecraft's roughly 30 years of writing.

Though many write about Lovecraft, no other single scholar has produced as much as S. T. Joshi has. Since editing his first Lovecraft publication, *Miscellaneous Writings* (1995), Joshi has ardently combed archives, other authors' correspondences, publishers' records, and other historical documents to piece together the story of Lovecraft and the birth of the Weird. Lovecraft scholarship and critical perspectives on pulp fiction have benefitted from Joshi's earnest attentions, facilitating a range of scholars with different theoretical and critical lenses to examine the popular imagination.

Though Lovecraft was a thorough scholar of horror, he was not a scholar of social justice, reform, or even human rights. It is overly generous to excuse his shortcomings as merely being a man of his times. To find someone who embraces the Weird with equal zeal but does not leave the reader with the same ethical misgivings, one must turn to Thomas Ligotti.

Thomas Ligotti: The Weird as Gateway to Realizing the Truth of Nihilism

Author, poet, essayist, and philosopher, Thomas Ligotti, born in 1953, entered no less of a tumultuous time than Lovecraft, but a radically different world. It is safe to label Ligotti's writings as a post-Lovecraftian Weird. Ligotti dedicates his short story, originally published in 1990, "The Last Feast of the Harlequin" (2015, p. 255) to Lovecraft and embeds Lovecraftian references and themes in several other works. But Ligotti is not an imitator, a parodist, or an adoring acolyte. The titular Harlequin is a naïve cultural anthropologist who discovers that a festival of clowns hides a far darker ritual of metamorphosis. Ligotti smirks as he takes Lovecraftian themes and transfers them into far more unsettling uncanny and abcanny configurations. If anything, Ligotti is darker than Lovecraft because he is exquisitely self-aware about the consciousness-twisting we all engage in to get through our days, and the horrendous consequences when those efforts inevitably crumble.

Where Lovecraft fears the mixing of races, Ligotti targets the puppet, the marionette, the lifeless doppelganger that comes to life. His philosophy comes out as one realizes this is no mere phobia but a statement on the paper-thin construction of identity and what passes for reality. We are puppets condemned to intuit or know of our manipulation at the hands of forces far exceeding our comprehension. At one point, with his "Dr. Locrian's Asylum" in *Songs of a Dead Dreamer* (2015, p. 189), originally published in 1987, Ligotti puts forth a shockingly poetic and unsettling agenda that merits a Foucaultian gloss. One of the horrifying revelations of the story—of which there are several—is that a psychiatrist had been attempting to enhance the insanity of his patients. He sought to, in fact, remove the futile vestiges of their "sanity" and allow to shine forth "a knowledge that was unspoken and unspeakable" (p. 195). One of these methods was, not surprisingly, to expose patients to nocturnal puppet shows through a secret panel in their rooms.

Ligotti scholarship is a growing field (e.g., Schweitzer, 2003). Through his stories, poems, interviews, collaborations with the likes of Current 93, and the occasional seemingly instructional essays that slowly dissolve into horror—for example, "Notes on the Writing of Horror: A Story" (Ligotti, 2015, p. 91) and "Professor Nobody's Little Lectures on Supernatural Horror" (p. 183)—Ligotti offers readers ample insights into his fundamental assumptions and attitudes to horror and life, such as it is. Nevertheless, like Miéville building his theory of the abcanny, Ligotti has offered a full statement of his fundamental philosophical stance in *The Conspiracy Against the Human Race* (2010).

In this ostensibly nonfictional work, Ligotti (2010) repeatedly describes the world as "malignantly useless." Consciousness itself is something of a sick joke in Ligotti's estimation. The more aware one is of the nature of the human condition, the more one is cursed to suffer the horrors of which this world is woven. Spinning together philosophy and fiction, Ligotti is pessimistic not only about life and meaning but also about the prospects of humans doing anything about it, such as ego death or voluntary extinction. The work is poetically written and bold. Ligotti's audience expanded when Nic Pizzolatto, writer for season 1 of *True Detective* (2014), admitted in an interview with the *Wall Street Journal*'s Calia (2014) that Ligotti's work served as an important inspiration for the bleak nihilistic dialogue of Matthew McConaughey's character, Rust Cohle (Pizzolatto, 2014).

Miéville and Ligotti would seem to agree: the widely held understandings of the world are shot through with countless misunderstandings, distortions, willful misdirections, ignorances, and contortions of consciousness. These serve as futile defenses against what is an incomprehensible reality beneath. Miéville insists on the abcanny un-meaning that this fundamental reality brings. Ligotti would emphasize that reality is incomprehensible because it doesn't mean anything other than a fundamental antipathy to human existence. Yet—and I risk oversimplifying their complex arguments here in my response—I cannot help but note once again: in the face of all this, they both choose to create.

The Return of the Monolith

As I was completing this chapter, my wife and I took a trip to Berlin. The thick layers of history do not stratify discretely in Berlin—they seem to mingle and transform as structures emerge and dissolve, leaving traces that themselves come to signify new irruptions. One need only look to the number of Weimar era–inspired speakeasies to wonder at how history can fold in on itself in that city.

Within our first few days, we visited the *Jüdisches Museum Berlin*. To attempt to describe the museum, as I have tried to with friends and colleagues since our return, is something of an exercise in futility. Architect Daniel Libeskind, the museum's curators, and the contributing artists create a flow of spaces that beget profound experiences of coming to the frontiers of meaning. Within the first floor one encounters a gap Libeskind calls the "Void of Voids"—a steel-doored darkness that extends up into a dim nothingness with a distant, almost-intuited opening to outside, letting in attenuated light and sound. Several other voids and stark surfaces bound and define the acute and obtuse angles of the museum.

The museum is not all spare darkness. Joy and defiance, richness and texture fill many of the galleries. The Ineffable edges the overall experience more than the Unspeakable. So do great disruptions and questions. Near the end of the museum's multistorey flow, three videos—including one of Hannah Arendt—offer some language to point to what has been a central juxtaposition of the museum: the Holocaust has no meaning. To proffer explanations or interpretation is to betray the horror, the shocking, nihilistic meaninglessness of it. Meaning is made by those who live, create, hope, remember, memorialize, respond—in short, meaning is made in living.

Growing from that experience, as our trip continued, the remnants of the Berlin Wall became ciphers. They revealed themselves as cryptic, meaningless monoliths that spun into the meaning-makings that were "East" and "West" Berlin—the shifting stories before, during, and after. We found ourselves frequently asking, "Was this the East?" or "Are we in the West?" Today, the only orienting indication in many parts of the city are the remaining differing pedestrian crossing signals. In some parts of the city, a brick line may pass along or through a sidewalk to mark where the Wall once stood. In others, long stretches of the Wall have become open-air art galleries. In still others, single slabs stand covered with graffiti and chewing gum. The meaning-making accretes in opposition, in juxtaposition, and in response to histories, present moments, and futures that are themselves constantly remade, rewritten, and reinterpreted. And over all this bristles a forest of construction cranes.

In short, my monolith—its inscrutability inscribed so long ago in my psyche—returned in the landscape of a Berlin constantly being built and rebuilt.

Applying the Abcanny

As I hope my brief travelog illustrates, discussions of the edges of meaninglessness and meaning-making are not best reserved for graduate seminars in continental philosophy. Yet in the free play China Miéville invites his audience into with his abcanny, one can blithely remain in the eldritch worlds of Weird fiction. Indeed, in this chapter, I have used fictional cinema as my central examples. Nevertheless, though their total word count still strongly favors the fictional, Miéville and Ligotti both stretch their discourse into an ostensibly nonfictional world. For Miéville, that is a Weird world, haunted by the uncanny, and undone at every front by the abcanny. For Ligotti, it is a world that is "malignantly useless." An imaginal psychologist such as myself might quibble whether we should erect any walls between the fictional and nonfictional when so much of each person's lived world is composed of stories. Nevertheless, the question remains: Is the abcanny merely a literary device? Can a concept that dances so adroitly with nihilism be of use to other fields?

Because the abcanny undoes definitions, it poses fundamental challenges when applying it outside of fiction. When Freud or Heidegger each offers their interpretations of the *uncanny* and when Kristeva gives readers the abject, there is—no matter how slippery or slimy—a substance to it. Unconscious, unacknowledged, threatening to consciousness or convention, but a substance nonetheless. In sharp contrast, Miéville's abcanny indicts and undoes substance. Indeed, Miéville (2012) says the abcanny "un-means" (p. 382). Thus, beyond the madness that threatens the hapless protagonists in Weird stories by Lovecraft, Ligotti, or VanderMeer, what would it mean to live in an ostensibly nonfictional world in which un-meaning erodes our always-already-provisional truths on every front?

From an initially fictional footing, can the abcanny stretch into the world of psychotherapy, philosophy, and theology? Perhaps the abcanny can, for a time, be a new taking up and remaking of themes once cultivated by the artists, philosophers, and activists of the sublime, surreal, situationist, existential, absurdist, and even those postmodern currents that did not entirely devour themselves in solipsistic cynicism.

Clinical Implications

The tension between a world that is meaningless versus life as the individual's responsibility for their own meaning-making is a classic existential tenet that unifies a range of existentially informed psychotherapies. According to existentialists like Jean-Paul Sartre (1905–1980), Viktor Frankl (1905–1997), Rollo May (1909–1994), and many others, one can choose to ignore, deny, or attempt to hand over the responsibility for one's own situation; but these ultimately ineffectual efforts can never negate one's own fundamental meaning-making. Those desperate efforts do, however, distort the nature of one's lived world, exacting a real cost in one's ability to be responsive to the present unfolding moment. Various ilk of anxiety or angst and the previously mentioned types of existential uncanniness accompany these deformations.

Many counselors and psychotherapists who might not label themselves as "existential" frequently find themselves in a phase of treatment in which the major focus is clients taking increased responsibility for their lives. When Dr. Phil McGraw challenges his guests with the signature line "How's that working for you?" he is pointing to this sort of accountability to oneself. In the non-television world, the nuance of "blame" versus "responsibility" can take up anywhere from a few minutes to months of therapy. And to clarify, existential responsibility does not imply that developmental and socioeconomic forces are somehow one's fault, or that they can be ignored with some force of will. Instead, one has no choice but to deal somehow with the present-moment realities into which these forces throw one. The existential question lies in how one chooses to do that. Clearly, one can make a shift to taking charge of one's choices and attributions without endorsing the fundamental meaninglessness of the world; but the ongoing question of how to make substantive change in one's life does seem to necessitate a shift in how one makes meaning.

As noted earlier, in this very same world that existentialists purport to be meaningless, neurobiologists still seek to subvert this existential given. So do those psychodynamic theorists who present early childhood experiences and inherited potentialities as adequately explanatory for why and how humans do what they do. Whether at the aforementioned first puzzle level or the second life lessons level of mysteries, these explanations can become a type of essentialism that addresses questions of meaning with a confident "That's just the way it is." And if that is, indeed, the way it is, then one should seek out either the appropriate pharmaceutical or brain stimulation or, alternately, psychoanalytic setting to address one's complaints.

From an existential viewpoint, these neurological and psychoanalytic discoveries and assertions may serve provisional purposes as milestones of the journey of shifts in perspective. After a typically arduous course of trial and error, a pharmaceutical might indeed help one gain some clarity in one's life. Alternatively, a course of psychoanalysis can help one accept one's lived world and get out of one's own way. But the danger comes when these approaches become fundamental explanations and endpoints to the journey. That is, one uses these essentialist explanations to foreclose the unavoidable questions of life as though they have, once and for all, been answered—or as though they don't matter. In doing so, one ignores the Ultimate Mysteries. If clutching to essentialist convictions as ultimately satisfactory hides a type of nihilism beneath it, then that is a scrupulously avoided realization for those who like answers better than questions.

Nonetheless, Miéville goes still further than the existentialist's assertion of the meaninglessness of the world and the individual's unavoidable responsibility for meaning-making in the face of it. Miéville's abcanny is not merely meaningless. The abcanny erodes meaning. In this perspective, any specific meaning cannot last long—it has an ephemeral shelf life, if it ever had life in the first place. The abcanny would seem to demand an ongoing repositioning, a reconfiguring, with a constant commitment to creativity and transformation. All permanence is illusory and shot through with the erosive groundlessness of the abcanny.

Therapeutically, this kind of impermanence poses some real challenges; but these are challenges of which any experienced clinical practitioner or researcher is aware. Most sufferers do not "get over" depression—or any other severe and pervasive mental illness—once and for all. There is no set of relationship skills so effective that one will never have another conflict. The self-care demands of one context or phase of life may not transfer effectively to another. What a childhood episode means to the 23-year-old in counseling may be significantly different than to the 48-year-old. Is one meaning "truer" or "wiser"? That is, would the 23-year-old be better served by coming to those realizations that resonate with the 48-year-old?

These shifting settings and demands become more complicated when the therapist's development and context come into play. As noted previously, therapists can indeed impose their interpretations so pervasively as to color or even construct the client's internality. Thus, a patient's therapy can become significantly more about the therapist's needs and pathologies than the patient's. Given this threat, ethical therapists acknowledge that they must be intensely involved in their own unfolding process, typically through receiving their own personal therapy and clinical supervision. But these efforts do not erase the practitioner's material from the patient's treatment room. They merely hope to raise these currents to the surface for the therapist. Thus, clinical authors in the "depth" tradition often refer to the therapist as "the other patient in the room."

Whether seen in the patient's shifting contexts and needs or the therapist's own unfolding personal and professional process, it should be clear that, like Heraclitus's river, one never steps into the same consulting room twice. Impermanence is the rule. Yet the clinical research record is overwhelmed by efforts to standardize and manualize treatment. The race in clinical science toward an abiding objectivity may express its greatest hubris in those efforts to establish inviolate definitions, causes, and treatment regimens for "diagnoses."

All clinical treatment begins with some form of the question, "What brings you here?" This question is equally valid for the therapist as the patient, but for the sake of this discussion, the focus will stay with the patient. Practitioners may take a while to get a full picture of why the patient has sought treatment. Furthermore, the reason for the patient coming in may evolve to the extent that the progression of the provisional answers to this question could prove the crux of therapy. Regardless of the flux and flow of the reasons, as I so often remind my students in clinical courses, patients don't come to treatment because they've had a lovely day, find existence deeply meaningful, enjoy fulfilling relationships, a rich vocational life, and robust health. In one form or another, the client enters therapy because of a symptom.

A *symptom* is a strange sort of certainty. Otherwise, why would someone subject themselves to sharing the most intimate parts of their life with a total stranger— that is, a mental health professional? Of course, the suffering that coalesces into a symptom can seem quite "uncertain," lead to confusion and bewilderment, discord, and a host of possible competing interpretations. But to the extent that it warrants the name, the symptom is a concrete literality. Simultaneously, the symptom is an unavoidable inscrutability.

Various meanings spin rapidly around the symptom, as noted earlier in discussing anxiety. The sufferer desperately wants to understand this seeming invasion into their lives. The patient may attach great significance to the meaning they make of the symptom. For instance, "I hurt in this specific way because of something that has been done to me," "I suffer because of the nature of my character," "I cannot feel normal because of a world that is fundamentally not made for someone like me," or "I need to suffer in this way for the sake of someone else." Yet as I also remind my clinical students, glossing Jung and Donald Winnicott (1896–1971), what the patient thinks is the answer to their problems when they enter therapy is probably part of the problem.

Even in those too-rare situations when offered adequate time to start examining questions about how the patient has made meaning of and with the symptom, the mental health industry too gladly plays into a prepackaged-meaning-proffering business. The public is reliably informed that "diagnosis" is a full-voiced explanation of any specific symptom. For instance, the consequences of a traumatic brain injury or those disorders strongly linked to biological, genetic—and epigenetic—etiology such as *schizophrenia, bipolar*, and *major depression* all seem to offer the patient a very clear reason for their suffering. The broad understanding is that trauma "causes" one to later suffer from various disorders. And a childhood rife with instability and abuse leads one to a range of characterological issues. Admixtures of these forms of explanation then transfer to all other mental health diagnoses. But is an "explanation" the same as "meaning"? In too many cases, the terms are antonyms. That sentiment bears some further examination.

As already noted earlier, causal explanations typically rest in material assumptions which ultimately demand a devil's bargain. Either the entirety of existence is explicable in a chain of materialist explanations or one must create—as did René Descartes (1596–1650) in just such a situation—another substance like "mind," "soul," or "spirit." One either teeters on the edge of nihilism with a purely materialist epistemology or falls into dualist spiritist esotericism. Facing the horns of this dilemma, most therapists retreat into comforting themselves that simply reducing symptom severity is likely a "good thing," and that all this philosophical navel-gazing isn't. Yet a diagnosis, with its unexamined explanation-as-meaning substrate, slaps a professional-sounding label onto what remains a distressing reality in its very occurrence, regardless of its attenuation.

Adding to the limited utility of a diagnosis, most diagnoses describe a syndrome, that is, a collection of symptoms that tend to appear together. Typically, quite a bit of variety exists within each diagnosis, and few diagnoses have a set etiology—a required cause and course. All this is not to say that a clear picture of symptoms might not be a useful step along the journey of the patient claiming increased responsibility in their lives. But too often the diagnosis is yet another form of foreclosing on those opportunities.

To put this all a bit more clearly: the symptom does not mean anything. In this inscrutability, the symptom demands one do something with it. A call to make meaning is the nature of the human kind of being in a meaningless world; but the symptom demands a new taking up of meaning in a pointed and intimate way. In most cases, this meaningless symptom forces the sufferer to spin into often-desperate compensatory meaning-searching. It's not that any interpretation, explanation, or causal chain is wrong, per se; it is simply not true forever—or for very long, for that matter. The meanings adopted along the way in a too-often-frenzied search for explanation are rarely fully satisfactory and never satisfactory for long. Thus, the symptom may be one of the clearest examples of the abcanny. The symptom undoes any meaning one has been making: it un-means. Moreover, in too many cases, the symptom becomes inexorably bound into the explanations, compensations, and efforts at amelioration. In this way, this symptom complex is a clutching to a meaning that the abcanny has already so thoroughly worm-eaten as to render the meaning toxic.

What, then, is the alternative? Some therapists are secure enough in the process to allow the symptom to be an invitation to wonder, but not to know. To actually listen to the symptom means making room for the Weird, because symptoms are Weird. Those symptoms that work perfectly well within a sick culture, family system, or relationship take much longer to show up in the consulting room, if they ever do. The symptom that leads someone to treatment is an undeniable disruption of those narratives that every person normally doubles, triples, and quadruples down on to keep moving through their day. Thus, in their indictment of outmoded meanings, the symptom, in its abcannyness, is an invitation to change.

Most of how the individual gets through life is through adopting roles and stories that conspicuously defend against the abcanny. "I" am my identity. Friends have relatively consistent personalities. Life has rules. Bad things happen for reasons. Good things happen for reasons. These defenses work, until they don't. Everything works until it doesn't, although each person typically continues to do those things well after the time that they served any purpose. The uncanny haunting and the abcanny Weirdness of life typically show up in between the things we insist are still working. They emerge between work and distractions, stimulants and exhaustion. They show up in loneliness, dissatisfaction, incongruity, doubt, and confusion. They also show up in unexpected forms of love, awe, wonder, hope, and joy.

Thus, a therapist committed to creating an environment in which the patient can undo their defensive structures against the ubiquitous abcanny commits to wonder and curiosity. This sort of companion notes the incongruous, the tensions, the juxtapositions, the interstitial, and the intersectional. They also notice often-unexpected signs of life. The goal of this sort of therapy cannot be getting back to work, or school, or the way a relationship used to be. There is no "getting back." The abcanny has already long ago undone what was. Only through bravely fostering creativity, imagination, vulnerability, and bewildered honesty can treatment embrace the Weird—that is, deal with life as it unfolds.

For those who have experienced marginalization, acknowledging the always-already-there Weird may prove easier. Life is always Weird if one is queer in a hetero- and cisgender-normative culture. Having the nuances of one's identity and cultural configurations paved over with hegemonic racial categories is also likely to create enough dissonance to show how Weird life already is. Living in a capitalist and, thus, materialist culture ought to be Weird for everyone, as haunted as Marx and Engels tell readers it is. But for some, the promise that they will one day be part of the small minority "on top," or at least "comfortable," adequately distracts them from or explains away their socioeconomic exploitation. Yet those aspirations aren't genuinely resonant for the majority. To be honest, simply trying to get by can keep one quite distracted from what surrounds one, with the racism, heteronormativity, and exploitation creating a constant strange gravitational distortion one unconsciously twists one's body to accommodate. Nevertheless, there are those who cannot help but see the fundamental monstrosity of a free-market, capitalist, racist, heteronormative society. In their marginalization, they may find constant adaptation more native. All the shifting constructions of ethnicity, heritage, skin tone, gender, neurodiversity, faith, religion, and spirituality can bring with them interstitial configurations in which some know they cannot participate in the dominant narrative without qualifying their position. Marginalization impacts access to basic needs, dignity, safety, and development. And for some, it can offer access to the realization that our lives are Weird in their in-betweenness, their shifting definitions and code switches, their unfulfilled promises, and their divergent narratives. When someone has had this sort of realization, it can offer the potential to make other changes more easily. And as noted earlier, it is likely that even for the "privileged," ethical therapy will necessitate acknowledging socioeconomic and environmental realities if it is to effect any sort of meaningful change.

The transpersonal or Jungian practitioner might embrace the 'Encounter with the Abcanny' as a sort of liminal space in which one dances with the shadow. But scripts of *bardos*, shamanic journeys through the World Tree, or other archetypal patterns, run the risk of leaning more toward George Lucas than Stanley Kubrick. Sure, the abcanny could be taken up as part of a sort of existential mysticism—a paradoxical grounding in epistemological frontiers. But the ever-present danger of reifying the inexplicable is strong.

The topic of a psychotherapy in which the abcanny is a central force merits its own volumes, and I have offered this preceding section simply to hint at some possibilities. To conclude, however, lest my enthusiasm for the abcanny outstrip the concept, perhaps it is best to let Thomas Ligotti have a last word to save us from any unqualified optimism or sense that discussions of nothingness are inherently salubrious to the therapeutic context. In the previously mentioned "Dr. Locrian's Asylum" (2015), originally published in 1987, the narrator reveals that he has been spinning his tale from a locked room in which he is gradually learning the secrets that Locrian had feverishly sought to distill by unencumbering the madness of his patients. Ligotti concludes the story with the narrator declaring, "Commending me to an absolute cure, he will have immured another soul within the black and boundless walls of that eternal asylum where stars dance forever like bright puppets in the silent, staring void" (p. 199).

Theological Implications

Apophatic theologians will likely recognize some aspects of the Ineffable in all this talk about epistemological frontiers. Nevertheless, emerging from Weird fiction, the abcanny equation leans rather more heavily toward the Unspeakable over the Ineffable. Thus, considering the abcanny, what theologians so often take up as the "problem of evil" perhaps ought to be about the "problem of meaninglessness" or "nihilism" instead. That is, rather than thinking about acts of hatred, abuse, exploitation, marginalization, falsification, and more as growing from some malignant substance (i.e., "evil"), how might discussions look were they to center on meaning-making in the face of a progressive, deteriorative meaninglessness? In such a framework, existential questions about taking up alterity, limits of knowledge, and concepts of the self and belonging move more to the forefront.

Nevertheless, the abcanny adds that any meaning made will only be provisional and for a time. Therefore, the meaning that was so existentially authentic in one context and time can become the reified, defensive inauthenticity of another.

Miéville (2012) freely admits that his abcanny seeks to bring back some of what once rested in the sublime. This sublime revival is part of Miéville's critique of the essentialism of Freud and Kristeva. The world of psychoanalysis has explained away much of the awe and wonder once contained in the encounter with the sublime. Theologians who seek to not entirely abandon the salience of Freudian explanations for the human mind seize upon the passing references to the oceanic feeling in Freud's work as evidence that one can make room for wonder and psychodynamic rigor. But does the sublime have something to offer that goes beyond a stimulus that elicits pre-egoic awe?

Too often, the is-ness of some phenomena calcifies into some sort of materialist explanation. This leaden weight quickly pulls attention away from the phenomena. The sublime may make one question oneself, or reality, or how one makes meaning; but the sublime does this in its undeniable and inscrutable is-ness. That this raw is-ness brings with it an abcanny sting that dissolves facile explanations ought to receive more attention. Thus, some sort of phenomenological sensibility is necessary to avoid essentialism and reification of the sublime.

To Buddhist scholars, much of this discussion likely seems humorous at best and cumbersomely wrong-headed at worst. Impermanence is a core tenet of Buddhism. *Sunyata*, translated as "emptiness" or "nothingness," is a fundamental doctrine that Buddhism inherited from its Indian origins. By the seventh century, the *Heart Sutra* already stated that form and emptiness are inexorably entwined. Thus, one might, perhaps audaciously, think of the abcanny as an aspect of the dharma, especially in its Zen currents. Certainly, *Butoh* dance would seem to be an expression of such an intersection.

As such Buddhist ideas have had well over a century to integrate into Western religious discourse, terms such as "nontheism," "post-theism," and Kearney's "anatheism" (2009) continue to propagate. Such linguistic and intellectual constructions seem deeply entangled with varying understandings of the verb "to be," the linguistic vector "God," and metaphors. Thus, Jean-Luc Marion can state, "The question of the existence of God, perhaps, has no more meaning than to ask 'what is the color of God?'" (Wallenfang, 2022, 5:50). Marion, once a student of Derrida, is deeply engaged in the intersections of phenomenology, mysticism, and theology. His works ask philosophers and theologians to profoundly shift their frame of reference when it comes to theological questions. Thus, if one engages in theological discourse for or against the existence of God, Marion sees a type of idolatry at work, bound up in a misapprehension of existence itself. As incongruous as it may seem, the abcanny can be seen actively at work when one takes up questions about the Divine in terms of existence rather than the phenomenology of being-toward-the-Divine. Absurd as it may be to try to wed Miéville's thought to the Hebrew Testament, the abcanny can be a sort of punishment for the idolatry of holding onto existence-based constructs of the Divine—or any "thing," for that matter.

An abcanny-informed theology cannot be simply apophatic. A suspicion of language and constructs as reifying what cannot be held in such boxes can only go so far. The abcanny demands a commitment to movement if one is not to fall into the idolatrous comfort of any convention. The yearning of the heart, the stretching toward hope, the belief in love, the lived knowledge that labels and categories do not adequately summarize life: these convictions can never be decided once and for all. New contexts, phases of life, relationships, challenges—even a new day—demand new configurations of one's orientation toward what matters most and most deeply. An abcanny-informed theology would be one of constant discernment, fueled by an abiding rejection of the adequacy of any label.

Philosophical Implications

This chapter has woven philosophical considerations throughout. For instance, Derrida's hauntology receives fresh considerations in Miéville's writing. It is also quite possible that Miéville's discussion may have much to do with the Lacanian idea of the *real*. Miéville, normally quite skeptical about the applicability of any psychodynamic theorizing, seems to drift between seeing Lacan as another essentialist and allowing for the possibility that Lacan may indeed have hit upon the abcanny when Miéville notes that the Weird is "usually implacably Real in Lacanian terms" (2008, p. 107). However, any attempt to bridge the abcanny to Lacan would necessitate a wholesale rapprochement of *jouissance*, the symbolic, the imaginary, and could lead to some marvelously creepy reinterpretations of the mirror phase. It must fall to interdisciplinary conversations with creative Lacan scholars, such as Hook (e.g., 2017), to deepen that discourse.

Although there are far too many philosophical directions one can go in connecting the abcanny to meaninglessness, nihilism, identity, and impermanence, one last comment on alterity merits mention. This chapter's discussions have all been playing with frontiers of otherness. The abcanny, after all, reminds one that every familiarity is a brittle crust atop a seething Weird alterity. Things, people, and oneself are all far stranger than anyone allows. Therefore, a deeper phenomenology of the abcanny would necessitate an extended consideration of the works of Emmanuel Levinas (1906–1995). Levinas makes alterity primary. The individual owes a fundamental debt to the Other—transcendent alterity. Most people encounter this Other in others—individuals we encounter outside ourselves. This debt to the Other, experienced with others, cannot be paid. In my depths, "I" am not some irreducible "self" but this debt to the Other.

Scholars of Levinas typically take his works as a bridge between the discourses of faith, psychology, and philosophy. As such, he is usually used as a gentle and intellectually rigorous proponent of the fundamentally ethical nature of life. That is, one does not come to ethics by way of philosophical mechanisms; rather, philosophy and psychology emerge from the unavoidably, primarily ethical configuration of the human condition. This grounding itself is found in the primacy of alterity.

As light-filled and life-affirming as Levinasian discourse typically is, the converse darkness ought not to be ignored. Rigid identities will always be defensive against alterity. "Othering"—a dark craft in which Lovecraft was a past master—is itself a defense against the primacy of the Other. The phenomenology of clutching to things, principles, intellectual justifications, and a self-as-primary is a study in pitch-black delusion. The inevitability of the primacy of alterity renders these defensive postures untenable. Thus, one must constantly reconfigure one's denial of the other if one is to not give in to the call of the Other. The threatened dissolution of one's certainties can seem indistinguishable from madness. Thus, an essay or text bridging the Weird and abcanny to Levinas's philosophy seems ready to be written.

A Return to the Theater: The Shabcanny

While the curtains close with a rattle and a thump, I invite readers to return with me to that movie palace in which I first saw Kubrick's *2001* (1968). Theaters, like meaning-making, need constant upkeep and renewal. The Palace Theatre of Canton, Ohio, where the screening occurred, opened in 1926 and has undergone several renovations since that mid-1970s showing. If I'm honest, I have a strong bias toward wanting to see these historical landmarks preserved, updated, used, and repurposed to remain parts of a changing urban landscape.

Simultaneously, I also have a weakness for run-down theaters—crumbling plaster, creaking floors, tattering carpets, and all. Most theaters were not built to last. They were hastily constructed to exploit an opportunity. If anything remains of them, their decaying bodies are artifacts of long-gone economic, cultural, and geographical configurations. When an empresario or theater company buys, rents, or squats in such spaces, they can create something like a temporary autonomous zone (TAZ). This transitory configuration is nothing new. Carnivals, circuses, Travelers, theatrical troupes, migrant laborers, artists' collectives, bootleggers, skate parks, film production companies, criminal gangs, disaster recovery crews, and musicians on tour—to name but a few—are more than familiar with the need to establish their own impermanent, temporary cultures. The TAZ will dissolve with their failure, the completion of their purpose, or the context changing adequately to force the crew to move on or break up.

One performance aesthetic giddily embraces this run-down, transitory intersection. Whether they find the crumbling theaters or bring the set with them, this subgenre is something like a "broken cabaret" that includes what is now roughly labeled "dark cabaret." Its provenance is deep and shabby and may stretch far further back than the Edwardian *Grand Guignol* and other salacious theatrical spectacles. But in its Weimar Republic–Berlin resonances from the works of Bertolt Brecht (1898–1956) and Kurt Weill (1900–1950), this aesthetic finds inspirations that were themselves already tenuous, tattered, and threadbare. That era's tension of nihilism, fascism, creative defiance, and resigned dissipation found voice in Isherwood's *Goodbye to Berlin* (1939). Van Druten's 1951 play *I Am a Camera* kept the story alive and led to the 1966 musical *Cabaret* (Kander et al.) and the 1972 film adaptation (Fosse & Allen). Thus, just as a divided Berlin was becoming an avant-garde cultural hotspot, the cabaret, gone but not forgotten, renewed its lease.

Cold War Berlin in the 1970s offered important counterculture influences with David Bowie (1947–2016), Iggy Pop, Nina Hagen, Nick Cave and the Bad Seeds, and others who made their way through the city. Hockenos tells this story well in his *Berlin Calling* (2017). Today, with arch-self-awareness, the television series *Babylon Berlin* (Tykwer et al., 2017–present) keeps the Weimar references fresh. But this story and aesthetic extend well beyond the Weimar Republic or the evanescence of the 1980s' divided Berlin.

For contemporary examples from the last 50 years, this aesthetic can be found in the music, stage productions, and "events" of Tom Waits, the Tiger Lillies, Rasputina, Squirrel Nut Zippers, Gogol Bordello, Sleepytime Gorilla Museum, the Dresden Dolls, Katzenjammer, Circus Contraption, Jill Tracy, Firewater, and Morphine, among many others. Productions tumble through elements of busking, burlesque, contemporary circuses like Cirque du Soleil, tent revivals, speakeasies, medicine shows, puppetry, and a host of other interstitialities. In addition to freely borrowing from classical, jazz, and rock cabinets, instrumentation can look like Duchamp ready-mades and found objects, calliopes, hurdy-gurdies, theremins, musical saws, accordions, relics of long-gone innovations like the Stroh violin, and other musical resurrections, reanimations, and zombifications.

Literary and art history resonances abound. In a classic example, the Tiger Lillies took a German children's book of over-the-top cautionary tales, *Der Struwwelpeter* (Hoffmann, 1845), to inspire their 1998 show *Shockheaded Peter* (Jacques et al.). Other sources run from the Medieval to the Romantic, Gothic, Decadent, Surreal, Dada, Absurdist, and beyond, encompassing Dante, Chaucer, Coleridge, Poe, Dickinson, Lovecraft, Gaiman, Moore, Burroughs, Bukowski, Wilde, Baudelaire, Rimbaud, Mallarmé, and many more. So deep are the homages and references that one might think that this broken cabaret is where liberal and fine arts majors end up, quaffing absinthe-forward artisanal cocktails.

This genre combines the ironic, punk, camp, goth, kitsch, glam, honkytonk, metal, Balkan, occult, klezmer, bleak nostalgia and longing, arch-theatrical, and retrofuturisms of Steampunk, neo-noir, and Dieselpunk, all with varying degrees of self-aware humor. The magical and banal wreak a strange temporary alchemy. With paradox offering its ritual power, in its conspicuous avoidance of ever entirely "playing it straight," the denizens of a broken cabaret can often point to an unexpected, heartbreaking sincerity.

Thus, I beg the reader for one last indulgence of a neologism, as I add to Miéville's (2012) tongue-in-cheek list of "not-cannies": the *shabcanny*. This is the shabby, threadbare, caked-makeup, decaying creativity that defies the inevitable extinguishing of the footlights with one more rough-throated encore. The shabcanny relates to Miéville's (2012) "postcanny," in which he describes the monstrosities of the past that have been thrown out. I think of junk stores with old toys that no one remembers anymore. But the shabcanny brings a defiant "Island of

Misfit Toys" (see *Rudolph the Red-Nosed Reindeer*, Roemer et al., 1964) rebellion with it, along with twinges of longing, nostalgia, irony, and camp and cool.

The shabcanny rebels against shiny novelty with genuine bricolage creativity. It indicts heteronormative culture with gleeful queerness. It shouts down fascism while goosestepping in moth-eaten uniforms, even as it is lined up against the wall. Through endless satire, it undoes itself even as it rages against hypocrisy. Stare too long and one will see a deep sadness, a grief for those lost and left behind, and a sorrow for the inevitable demise of all that is beautiful, pure, and true—maybe including oneself. Only in this vulnerability does the scandalously gorgeous, the heart-wrenchingly broken, the blasphemously sacred have an ever-so-brief time and space to emerge. In its aftermath, one must move on. Holding on to what has passed leaves one in cliché, hypocrisy, empty nostalgia, and dissipated decay.

This is territory familiar to Ligotti. As Harris notes in his 2012 article and elsewhere in this current volume, Ligotti's stories offer uncanny puppets, run-down neighborhoods and worlds, cults of clowns, harlequins, and carnival sideshows. Miéville, too, offers ghetto-dwelling artists and inventors of all kinds intersecting for fleeting moments of the effulgent. If there is a whiff of sulfur in Ligotti's tales or the distant echo of jackboots in Miéville's, it is only because they know this will all pass away. It may well end in tears. But still they create.

While discussing these ideas with author Susan Rowlands at a London Arts-Based Research Centre event (October 18, 2023), she observed that the nihilism-tinged Weird was rife with the inevitable tragedy of an Oedipally obsessed patriarchal world. She offered that comedy must be the response. "In tragedy we fall," she noted, "but in comedy, we keep getting back up." This sums up much of the tension I believe the shabcanny may convey.

The abcanny demands an answer. The abcanny demands we do something with the constant change we snapshot into false permanence. A shabcanny creativity shot through with this awareness may be an answer. For now.

Everything Changes

The themes this chapter has played with are not new. Camus broaches all these issues in a way that spoke to his time. I have cited many existentialists as pointing toward these tensions throughout this chapter. Today, the transition from Gen X to millennials to postmillennials brings forth similar discussions. Irony, pessimism, cynicism, misinformation, disaffection, and nihilism are frequent topics in those generations, for whom postmodernity is both a well-established condition and a philosophy more likely experienced in animated comedies than the works of Foucault or Derrida.

Thus, what a delight so many experienced when the Daniels released *Everything Everywhere All at Once* (Kwan et al., 2022). In this multi-award-winning film, a bagel with—literally—everything on it becomes a concretization of the nihilistic entropy of a multiverse too vast to mean anything. The film pits a family running a laundromat against this multi-cosmic force. By the end, the emptiness has not been explained away. No single meaning carries the day. But an in-the-moment taking up of the invitation to be truly present to another in one's best ability to love does.

The film (Kwan et al., 2022) offers one species of an emerging response to both modernity and postmodernity: the metamodern. Not repudiating the brutal legacy of modernity or denying the absurdity of the postmodern condition, the metamodern offers the individual and communities an opportunity to ask, as if for the first time, "How shall we live?" Though words like "hope" and "love" may still carry an asterisk as metamodern advocates separate their meaning-making from those who have abused these terms, the metamodern seeks to live in ways that embody what a choice to live entails.

Acknowledging the abcanny does not demand that we defeat nihilism. We cannot defeat the absurdity of life, its indeterminacy, its breathtaking indifference. The abcanny strips life back to nothing, and each person is left to ask what matters. Choosing to live, how shall we go about our lives? What mattered once will not matter ever again in the same way. We cobble together scraps, traces, references, homages, reconstructed "memories," and pocket lint to make new lives.

This chapter sits in a volume of essays originally offered at a conference. In its conventions, these essays roughly participate in a type of "scholarly record." We authors define our subject and perspectives, cite our sources, explain our cases, and offer our conclusions. I am left a little uneasy about where this writing has taken me in the face of those academic conventions, since "everything changes" seems to be one of the abiding impacts of the abcanny. Everything changes: conferences, professional organizations, professions, relationships, families, definitions of families, definitions of relationships, ethical codes, identities, genders, languages, faiths, gods, definitions of faiths and gods . . . and on and on. Like a Tibetan Buddhist sandpainting, I am tempted to burn this essay as soon as I finish it. (If you are reading this, apparently, I didn't.)

I don't know if any of what I've said in this chapter is what China Miéville meant with his coining of the *abcanny*. What I have offered here is where playing with some of his sources and his writing has taken me when applied to fields in which I more typically roam.

So with the curtain closed, the house lights are turned up. I can no longer see the stars or the black spaces between them. But I remain haunted by the inscrutable presence of that monolith. As the inscrutably alien continues to emerge around me, I hope that I will continue to be baffled, intrigued, and full of wonder.

References

Aronovsky, D. (Director, Writer, Story), Gullette, S. (Story), Watson, E. (Story & Producer), Vogel, S. (Producer). (1998). π [Film]. Protozoa Pictures.

Aster, A. (Director & Writer), Andersson, P., & Knudsen, L. (Producers). (2019). *Midsommar* [Film]. Square Peg; B-Reel Films; A24.

Blomkamp, N. (Director & Writer), Tatchell, T. (Writer), Jackson, P., & Cunningham, C. (Producers). (2009). *District 9* [Film]. QED International; WingNut Films; TriStar Pictures.

Bould, M. (2000, September/October). Blowing raspberries: An interview with China Miéville. *Vector*, *213*, 4–8.

Butler, A. M. (2000, September/October). Abjection and *The Thing*. *Vector*, *213*, 9–12.

Calia, M. (2014, February 2). Writer Nic Pizzolatto on Thomas Ligotti and the weird secrets of "true detective". *The Wall Street Journal*.

Campbell, J. (1949). *The hero with a thousand faces*. Pantheon Books.

Carpenter, J. (Director), De Luca, M. (Writer), King, S. (Producer). (1994). *In the Mouth of Madness* [Film]. New Line Cinema.

Carpenter, J. (Director), Lancaster, J. (Writer), Foster, D., & Turman, L. (Producers). (1982). *The Thing* [Film]. The Turman-Foster Company.

Chiang, T. (2002). Story of your life. In T. Chiang (Ed.), *Stories of your life*. Vintage Books (Original story published 1998).

Clarke, A. C. (1982). *2010: Odyssey two*. Ballantine Books.

Clarke, A. C. (1987). *2061: Odyssey three*. Del Rey.

Clarke, A. C. (1997). *3001: The final odyssey*. Del Rey.

Clover, C. J. (1992). *Men, women, and chainsaws: Gender in the modern horror film*. Princeton University Press.

Creed, B. (2015). Horror and the monstrous-feminine: An imaginary abjection. In B. K. Grant (Ed.), *The dread of difference: Gender and the horror film* (2nd ed.). University of Texas Press (Original work published 1996).

Daniels, A. B. (2011a). *Imaginal reality, volume one: Journey to the voids*. Aeon Books.

Daniels, A. B. (2011b). *Imaginal reality, volume two: Voidcraft*. Aeon Books.

Daniels, A. B. (2014). *Jungian crime scene analysis: An imaginal investigation*. Routledge.

Daniels, A. B. (2021). "1321: A space odyssey": A response to Franke. In A. B. Daniels (Ed.), *Dante & the other: A phenomenology of love*. Psychology & the Other Series. Routledge.

Demme, J. (Director), Tally, T. (Writer), Utt, K., Saxon, E., & Bozman, R. (Producers). (1991). *The Silence of the Lambs*. Strong Heart Productions.

Derrida, J. (1994). *Specters of Marx: The state of the debt, the work of mourning and the new international*. Routledge (Original work published 1993).

The Doors. (1978). *An American prayer* [Album]. Elelktra & Asylum Records.

Doyle, A. C. (1902). *The hound of the baskervilles*. George Newnes Ltd.

Duffer, M., & Duffer, R. (Creators & Executive Producers), Levy, S., Cohen, D., Wright, B., Holland, C., Mecklenberg, J., Thunell, M., Gajdusek, K., Paterson, I., & Gwinn, C. (Executive Producers). (2016–present). *Stranger Things* [TV series]. 21 Laps Entertainment; Monkey Massacre Productions; Upside Down Pictures (season 5).

Ersoy, G. (2019). Crossing the boundaries of the unknown with Jeff VanderMeer: The monstrous fantastic and "abcanny" in *Annihilation*. *Orbis Litterarum: International Review of Literary Studies*, *74*(4), 251–263.

Fincher, D. (Director), Giler, D., & Hill, W. (Writers & Producers), Ferguson, L. (Writers), Ward, V. (Story), Carroll, G. (Producer). (1992). *Alien3*. Brandywine Productions.

Forbes, B. (Director), Goldman, W. (Screenplay), Scherick, E. J. (Producer). (1975). *The Stepford Wives*. Palomar Pictures.

Fosse, B. (Director), Allen, J. P. (Screenplay). (1972). *Cabaret* [Film]. ABC Pictures; Allied Artists.

Foucault, M. (2006). *History of madness* (J. Murphy & J. Khalfa, Trans.). Routledge (Original work published 1961).

Freeman, M. (2023). *Toward the psychological humanities: A modest manifesto for the future of psychology*. Routledge.

Freud, S., Strachey, J., Freud, A., & Rothgeb, C. L. (1953). *The standard edition of the complete psychological works of Sigmund Freud*. Hogarth Press and the Institute of Psycho-Analysis.

Gaiman, N. (1996). *Neverwhere*. BBC Books.

Gaiman, N. (1999). *Stardust*. DC Comics.

Gaiman, N. (2002). *Coraline*. HarperCollins.

Garland, A. (Director & Writer), Rudin, S., Macdonald, A., Reich, A., & Bush, E. (Producers). (2018). *Annihilation* [Film]. Skydance; DNA Films; Scott Rudin Productions; Huahua Media.

Glazer, J. (Director & Writer), Campbell, W. (Writer), Wilson, J., & Weschler, N. (Producers). (2013). *Under the Skin* [Film]. BFI; Film 4; Silver Reel; Creative Scotland; JW Films; FilmNation Entertainment.

Goddard, D. (Director & Writer), Whedon, J. (Writer & Producer). (2011). *Cabin in the Woods* [Film]. Mutant Enemy Productions.

Green, M. (Developer & Executive Producer), Abrams, J. J., Peele, J., Demange, Y., Knoller, D., Carraro, B., Stephenson, B., & Sackheim, D. (Executive Producers). (2020). *Lovecraft Country* [TV Series]. Afemme; Monkeypaw Productions; Bad Robot Productions; Warner Bros. Television Studios.

Hardy, R. (Director), Shaffer, A. (Writer), Snell, P. (Producer). (1973). *The Wicker Man* [Film]. British Lion Films.

Harris, J. M. (2012). Smiles of oblivion: Demonic clowns and doomed puppets as fantastic figures of absurdity, chaos, and misanthropy in the writings of Thomas Ligotti. *The Journal of Popular Culture, 45*(6), 1249–1265.

Heidegger, M. (1996). *Being and time. A translation of Sein und Zeit* (J. Stanbaugh, Trans.). State University of New York Press (Original work published 1927).

Higochinsky (Director), Niita, T. (Screenplay), Miyake, S. (Producer). (2000). *Uzumaki* [Film]. Omega Micott.

Hockenos, P. (2017). *Berlin calling: A story of anarchy, music, the wall, and the birth of the new Berlin*. The New Press.

Hoffmann, H. (1845). *Der Stuwwelpeter*. Literarische Anstalt.

Hook, D. (2017). *Six moments in Lacan: Communication and identification in psychology and psychoanalysis*. Routledge.

Isherwood, C. (1939). *Goodbye to Berlin*. Hogarth Press.

Jacques, M. (Music & Lyrics), Huge, A., & Stout, A. (Music), Bleach, J., Cairns, A., Gilmour, G., & Griffin, T. (Book). (1998). *Shockheaded Peter* [Musical].

Jonze, S. (Director), Kaufman, C. (Writer), Stipe, M., Stern, S., Golin, S., & Landay, V. (Producers). (1999). *Being John Malkovich*. Gramercy Pictures; Propaganda Films; Single Cell Pictures.

Kander, J. (Music), Ebb, F. (Lyrics), Masteroff, J. (Book). (1966). *Cabaret* [Musical].

Kaufman, P. (Director), Richter, W. D. (Screenplay), Solo, R. H. (Producer). (1978). *Invasion of the Body Snatchers*. Solofilm.

Kearney, R. (2009). *Anatheism: Returning to god after god*. Columbia University Press.

Korzybski, A. (1933). *Science and sanity: An introduction to non-Aristotelian systems and general semantics*. Science Press Printing Co.

Kristeva, J. (1982). *Powers of horror: An essay on abjection*. Columbia University Press (Original work published 1980).

Kubrick, S. (Director), Kubrick, S., & Clarke, A. C. (Producers & Writers). (1968). *2001: A space odyssey* [Film]. Metro-Goldwyn-Mayer Corp.

Kwan, D., & Scheinert, D. (Directors, Writers, & Producers), Russo, A., Russo, J., Larocca, M., Wang, J., & Peter, T. L. (Producers). (2022). *Everything everywhere all at once* [Film]. IAC Films; Gozie AGBO; Year of the Rat; Ley Line Entertainment.

Langley, T. (2023). *Stranger things psychology: Life upside down*. Wiley.

Leman, A. (Director & Producer), Branney, S. (Screenplay & Producer). (2005). *The Call of Cthulhu*. H. P. Lovecraft Historical Society.

Ligotti, T. (2010). *The conspiracy against the human race*. Viking Press.

Ligotti, T. (2015). *Songs of a dead dreamer and Grimscribe*. Penguin Classics.

Lovecraft, H. P. (1995). *Miscellaneous writings* (S. T. Joshi, Ed.). Arkham House.

Lovecraft, H. P. (2008). *The complete fiction*. Barnes & Noble.

Lucas, G. (Director & Writer), Kurtz, G. (Producer). (1977). *Star Wars* [Film]. Lucasfilm Ltd.

March-Russell, P. (2017). The abcanny politics of landscape in Lucy Wood's Diving Belles. *Short Fiction in Theory & Practice, 7*(1), 53–65.

Miéville, C. (2004). *Between equal rights: A Marxist theory of international law*. Brill Academic Publications.

Miéville, C. (2008). M. R. James and the Quantum Vampire: Weird; Hauntological: Versus and/or and and/or or? *Collapse, 4*, 105–128.

Miéville, C. (2009). *The city & the city*. Macmillan.

Miéville, C. (2010). *Kraken*. Macmillan.

Miéville, C. (2011). *Embassytown*. Pan Macmillan.

Miéville, C. (2012). On monsters; or, nine or more (monstrous) not cannies. *Journal of the Fantastic in the Arts, 23*(3), 374–392.

Miéville, C. (2016). *The last days of new Paris*. Del Rey Books.

Miéville, C. (2017). *October: The story of the Russian revolution*. Verso.

Miéville, C. (2022). *A spectre, haunting: On the communist manifesto*. Haymarket Books.

Nautilus English Books. (2012, April 30). *The anatomy of the city: China Miéville's "Kraken"*. https://nautilusenglishbooks.wordpress.com/2012/04/30/the-anatomy-of-the-city-china-mievilles-kraken/

Nolan, C. (Director, Writer, & Producer), Nolan, J. (Writer), Thomas, E., & Obst, L. (Producers). (2014). *Interstellar* [Film]. Legendary Pictures; Syncopy; Linda Obst Productions.

Peele, J. (Director, Writer, & Producer), McKittrick, S., Blum, J., & Hamm, Jr., E. H. (Producers). (2017). *Get out* [Film]. Blumhouse Productions; QC Entertainment; Monkeypaw Productions.

Pike, D. L. (2019). China Miéville's Fantastic Slums and the urban abcanny. *Science Fiction Studies, 46*(2), 250–267.

Pizzolatto, N. (Creator, Executive Producer, & Writer), Fukunaga, C. J., Stephens, S., McConaughey, M., Harrelson, W., Golin, S., & Brown, R. (Executive Producers). (2014). *True detective* (Season 1) [TV Series]. Anonymous Content; Parliament of Owls; Passenger; Neon Black; Lee Caplin/Picture Entertainment; HBO Entertainment.

Ramis, H. (Director, Screenplay, & Producer), Rubin, D. (Screenplay & Story), Albert, T. (Producer). (1993). *Groundhog day*. Columbia Pictures.

Roemer, L. (Director), Muller, R. (Writer), Rankin, Jr., A. (Producer). (1964). *Rudolph the red-nosed reindeer* [Television Special]. Videocraft International.

Roscoe, A. (2023, May 14). *Fake studies in academic journals may be more common than previously thought* [Radio broadcast]. NPR. www.npr.org/2023/05/14/1176062276/fake-studies-in-academic-journals-may-be-more-common-than-previously-thought

Ruff, M. (2016). *Lovecraft country*. HarperCollins.

Sagan, C. (1985). *Contact*. Simon & Schuster.

Schweitzer, D. (Ed.). (2003). *The Thomas Ligotti reader*. Wildside Press.

Scott, R. (Director & Producer), Goddard, D. (Screenplay), Kinberg, S., Schaefer, M., & Huffman, M. (Producers). (2015). *The Martian* [Film]. Scott Free Productions; Kinberg Genre; TSG Entertainment.

Scott, R. (Director), O'Bannon, D. (Writer & Story Writer), Shusett, R. (Story Writer), Carroll, G., Giler, D., & Hill, W. (Producers). (1979). *Alien* [Film]. 20th Century Fox; Brandywine Productions.

Shenk, J. (director) (2001). *The beginning: Making Star Wars: Episode I the Phantom Menace* [Documentary Film]. Lucasfilm Ltd.

Shyamalan, M. N. (Director, Writer, & Producer), Kennedy, K., Marshall, F., & Mercer, S. (Producers). (2002). *Signs*. Touchstone Pictures; Blinding Edge Pictures; The Kennedy/Marshall Company.

Shyamalan, M. N. (Director & Writer), Marshall, F., Kennedy, K., & Mendel, B. (Producers). (1999). *The Sixth Sense*. Hollywood Pictures. Spyglass Entertainment. The Kennedy Marshall Company; Barry Mendel Productions.

Sorokin, V. (2011). *Ice Trilogy*. New York Review Books Classics.

Spielberg, S. (Director), Crichton, M., & Koepp, D. (Screenplay), Kennedy, K., & Molen, G. R. (Producers). (1993). *Jurassic Park*. Universal Pictures. Amblin Entertainment.

Tarkovsky, A. (Director & Writer), Gorenstein, F. (Writer), Tarasov, V. (Producer). (1972). *Solaris* [Film]. Mosfilm.

Tarkovsky, A. (Director), Strugatsky, A., & Strugatsky, B. (Writers), Demidova, A. (Producer). (1979). *Stalker* [Film]. Mosfilm.

Tennyson, A. (1850). *In memorium, A. H. H.* www.online-literature.com/tennyson/718/

Topolsky, J. (2012, September 2). The classics: John' Carpenter's "apocalypse trilogy". *The Verge*. www.theverge.com/2012/9/2/3279482/the-classics-john-carpenter-apocalypse-trilogy

Tranter, K. (2012). An interview with China Miéville. *Contemporary Literature*, *53*(3), 416–436.

Tykwer, T. (Creator & Writer), Handloegten, H., & von Borries, A. (Writers), Arndt, S., Schott, U., & Polle, M. (Producers). (2017–present). *Babylon Berlin* [Television Series]. ARD Degeto; Sky Deutschland; X Filme Creative Pool; Beta Film.

VanderMeer, J. (2011). Conversation #1: China Miéville and the monsters. In J. VanderMeer (Ed.), *Monstrous creatures: Explorations of fantasy through essays, articles, and reviews* (pp. 55–63). Guide Dog Books (Original interview published 2008).

Vandermeer, J. (2014). *Area X: The southern reach trilogy: Annihilation; authority; acceptance*. FSG Originals.

Van Druten, J. (1951). *I am a camera* [Play]. Random House.

Venezia, T. (2010). Weird fiction: Dandelion meets China Miéville. *Dandelion: Postgraduate Arts Journal and Research Network*, *1*(1), 1–9. https://doi.org/10.16995/ddl.221

Villeneuve, D. (Director), Heisserer, E. (Writer), Levy, S., Levine, D., Ryder, A., & Linde, D. (Producers). (2016). *Arrival* [Film]. FilmNation Entertainment; Lava Bear Films; 21 Laps Entertainment.

Wachowskis (Directors & Writers), Silver, J. (Producer). (1999). *The Matrix*. Warner Brothers; Village Roadshow Pictures; Groucho II Film Partnership; Silver Pictures.

Wallenfang, D. (2022, June 5). *Jean-Luc Marion on the question of 'god's existence* [Video]. YouTube. www.youtube.com/watch?v=oDN6MuS4TqQ

Weir, P. (Director), Niccol, A. (Writer & Producer), Rudin, S., Feldman, E. S., & Schroeder, A. (Producers). (1998). *The Truman Show*. Scott Rudin Productions.

Whipp, G. (2018, January 4). Q&A: Christopher Nolan on the power of the people and why "2001" should be required preschool viewing. *Los Angeles Times*. www.latimes.com/entertainment/envelope/la-en-mn-christopher-nolan-20180104–htmlstory.html

Witzel, G. (2018). Abcanny waters: Victor LaValle, John Langan, and the weird horror of climate change. *Science Fiction Studies*, *45*(3 [136]), 560–574.

Wolf, V. (1981). *To the lighthouse*. Harcourt Brace & Company (Original work published 1927).

Wright, E. (Director & Writer), Pegg, S. (Writer), Park, N., Bevan, T., & Fellner, E. (Producers). (2013). *The world's end*. Relativity Media; Working Title Films; Big Talk Pictures; Dentsu.

Yalom, I. (1980). *Existential psychotherapy*. Basic Books.

Yalom, I. (1989). *Love's executioner and other tales of psychotherapy*. Basic Books.

Zemeckis, R. (Director & Producer), Hart, J. V., & Goldenberg, M. (Writers), Sagan, C., & Druyan, A. (Story Writers), Starkey, S. (Producer). (1997). *Contact* [Film]. South Side Amusement Company.

Chapter 2

The Divinalien

On Divine Alterity

Emily McAvan

Emma Baranowski, Naomi Anbar, and Amelia Maybrun provided copyediting for this chapter as part of the Northeastern University Psychological Humanities Workgroup.

This chapter investigates what it means that our culture has a place for aliens among other forms of fantastic beasts and monsters. Aliens have been a popular figure in science fiction narratives, and such representations have fueled belief in their real-world existence. According to the Pew Center, 65% of Americans believe in the existence of aliens (Kennedy & Lau, 2021), while 90% of Americans believe in some kind of higher power (Fahmy, 2018). About 56% of those profess faith in the God of the Bible, while another 33% say they believe in some kind of higher power or spiritual force. What, then, does this confluence between the alien and the divine signify, and what might that mean for us in tracing its relationship to alterity? If *both* God and aliens exist, did God create aliens? Or are they, in some circumstances, more like God than us?

I want to begin examining these questions by coining a phrase: the *divinalien*. I take inspiration for this term from Jacques Derrida's (1930–2004) term the "divinanimal," (1997/2008, p. 132) which he proposed in the posthumously published *The Animal That Therefore I Am*. Derrida coins the term as a means to discuss the confluence between the animal and the divine. For this chapter, I offer the *divinalien* to signal the way that representations of aliens meet long-standing ideas of the divine in the way they pursue transcendence as a goal, in the way that alien alterity comes to take on some of the cultural functions that God or angels have historically had in countries with a Christian past—and perhaps present. Arthur C. Clarke (1917–2008) famously formulated the law that "any technology sufficiently advanced is indistinguishable from magic" (1962/1973, p. 21), and it is arguable that the advanced technologies of aliens in science fiction intersect with the divine, the magical, and the strange.

At the beginning of the twentieth century, Rudolph Otto (1869–1937), in *The Idea of the Holy* (1917/1923), influentially addressed what he called the numinous, an otherworldly essence in which something beyond the everyday shows itself to us. Midcentury, Mircea Eliade (1907–1986) supplemented this with the idea of a

DOI: 10.4324/9781003519102-2

hierophany (1959, p. 11), an instance of the sacred intervening into the everyday profane world that we see across religious traditions. Both of these writers sought to explain the continued persistence of religious feeling after the Enlightenment and perhaps unsurprisingly saw the appearance of the sacred in everyday life as a profoundly irrational "subjective" experience that is rarely shared collectively. Just as the numinous, a phenomenological experience of the divine is profoundly subjective. I argue that the idea of a real encounter with an alien is itself subjective too. As examined by Scribner and Wheeler elsewhere in this volume, testimonies of alien abductions, whilst familiar to us from science fiction, are not generally understood to be describing physical realities so much as the psychological states of the witnesses—say, as a psychotic episode—and these are not considered widely authoritative in defining the nature of physical reality in the same way that the work of quantum physicists might.

In this sense, the alien and the divine in culture emerge as non-realistic narratives whose cultural work is, in many senses, metaphorical—a metaphoricity that bleeds into the beliefs of the vast majority of Americans who profess belief in both aliens and God. A "higher power," or even "God," can often mean, strictly, a belief in providence, in an order to the universe in which events happen for a reason, or it might even signal a desire for that to be true—just as "belief" in aliens might signal a desire for their existence and, perhaps, for the kinds of completion and wholeness at work in their popular culture depictions. Martin Hagglund has persuasively contended that many religious people are motivated as much or even more by this worldly care for the finite rather than the eternal, a practice that he calls "secular faith" (2019, p. 5). But it is also clear to me that the transcendent, as I prefer to call it rather than the eternal, functions in many instances of apparently secular life, even among atheists, from belief in the invisible power of the market or romantic love or Christmas to the narratives of popular fiction. Both the disenchantment of the world described by Max Weber (1864–1920) and Nietzsche's (1844–1900) death of God were arguably incomplete processes, perhaps inherently so. As well as the return of various forms of fundamentalisms in the late twentieth century, new forms of irrationalism now circulate, such as disbelief in the power of vaccines or climate science, or a messianic belief in certain politicians or the power of technology to save us from a warming world. Here I situate myself firmly amongst those writers who see our society as "post-secular," as being marked by an unpredictable mix of secular and profane not strictly defined by traditional categories of belief or religious practice. Charles Taylor has described this cultural milieu as a "pluralist world, in which many forms of belief and unbelief jostle" (2007, p. 531), and it is precisely through ambivalence and incoherence that we experience the contradictory terrain of contemporary life.

In coining the divinalien as a concept, then, I'm interested in thinking through the cultural confluences between the divine and the alien as a deconstructive concept that troubles the boundaries between these two images, that tells us something about how images of alterity and transcendence function, culturally speaking. I argue that the divinalien is specifically an image of transcendence, that it comes from above and contains a sense of abundance that overflows the boundaries of the physical world. Emmanuel Levinas (1906–1995), in *Of God Who Comes to Mind* (1982/1998), defines *transcendence* as the idea of being plus height, which has quite specific resonances in his post-phenomenological ethics of responsibility, but which I think works very well to encapsulate what is at stake in how we might turn our gaze to see aliens. In their alterity, images of aliens promise fulfillment, complete presence, complete meaning. They signal an understanding of the universe and a capacity to affect it in ways that humans cannot. They often even presage the end of history—sometimes its messianic completion, sometimes its apocalyptic destruction. Though, in many ways, the contemporary fields of literary fiction and cultural theory are defined by their emphasis on the immanent, there is ultimately no entire eliminating of the transcendent, which emerges in unexpected arenas like science fiction to adulterate categories like sacred and profane, fiction and truth, real and unreal.

The Divinalien

If we look at some of the images of the alien in science fiction, we can note a number of different thematics emerging. These are:

1. A saturation of white light
2. Images of hovering or flying
3. An affective relation of awe, wonder, and terror

These images occur over and over in science fiction films and TV series, from *Close Encounters of the Third Kind* (Spielberg, 1977) to *The X Files* (Carter, 1993–2002). It is my argument that these images show that the alien is one of the sites for "transcendence" in our culture, one place in which there is imagined to be an otherness to reality whose excess moves us beyond the limits of how we take up the human and everyday matter.

There are numerous examples of this to be found in visual media, in film and TV, and even in the imagery used to accompany stories in popular press. The image of a flying saucer hovering above the Earth, lit up with dazzling lights and powered by unknown fuel sources—the movement of flying saucers is often uncannily fast and quiet—has been a staple of science fiction since the 1950s. Appearing in B movies like *The Day the Earth Stood Still* (Wise, 1951) and *Plan 9 from Outer Space* (Wood, 1959), the flying saucer has become emblematic of our encounter with aliens and continued throughout the late twentieth century into the twenty-first. Spielberg's *Close Encounters of the Third Kind* (1977), for instance, depicts a flying saucer above the Earth whose lights have a kind of luminous quality. Emmerich's *Independence Day* (1996) depicts a similar image, with another circular spaceship, but this time marked by destruction, with a bright light laser destroying such iconic landmarks as the White House. Similar images of spaceships can be found in late-90s TV series *Stargate SG-1* (Glassner, 1997–2007) and the pulp parody *Mars Attacks* (Burton, 1996).

But it is not only spaceships which come from a position of height, with the humans that interact with aliens often flying through the air themselves. This famously occurs in Spielberg's *E.T. the Extra-Terrestrial* (1982), where ET causes Elliott and his friends' bikes to fly through the air. In *The X Files* (1993), a scene depicted Agent Fox Mulder's sister Samantha being abducted by aliens and shows her suspended in mid-air as she leaves through her bedroom window. The image of the alien abduction by tractor beam was familiar enough by the early 90s to be parodied by *The Simpsons* (Brooks, 1989–present) in many of their Halloween "Treehouse of Horror" episodes.

If we start to think about these images and their relationship to divinity, we might first of all note the other place in our culture where images of saturated white light take place—familiar to us in representations of heaven or near-death experiences. In the case of the near death, one can note another place where transcendence irrupts. These shining celestial spaces are found in popular culture images of heaven, as in the movie *Bruce Almighty* (Shadyac, 2003), or even in the saturated light of Harry Potter's near-death experience in *Harry Potter and the Deathly Hallows, Part 2* (Yates, 2011). Popular press outlets like Newsweek accompany stories on heaven with images of pearly gates and saturated white light (Almond, 2018).

Thus, a first major point of the divinalien intersection is that there is a usually unacknowledged confluence between the tropes that signify the divine and those that signify the alien. In numerous science fiction texts, the depiction of aliens is in the realm of what Rudolph Otto in *The Idea of the Holy* (1917/1923) once called the numinous, an otherworldly essence in which something beyond the everyday shows itself to us. What might it mean that all these images are typically bathed in white? There is a sense that the saturation of white signifies a purity of matter beyond the quotidian, that they represent being in its purest essence. Aristotle famously imagined that all light color came from either lightness or darkness (Smithsonian, 2021), sent by God from heaven, while Newton replaced this model by demonstrating through the use of a prism that sunlight was composed of seven colors. Thus, whiteness has arguably an archetypal relationship to transcendence, it has been imagined to be the origin of all light, and the more of it that saturates a screen, the more a scene is pointing us toward or beyond the material world. This is, I argue, an idea that suggests an excess of being in the alien, an originary overflowing that goes beyond the everyday into the realm of the supernatural, the otherworldly, the divine.

We can supplement this idea of transcendence in the alien by thinking further about the images of hovering that are so familiar to viewers of science fiction. Again, there is a relationship between the idea of height and ideas of the divine in Christian theology. Ask any 5-year-old—or 50-year-old, for that matter—where heaven is and they'll inevitably point you up to the sky. The word "heaven" in English originates in the Old English *heofon*, meaning, the home of God. This is more or less an accurate rendering of much of the history of the word, though in foregrounding the presence of God, it loses the associations of height. The Hebrew

Bible uses a number of words to describe heaven, notably the word for heaven, which is *shamayim*, a plural form related to the idea of water—*mayim*. In its earliest sense, in Genesis 1:1, it designates an original upper water, though this is soon distinguished from the waters below as *rakia*, firmament (Genesis 1:8). *Shamayim* then begins to take on the more familiar senses associated with heaven of height and God's presence. The term *marom* also appears, as in Psalm 68:18, as "on high," while God himself is described as *elyon* (God most high) in Jewish liturgy. The sense of the height of heaven is so pervasive that the New International Version even talks about "him who rides across the highest heavens" (Psalm 68:33), though Jewish translations render that verse with "ancient heavens."

When we get to Christian interpretations of heaven, we see heaven continuing to be associated with height, without any of the connection to water. The New Testament uses the Greek *ouranos*, meaning "sky," which is linked to the Greek god Uranus, the god of the sky.

In the Latin Vulgate, *rakia* is rendered as *firmamentum*, which has the implication of support, of holding up, or even of the main crux of an argument. In the New Testament, 1 Thessalonians depicts life after death through images of the sky:

> For the Lord himself will come down from heaven, with a loud command, with the voice of the archangel and with the trumpet call of God, and the dead in Christ will rise first. After that, we who are still alive and are left will be caught up together with them in the clouds to meet the Lord in the air. And so we will be with the Lord forever.
>
> (4:16–17, NIV)

Note that God initially comes *down* from heaven—so his proper place is above us—and that Christian believers meet up with the dead in the clouds. This verse, I should note, has helped inspire the more recent evangelical idea of the rapture as well as more historic associations between the sky and the divine.

There are a number of ambivalences in the etymology of the word "heaven" worth highlighting in this context then. If we think of *firmamentum*, of holding up or support, then we are entered into a sense of relationality to the heavens. Is it the sky that is held up, and if so, how or by whom? Or conversely, might that heaven also be holding *us* up? Are we bound up from the start in a relationship to the transcendent? *Shamayim* raises other, interesting questions about relationality, in which the distinction between upper and lower waters suggests the difference between the two to not be a categorical difference of ontological composition so much as height. This is perhaps a somewhat-dissonant idea that has largely been discarded in the history of the idea of heaven—an immanence that has been ignored in the depiction of heaven as a transcendence that is both height *and* being. And if *shamayim* is a plural—"heavens"—then perhaps we can see this as signaling to a broader sense beyond simply that of our earth. If there are heavens, then perhaps there are multiple earths. And in *ouranos*, we get the sense of a polytheism sneaking into Christianity, of "gods," again plural. All this would seem, therefore, to be fertile ground for the space of the divinalien, which displaces the singularity of the biblical God into a multiplicity above.

After all, popular culture depictions of heaven tend to situate it in the clouds, above us. So if we think of the alien as being above us, too, as coming down from beyond the Earth's atmosphere, then really it's coming down from heaven. What is significant about the science fiction recurrence of images of alien hovering is that they transcend gravity; they transcend our place on the earth—and the earth has been historically associated with the human, of course, right from the narrative of Adam being made from the "dust of the earth" in Genesis 2:7, JPS. In their height above us, they occupy the space of the divine.

Alien Alterity

With our eyes cast upward, we can clearly see that there is something happening here in the association between the alien and the divine, and the ways in which the divine alien transcends matter, gravity, categories of earthly being, and emotional response. What I want to get at in coining the phrase "the divinalien" is the idea that these categories are in fact overlapping, are in fact different ways of expressing a relationship to alterity. We sometimes use the word "alienate" to describe an estrangement, some sort of disconnection, or disconnection between self and other. Indeed, the word "alterity" comes from the Latin *alter* (two)—it's a relationship between self and other. Post-structuralist thinkers have fleshed out our understanding of this relationship, showing the way that it is constructed through language—for Lacan—or sexual difference—for Irigaray. But it is Levinas whose work shows what is at stake most of all in alterity. For Levinas, the other always asserts an ethical demand upon us. And upon Levinas's work, Derrida builds, complicating the linguistic dimensions through which otherness becomes known to us. In other words, Derrida insists upon the strangeness of the other, of the ways we cannot control or predict or fully account for their alterity. In light of this, I argue, therefore, that the divinalien is most of all an image of the stranger, of the strangeness of the stranger.

An *alien* can be, as well as an extraterrestrial, a foreigner, someone from another land. Of course, the chief means through which the Bible talks about alterity is the idea of the stranger. In the Torah, the word *ger*, Hebrew for "stranger," is mentioned almost 50 times. Exodus 23:9, for instance, says that "you know the feelings of a stranger, having yourselves been strangers in the land of Egypt" (JPS). This is taken up in the New Testament, with Matthew 25:35, for example, having Jesus say, "I was hungry and you gave me something to eat, I was thirsty and you gave me something to drink, I was a stranger and you invited me in" (NIV). These invocations of the stranger are bound up in a discourse of hospitality, which Derrida has argued can be seen as one of the foundational elements of human civilization (Derrida & Dufourmantelle, 1997/2000). But these strangers remain ostensibly human and, as such, can be seen to function within a field of intelligibility that the truly alien does not. We can know these strangers' feelings and can invite them in for food and drink. The stranger has a face in the sense that Emmanuel Levinas has given it in *Totality and Infinity* (1961/1985) and is able to exert an ethical demand upon us. And they almost certainly have a language of some kind. In short, the human stranger is intelligible.

The divinalien, however, is not precisely intelligible in the same way. Firstly, it exists as a transcendence of the limitations of form. Science fiction imagines aliens in a multitude of ways, as monstrous hybrids of familiar forms, cutting together aspects of plants, insects, mammals, and the humanoid. They may be, as in the infamous "little gray" or "little green" men, somewhat like us. Or they may be, as in the titular alien of the *Aliens* series, beginning with Scott's *Alien* (1979), more animalistic than us. They may require different atmospheres to survive and modify their corporeal form in ways we cannot, as in *Arrival* (Villeneuve, 2016). They may be faster than us, as in the film series *Species*, beginning with Donaldson's 1995 release, or *Predator*, first appearing in McTiernan's 1987 film. Or they may be symbiotes whose lives stretch for thousands of years or "ascend" to a higher plane of existence beyond the corporeal, as in the TV series *Stargate SG-1* (Glassner et al., 1997–2007). But in any case, in their violations of our categories for mere strangers, these aliens collapse our boundaries between the human and the non-human emphatically. While they may be enough like us to communicate at times, they are ultimately not bound by the same corporeal limits as humanity; thus, they overrun the boundaries of category, fixity, and measurement through which we create the idea of the human.

Moreover, the alien comes to us from beyond language—it transcends it. The "universal translator" in *Star Trek* (Roddenberry, 1966–1969) allows humans to communicate with not-too-alien races like the Klingons, Vulcans, and Ferengi. In *Arrival* (Villeneuve, 2016), the process of coming to understand the language of the distinctly alien "heptapods" unlocks the ability to foresee the future, challenging our ideas of what temporality and causality mean. Perhaps more radically, Stanislaw Lem's evergreen *Solaris* (1961/2002) imagines an alien life-form as an ocean, profoundly foreign to human ideas of embodiment, intelligence, and even "encounter." The alien appears to "communicate" through behavior to its human observers, by creating spontaneous structures on its surface. But it also communicates through its knowledge of the human mind when it recreates the dead wife of the protagonist Kelvin from his memories. Lem probes the limits of materiality and cognition with a truly alien difference to what it means to know and to act. The divinalien does not communicate in the way that we do and, in doing so, shows us powers beyond our comprehension—and comprehension beyond our powers.

Following Jacques Derrida's famous formulation in *The Gift of Death* that "every other is a little bit Other" (1992/1994, p. 82), I argue that the alterity of the alien collapses the boundary between alien others, divine others, and human others. Like God, the divinalien is not bound by the rules that limit humanity. Some aliens are immortal, some omnipotent, and some know the secrets of the universe. I have, in my book *The Postmodern Sacred* (McAvan, 2012), used the term the "transcendental signifier," talking about the way that depictions of transcendence in science fiction signify to the sky, and to an authenticity of being beyond the everyday world marked by the play of difference. This is an adaptation of Derrida's idea of the "transcendental signified" (1972/2002, p. 19), in which God is a super-eminent plenitude of presence that guarantees the order of meaning. The transcendental signified is outside of the world of *différance*, of interpretation, and is the dream of "absolutely pure, transparent and unequivocal translatability" (Derrida, 1972/2002, p. 19). In other words: perfect meaning.

The divinalien signals upward, to a world of perfect understanding. Like God, the divinalien is able to be understood across linguistic divides. Like God, the divinalien is both absolutely other to our sense of ontology, of what a being "is," *and* in possession of an understanding that makes the universe absolutely comprehensible. These aliens have a messianic function, as harbingers that promise redemption and a fullness of meaning that have a proximity to the divine, but as others whose alterity can never be fully grasped.

Their otherness is always bound up in an otherness to finitude. If, as Judith Butler has noted, the human is always a matter of calculation (2016, p. 7), of rules through which the human becomes legible and understandable, then the divinalien, by contrast, cannot be measured or accounted for entirely. Where Spinoza once said that "no one has yet determined what the [human] body can do" (1677/1996, p. 71), this is doubly true for the divinalien, whose unknown capacities are a matter of ontology. What the alien "is," we do not know—indeed, trying to work out some understanding of alien alterity, including a way to control or defeat it, is often the narrative device through which encounters with the alien work in science fiction.

The strangeness of the alien then exists in a tension with "the true," with post-Enlightenment ontologies of the knowable, of verifiable reality, an implicit context for the non-Realist genre of science fiction. Darko Suvin (1979) famously defined *science fiction* as the literature of extrapolation, of taking an element of commonly understood reality and intensifying that element into something new. The "science" of science fiction would seem to be in question with the appearance of the truly alien, being more fantastic than realistic, less an extrapolation than an insertion of alterity. If the alien is strange, then it is not true vis-à-vis the dominant Realist narrative; but if the alien somehow became true, then it would no longer be strange—because it would have changed our epistemologies of what truly exists. This would be a domestication of the alien's alterity and would profoundly change our entire sense of what constitutes "reality." The slippage between unidentified flying objects (UFOs) and aliens, extraterrestrials from other planets, suggests that what the alien names is *unknowability.*

This is, I think, also the space of God, whose presence is imagined by some to lie behind human events, but for whose direct presence is largely imagined to have disappeared from the world, the aforementioned disenchantment of modernity famously described by Max Weber. While many people of course believe that God exists, even most of those believers would look for scientific explanations—disease, unwellness, or mental illness—for someone who claimed to be hearing the voice of God. Or we might consider the moralizing of the natural world engaged in by some members of the US Christian Right, as when Pastor John Hagee said that Hurricane Katrina was a result of "the judgment of God" (Gross, 2006) because of their sins, yet his declaration was widely condemned. Although I acknowledge that such beliefs have significant traction—Kennedy and Lau (2021) note that 48% of American adults believe God determines what happens to them most or all the time—I think that a post-Enlightenment epistemological rationalist belief system remains, in many senses, dominant. One does not hear religious explanations given for natural disasters much in the media, for instance; nor do most of us take a sick person to a priest rather than a doctor, regardless of our religious beliefs. The idea of a personal, theistic God coexists uneasily with the God of theodicy in a kind of semantic incoherence, and the movement between the two poles of the strange and the true then signals the ways in which the sacred interrupts the everyday as an instance of the impossible. Both God and alien are strange and often believed to be simultaneously true and untrue.

The divine and the alien are not so far apart anymore, and Derrida's gloss on the God of the Torah in *The Gift of Death* (1992/1994) shows the alienness of the divine. If aliens are divine, perhaps, too, the divine is alien. Is there anything more alien than the command of God in Genesis 22, the *Akedah*, in which he asks Abraham to sacrifice his son Isaac? Many readers, notably including Kierkegaard in *Fear and Trembling* (1843/1986), have struggled with the passage as an instance of a divine alterity whose command—and desire—appears monstrous, murderous even. The God of the Book of Job, who afflicts Job at the goading of a being simply called the Adversary—are not his motivations marked by an indecipherable alterity? And isn't Jesus, born without sin from a virgin birth, who transcends even death, incredibly alien in composition too? I would argue that part of the pleasure of the supernatural narratives in the Jewish and Christian traditions, which seem so deeply implausible to our modern eyes, is that they are really about the divinalien, the absolute alterity of the divine, which cannot be mastered or understood.

On Awe and Terror

And what this means for us, as humans, is our relationship to this divine alien is like the relationship to the divine that Otto (1917/1923) described so well— a co-mingling between awe and wonder, dread, reverence, and fear. Otto talks about how "feeling" remains even after our concepts have faded, an interesting phrase in the present, given the affective turn of much recent critical theory. Our encounter with the divine is a *mysterium tremendium*, a response to "the presence of that which is a Mystery inexpressible and above all creatures" (Otto, 1917/1923, p. 13). I note here both the alterity of the divine, a mystery that cannot be fully expressed in language, and of the image of height which appears too. We cannot make sense of an encounter with the alien within our post-Enlightenment scientific rationality, just as we cannot make sense of the divine. Indeed, the attempt across modernity to make religion more rational by reformers of all kinds has, in many ways, ultimately failed.

The alien often appears as a messianic figure, a stranger in whom we might find the redemption of history. The arrival of the Vulcans in *Star Trek: First Contact* (Frakes, 1996), humanity's first encounter with an alien race, heralds the beginning of a new utopian era in which war and conflict on Earth are over. More modestly, in *The X Files* (Carter, 1993), Mulder is convinced not only of alien existence but also of how the alien might redeem his lifelong search for his missing sister Samantha. The alien in *E.T. the Extra-Terrestrial* (Spielberg, 1982), too, evokes a sense of wonder at his otherness, at his ability to revive flowers simply from his thought— shades of the miraculous power of Jesus. As a children's movie, *E.T.* specifically is bound up in the production of cuteness, which Sianne Ngai has noted involves a power imbalance between the viewer and a dominated object, for "there is no judgment or experience of an object as cute that does not call up one's sense of power over it as something less powerful" (2012, p. 11). This is a rare instance of the alien's power being less than ours—with ET as a sick alien, his sense of threat to us is diminished, though the wonder remains. The divinalien often redeems; it saves—or is imagined to save.

We must remember, however, that there is always a sense of a potential threat from the alien too. The physicist Stephen Hawking famously said, "[I]f aliens ever visit us, I think the outcome would be much as when Columbus landed in America, which didn't turn out well for the Native Americans" (Williams, 2010, 42:05). We can see this violence at work in films like *Independence Day* (Emmerich, 1996), where there is a swift move from the awe of encountering the alien above to the dread of mass destruction. There's a scene in the movie of a rooftop party underneath the flying saucer, filled with people carrying signs saying, "Welcome" and "Take me away." The aliens are imagined here to be redeemers, to be saving mankind. As the scene progresses, the saucer opens up, bathed in an eerie blue light. "So pretty," says a female bystander in awe, while others look on agog. Then, of course, the blue light turns out to be a weapon, a laser which destroys the building underneath it instantly. Another example occurs in the film *The 5th Wave* (Blakeson, 2016), where an alien race simply termed "the others" lets loose several waves of attacks on Earth from its orbiting spaceship—an electromagnetic pulse which disables electrical power, unleashes earthquakes and a wave of avian influenza, and causes the possession of human bodies which go on to kill other humans. One should note the way the aliens are literally called "others" in this film, as well as the apocalyptic encounter with those aliens. The divinalien, then, can move redemption to destruction, can herald the end of the world rather than the beginning of a new one.

The way we experience the alien is with the same mix of emotions that we see in the divine, of transcending the realm of the rational, contained emotions— emphatically nonrational affective relations to alterity. "Be not afraid" is the phrase that occurs in the Bible anytime humans encounter the divine—especially angels—an idea which suggests maybe we *should* be a little afraid. This is a warning Hawking would undoubtedly affirm. The cluster of promises found by the alien is overlaid with fear, for the divinalien, this other, could either deliver or destroy, bring salvation or destruction—just as God brings both of those things to the people of Israel in the Tanakh and promises them to Christians in the New Testament.

In other words, the rationality that I have described that inflects our everyday practices cannot be strictly divided from either the irrationality of the religious or science fiction. Our affective responses to the divine, our *mysterium tremendium*, are not so easily distinguished from our responses to the alien. We desire and fear the alien, just as we desire and fear the divine. As a figure, the alien incarnates a whole host of characteristics that intersect with the divine, and as such, it is perhaps unsurprising, then, that belief in God—or at least a higher power—coexists with a belief in the alien in a significant number of people, even given the way that many traditional religions have discouraged a belief in the alien.

Conclusion

To conclude, I think the analysis of alterity which has been advanced by post-structuralists like Derrida and Levinas needs to be recalled in this context. If, as Levinas (1982/1998) argues, *transcendence* is "being plus height," this works very well to describe what is going on in the images of the alien above us. The alien has being, is finally fully present, and is above us at a height. It is a divine stranger who cannot be fully understood and cannot be totally assimilated to the realm of the quotidian, the mundane, the rational, or the order of the same. Derrida's (1997/2008) reaction to the other is one that calls for a hospitality to otherness, that demands an unconditional openness to that otherness. We cannot anticipate or control the otherness of the divinalien, cannot tell when whatever you call the sacred—the numinous of Otto, the hierophany of Eliade, the alterity of the other— will appear, or what it will do. While the alien may understand the secrets of the universe, we do not. Though in its transcendence of the everyday it promises the redemption of the utterly other, the divinalien is radically open in its consequences. Ultimately, we do not know when it will come, or what the alterity of the alien will bring, whether it be rapture or destruction, but in its inscrutability it brings with it the possibility of a transcendence of the everyday that remains significant.

References

Almond, P. (2018, June 8). What is heaven like? *Newsweek*. www.newsweek.com/heaven-afterlife-christianity-islam-judaism-966354

Blakeson, J. (Director), Grant, S., Goldsman, A., & Pinker, J. (Screenplay), Maguire, T., King, G., Plouffe, M., & Harris, L. (Producers). (2016). *The 5th wave* [Motion Picture]. Columbia Pictures.

Brooks, J. L., Groening, M., Jean, A., Selman, M., Frink, J., Simon, S., Reiss, M., Mirkin, D., Oakley, B., Weinstein, J., Scully, M., Cohen, D. X., Meyer, G., Omine, C., Long, T., & Maxtone-Graham, I. (Executive Producers). (1989–present). *The Simpsons* [Television series]. 20th Television.

Burton, T. (Director, Screenplay, Producer), Gems, J. (Screenplay), Franco, L. J. (Producer). (1996). *Mars attacks!* [Motion Picture]. Warner Bros. Pictures.

Butler, J. (2016). *Frames of war: When is life grievable?* Verso.

Carter, C., Goodwin, R. W., Gordon, H., Spotnitz, F., Gilligan, V., Shiban, J., Manners, K., Morgan, G., Wong, J., MacLaren, M., Watkins, M. W., & Greenwalt, D. (Executive Producers). (1993–2002). *The X files* [Television series]. Fox.

Clarke, A. C. (1973). *Profiles of the future: An inquiry into the limits of the possible*. Indigo (Original work published 1962).

Derrida, J. (1994). *The gift of death* (D. Willis Trans.). University of Chicago Press (Original work published 1992).

Derrida, J. (2002). Semiology and grammatology: Interview with Julia Kristeva. In *Positions* (A. Bass, Trans., pp. 15–34). Continuum (Original work published 1972).

Derrida, J. (2008). *The animal that therefore I am* (M.-L. Mallet, Ed.; D. Willis, Trans.). Fordham University Press (Original work published 1997).

Derrida, J., & Dufourmantelle, A. (2000). *Of hospitality: Anne Doufourmantelle invites Jacques Derrida to respond* (R. Bowlby, Trans.). Stanford University Press (Original work published 1997).

Donaldson, R. (Director), Feldman, D. (Writer & Producer), Marcuso, Jr., F. (Producer). (1995). *Species* [Motion Picture]. Metro-Goldwyn-Mayer Picture; Frank Marcuso Jr. Production.

Eliade, M. (1959). *The sacred and the profane: The nature of religion* (W. Trask, Trans.). Harcourt.

Emmerich, R. (Director & Writer), Devlin, D. (Writer & Producer) (1996). *Independence day* [Motion Picture]. 20th Century Studios.

Fahmy, D. (2018). *Key findings about Americans' belief in God*. Pew Research Center.

Frakes, J. (Director), Braga, B., & Moore, R. D. (Screenplay), Berman, R. (Producer). (1996). *Star Trek: First contact* [Motion Picture]. Paramount Pictures.

Glassner, J., Wright, B., Cooper, R. C., Mallozzi, J., Mullie, P., Anderson, R. D., & Greenburg, M. (Executive Producers). (1997–2007). *Stargate SG-1* [Television series]. MGM Domestic Television Distribution.

Gross, T. (2006). *Pastor John Hagee on Christian Zionism* [Radio broadcast]. NPR. www. npr.org/programs/fresh-air/2006/09/18/13077578/

Hagglund, M. (2019). *This life: Why mortality makes us free*. Profile.

Kennedy, C., & Lau, A. (2021). Most Americans believe in intelligent life beyond Earth; few see UFOs as a major national security threat. *Pew Research Center*. www. pewresearch.org/fact-tank/2021/06/30/most-americans-believe-in-intelligent-life-beyond-earth-few-see-ufos-as-a-major-national-security-threat/

Kierkegaard, S. (1986). *Fear and trembling* (A. Hannay, Trans.). Penguin (Original work published 1843).

Lem, S. (2002). *Solaris* (J. Kilmartin & S. Cox, Trans.). Harcourt (Original work published 1961).

Levinas, E. (1985). *Totality and infinity: An essay on exterity* (A. Lingis, Trans.). Duquesne University Press (Original work published 1961).

Levinas, E. (1998). *Of god who comes to mind* (B. Bergo, Trans.). Stanford University Press (Original work published 1982).

McAvan, E. (2012). *The postmodern sacred: Popular culture spirituality in the science fiction, fantasy and urban fantasy genres*. McFarland.

McTiernan, J. (Director), Thomas, J., & Thomas, J. (Writers), Gordon, L., Silver, J., & Davis, J. (Producers). (1987). *Predator* [Motion Picture]. 20th Century Fox; Lawrence Gordon Productions; Silver Pictures; Davis Entertainment; Amercent Films; American Entertainment Partners L. P.

Ngai, S. (2012). *Our aesthetic categories: Zany, cute, interesting*. Harvard University Press.

Otto, R. (1923). *The idea of the holy: An inquiry into the non-rational factor in the idea of the Divine and its relation to the rational* (J. W. Harvey, Trans.). Oxford University Press (Original work published 1917).

Roddenberry, G. (Executive Producer). (1966–1969). *Star trek* [Television series]. NBC.

Scott, R. (Director), O'Bannon, D. (Writer), Carroll, G., Giler, D., & Hill, W. (Producers). (1979). *Alien* [Motion Picture]. 20th Century Fox; Brandywine Productions.

Shadyac, T. (Director & Producer), Koren, S., & O'Keefe, M. (Screenplay & Producers), Oederkerk, S. (Screenplay), Carrey, J., Brubaker, J. D., & Bostick, M. (Producers). (2003). *Bruce almighty* [Motion Picture]. Universal Pictures.

Smithsonian Libraries. (2021). *The science of color.* https://library.si.edu/exhibition/color-in-a-new-light/science

Spielberg, S. (Director & Producer), Mathison, M. (Writer), Kennedy, K. (Producer). (1982). *E. T.: The extra-terrestrial* [Motion Picture]. Universal Pictures.

Spielberg, S. (Director & Writer), Phillips, J., & Phillips, M. (Producers). (1977). *Close encounters of the third kind* [Motion Picture]. Columbia Pictures.

Spinoza, B. (1996). *Ethics* (E. Curley, Ed. & Trans.). Penguin Classics (Original work published 1677).

Suvin, D. (1979). *Metamorphosis of science fiction: On the poetics and history of a literary genre.* Yale University Press.

Taylor, C. (2007). *A secular age.* Harvard University Press.

Villeneuve, D. (Director), Heisserer, E. (Screenplay), Levy, S., Levine, D., Ryder, A., & Linde, D. (Producers). (2016). *Arrival* [Motion Picture]. Paramount Pictures.

Williams, M. (Director), Hawking, S. (Writer). (2010). Aliens (Season 1, Episode 1) [Television series episode]. In J. Smithson (executive producer), *Into the universe with Stephen Hawking.* Darlow Smithson.

Wise, R. (Director), North, E. H. (Screenplay), Blaustein, J. (Producer). (1951). *The day the earth stood still* [Motion Picture]. 20th Century Fox.

Wood Jr., E. D. (Director, Writer, & Producer). (1959). *Plan 9 from outer space* [Motion Picture]. Reynolds Pictures Inc.

Yates, D. (Director), Kloves, S. (Screenplay), Heyman, D., Barron, D., & Rowling, J. K. (Producers). (2011). *Harry Potter and the deathly hollows-part 2* [Motion Picture]. Warner Bros. Pictures.

Chapter 3

The Alien Other
Cosmology and Social Transmission
of UFO Narratives

Scott R. Scribner and Gregory J. Wheeler

Hayley Dording, Emma Baranowski, and Mckenna Dahlen provided copyediting for this chapter as part of the Northeastern University Psychological Humanities Workgroup.

In 1927, J. B. S. Haldane (1892–1964) observed that "[t]he Universe is not only queerer than we suppose, but queerer than we *can* suppose" (p. 286). This quotation and its epistemological implications serve as a fitting epigraph for this examination of phenomena that fundamentally challenge the human capacity to make sense of the world and the cosmos.

Reports of unidentified flying objects (UFOs), more recently labeled "unidentified anomalous phenomena" (UAPs), underlie a substantial popular belief that Earth has been visited by alien beings. Over the past several decades, polls continue to show about a third of US and UK respondents believe that UFO reports are proof of alien life. In addition, alien abduction narratives (AANs) have achieved considerable social prominence since the late twentieth century (Scribner, 1999, 2003). Existing literature offers many proposed explanations for these phenomena; most interpret them as some type of physical, psychosocial, or religious event, thereby implicitly granting them ontological status.

Further examination reveals distinct differences in perceiver and content between these two categories of texts. For example, formal UFO sighting reporters tend to be extraverted and realistically oriented and to publish and socialize similarly, whereas originators of AANs tend to be more introverted, artistic, and may be discovered by UFO researchers or publicists (Mack, 1994). Wheeler (2000, p. 96) characterized such differences as discriminating between *Weldbild* (world picture, or "etic" science) and *Weltanschauung* (worldview, or "emic" folk belief) concerns. For example, UAP observations could be noted as "unidentified" but also suggestive of new technologies, whereas AANs primarily raise the possibility that non-human intelligences are in direct contact with humans.

An alien abduction narrative can describe a single experience or a group of experiences. AANs involve a claim that strange beings took the storyteller out of a bed or automobile—typically at night—and subjected them to quasi-medical examinations and other bizarre treatment. Frequently, these accounts include expressions of

DOI: 10.4324/9781003519102-3

terror as the victim is kidnapped and undergoes painful or humiliating procedures. Sometimes the alleged beings offer advice, philosophical or religious teachings, or warnings about Earth's precarious condition. An AAN storyteller may go public by themselves, or they contact and are interviewed by a professional writer or UFO researcher. The resulting narrative consists of a report of their being seized, transported, and experimented upon by alien creatures. Based on a controversial interpretation of data from a Roper Poll, some UFO abduction researchers have claimed that two million Americans may have been abducted by aliens (Hopkins et al., 1992).

Considering such extraordinary reports, one might ask why the study of UFOs and AANs could be important in this modern world, where "real" social problems need attention. Our response is that the claim that a personal report is simultaneously "strange" and "true" underlies both scientific and religious inquiry. "Strangeness"—a term of art in ufology—reflects a degree of deviation from what most people would consider the normal world picture, that is, the quality of anomalous content in the story. A truth claim implies a possibility of new knowledge and implications for the accepted worldview. A method that can improve our understanding of UFO reports and AANs might be generalized to shed light on other types of controversial narratives and claims, including those that influence the development of belief systems. Such a method could be termed *intersubjective*, a way to evaluate subjective reports and related claims while still being within the paradigm of accepted scientific consensus. Many theories have been proposed to account for the occurrence of alien abduction narratives. There are, in fact, too many possible explanations rather than too few (Scribner, 2003; Chapter 2).

The Night Sky in Antiquity

In *The idea of the holy* (1917/1923), Rudolf Otto (1869–1937) proposed a schema for understanding the human religious impulse, which also occurs in humankind's relationship to the sky. For many of us today, the night sky is dimmed by urban light pollution, so it may be difficult to grasp the emotional impact of a dark night sky. Otto's concept of *Mysterium tremendum et fascinans* described prehistory's interpretation of the sky as a habitation of various gods and the source of human meaning. *Mysterium tremendum*, a feeling of overwhelming awe and majesty of the "wholly other" in the night sky, leads to Otto's other pole of the numinous, *Mysterium fascinans*, an object of intense fascination and a desire to understand and absorb its mystery. Otto wrote:

> These two qualities, the daunting and the fascinating, now combine in a strange harmony of contrasts, and the resultant dual character of the numinous consciousness . . . may appear to the mind an object of horror and dread, but at the same time it is no less something that allures with a potent charm, and the creature, who trembles before it, utterly cowed and cast down, has always at the

same time the impulse to turn to it, nay even to make it somehow his own. The 'mystery' is for him not merely something to be wondered at but something that entrances him; and besides that in it which bewilders and confounds, he feels a something that captivates and transports him.

(p. 31)

Strangers in the Night

Systematic speculation about the sky goes back to the early Greeks, and their ideas were taken up by later philosophers and theologians through the centuries. However, Crowe (2008) noted that their underlying cosmological world picture had no support beyond speculation. As *tremendum* gave way to *fascinans*, the study of the stars, the "wanderers" (planets), meteors, comets, eclipses, and other bright lights led to the observational astronomy of each culture. Ancient traditions were drawn upon by Ptolemy in the first systematic cosmology of the West, the *Almagest*, written in the second century CE and influential to readers for another 14 centuries. His method, "saving the phenomena" of planets "wandering" or even moving backward on consecutive nights, placed Earth at the center of the universe, with everything moving in perfect circles around it.

In the sixteenth century, cosmographer Petri Apiani's diagram of the spheres[1] was the dominant medieval cosmological conception, with the sun, the moon, and the five known planets embedded within moving celestial spheres. Above these was the fixed sphere of the stars and constellations, and finally the Empyrean sphere, "a purely theological construction . . . immobile, and to be the place and ultimate container of the universe . . . the dwelling place of God and the elect" (Grant, 1993, p. 194). This is the destination of those "taken up into heaven," as described in 2 Kings 2:11 (NIV): "As they were walking along and talking together, suddenly a chariot of fire and horses of fire appeared and separated the two of them, and Elijah went up to heaven in a whirlwind."

The religious conception of the cosmos survives today in such everyday expressions as "the man upstairs" and "heavens above," thus subtly and subconsciously retaining the sky's *mysterium tremendum et fascinans* of earlier ages. The sky as spiritual home and destination underlies such concepts as "the Rapture," the taking up into the sky of the Christian faithful (cf. Lindsey, 1983). In addition, the double meaning of the *sky* as both outer space and spiritual destination is still implicit in the term "heaven."

Ptolemy's observations of the sky permitted the development of calendars that were essential to the Church, agriculture, trade, and daily life. Many monasteries sent young novices to new colleges to learn accurate observation of the sky for the correct timing of important ritual events, such as Easter (Falk, 2020). However, Earth's central position in the dominant theology and philosophy of the era remained largely unchanged, until more precise observations began to reveal discrepancies in the Ptolemaic system.

The Sundance of Nicolaus Copernicus

Copernicus's (1473–1543) novel solution to the Ptolemaic discrepancies shifted the sun to the center of his model, with the Earth moving around it in a circular orbit, thus stimulating a slow but profound shift in cosmological perspective. In his preface to Copernicus's work (1543/1952), the Lutheran theologian Andreas Osiander cautioned that "it is not necessary that these hypotheses should be true" (p. 505), implying merely a convenient technique for increasing astronomical accuracy, but others soon began to grasp their significance.

Giordano Bruno (1548–1600) was among the first to realize those implications. Extrapolating from the recognition that the Earth was a habitable body rotating around its sun, Bruno came to the conclusion that the stars in the sky might also be suns which, by analogy, had their own Earths with their own inhabitants. Bruno's ideas, along with his audacity to propose a new spirituality based on these concepts, placed him in peril with the ruling authority of the Church. Mendoza (1995) notes that rather than any heresy or Hermetic occultism Bruno practiced, "it was clearly his cosmology that worried the Church theologians the most" (p. 57). Bruno was burned at the stake on February 17, 1600. Shortly thereafter, Galileo Galilei (1564–1642) pointed his telescope skyward and discovered that the moon had geographical features and Jupiter had moons. In his history of cosmology, Danielson notes that Galileo modestly asserts that his assertions were "Neither Known nor Observed by Anyone Before" (Danielson, 2000, p. 145). Galileo then also became subject to ecclesiastical censure, but his observational records and techniques began the era of the telescope.

The Looking Glass Cosmos

Where previously the unaided eye had seen a mysterious "heaven," dwelling place of the gods, the telescope and new observational techniques revolutionized the sky. Telescopic observations started finding amazing new objects and leading to the discovery of new planets around the sun, further developing the concept of "space" as a place within which local planetary bodies revolved and distant stars ranged to the limits of the known. As Carl Sagan (1934–1996) remarked:

> For thousands of years, observers knew of just five planets. The astronomical world shook when William Herschel's telescope revealed a new one— Uranus. . . . Who can tell what might be found if a multitude of new worlds is hiding in the dark?
>
> (1995, p. 37)

Crowe (2008) cites multiple sources from the eighteenth century to assert that "in the period from 1750 to about 1800, aspects of the growing conviction that intelligent life is widespread in the universe had important effects on astronomy" (p. 129). Astronomers and philosophers began to advocate for the ideas that Giordano Bruno first elaborated 150 years earlier, but now with a developing cosmological model that could more readily support such a claim.

Another revolution in thought took place in the nineteenth century, laying the groundwork for further conjectures about life beyond Earth. Charles Darwin's theory of evolution introduced a new model for life's origin and became an undercurrent for speculation about life evolving elsewhere. Close observations of Mars by the nineteenth-century astronomer Schiaparelli led him to describe *canali* (channels), which was misinterpreted by astronomer Percival Lowell, who thought this meant "canals" constructed by a race of Martians (Danielson, 2000, p. 334).

"You're Going to Need a Bigger Sky"

At the turn of the twentieth century, remarkable changes in understanding the cosmos were happening apace. While Albert Einstein (1879–1955) was developing his gravitational theory of warped time and space, Edwin Hubble's (1889–1953) studies in the 1920s confirmed that a nebula thought to be nearby was in fact millions of light-years away, revealing that the universe was much larger than our own galaxy. Then, when the Andromeda galaxy came into clearer view, the universe expanded again, with each successive galaxy recognized as another entire Milky Way.

In 1930, our solar system expanded further with the discovery of Pluto. Space now began to be perceived as a place where other civilizations might flourish and perhaps threaten Earth, as in H. G. Wells's (1866–1945) *War of the Worlds* (1898), later puckishly dramatized by Orson Welles (1915–1985) in a 1938 Halloween radio program. As America recovered from a brutal financial collapse and war brewed in Europe, the age of the superhero began with the debut of the comic book characters the Phantom in 1936 and Superman and Flash Gordon in 1938 (Kinnard, n.d.). Likely the first costumed superhero, the Phantom ("the ghost who walks") brought a certain eldritch quality. However, Superman—Kal El from the planet Krypton—is truly alien, although a pair of eyeglasses and a smart suit seem adequate to disguise him as human. The 1938 radio series *Flash Gordon's Trip to Mars* further inculcated the alien threat which the Red Planet has posed since being identified with Mars, the god of war. By the early 1940s, the list of aliens acting in the world as superheroes and villains would grow. The psychology of superheroes coming from alien worlds and intervening in human society is still an archetype of our era, as McAvan (2012) ably notes.

The Cosmic Other, Descending

The continually expanding awareness of the scale of the cosmos and the concomitant insignificance of our place within it was accompanied by increasing reports of sightings in the sky and anomalous encounters. Only two years after the invention and first use of nuclear weapons in World War II, highly publicized reports of strange aerial phenomena occurred with the June 1947 sighting of "flying saucers" over Mount Rainier in Washington State, followed shortly afterward by the Roswell incident in July of 1947. As both the United States and the USSR developed ICBM capabilities, rockets reached near-Earth orbit, setting another precedent for outer space as a region ripe for travel.

It Came From Above

UFO and AAN reports—although often met with skepticism—have generated a wide range of opinions and beliefs. Some of these reports derive from unusual personal experiences or contemplation of scientific developments, and some have developed into more formalized religious forms, such as the Aetherius Society (Scribner & Wheeler, 2003). A growing body of writers have provided a wide range of theories and explanations about alleged encounters with numerous varieties of anomalous experience.

Although interpretations have changed, questions about extraterrestrial life are not new. Reports of fear and awe during wondrous events in the sky have occurred throughout human history. Stories of human contact with mysterious beings are universal across cultures. The Celtic cultures of Europe have their leprechauns (Vallee, 1969), and Indigenous people talk of "the little people" from the stars (Eliade, 1951/1964; Hirschfelder & Molin, 1992). These apparent cultural parallels inspired Thomas Bullard (e.g., 1982, 1991) to investigate whether the narrative structure of AANs resembled traditional folklore.

The most psychologically relevant cosmological concepts center on the question "Are we alone in the universe?" As long as this question remains unanswered, what are the implications for a lonely existence in such a vast universe? If we are not alone, what might the alien Other resemble, and could "they" pose a threat, either physically or culturally? At a deeper level, the problem of defining life still remains elusive and subject to our planetary biases (Mastrogiovanni, 2023). If we lack firm answers, our conjectures and speculations can reveal our deepest psychological beliefs and fears.

Before First Contact: We Are Still Alone

The contemporary motivation to study the social impacts of a definitive declaration that signs of life—intelligent or otherwise—have been detected beyond Earth's ecosystem also stems from the publicity surrounding UFOs/UAPs. In a 2019 commentary in the *Washington Post*, Drezner attempts to unravel public opinion from political implications and viable reportage relative to the very idea of UFOs. The recent Director of National Intelligence Report on UAPs[2] acknowledged that the data investigated was "reliable but inconclusive." The so-called extraterrestrial hypothesis (ETH) explanation of UAPs is still unconfirmed and remains an ambiguous notion unconvincing to most scientists (Matthews, 2021). Some have called for abandoning the search, because no evidence supporting the ETH has been found (Sutter, 2021).

One can find in the history of astronomy a growing set of facts that "we are not alone" as a planet or as a biological development in the universe, building a wave of expectation that such a finding will eventually occur. Most scientists still dismiss UFO-related phenomena, while a few pursue the possibility of finding extraterrestrial life through detection of radio emissions but discount the likelihood of interstellar travel and the anomalous flight characteristics common to UFO reports. Despite scientific caution and even derision, discoveries of extrasolar planetary systems—over five thousand as of this writing—lead to the expectation of finding evidence of life beyond Earth. According to a recent Pew Research poll,[3] over two-thirds of Americans believe in extraterrestrial life.

Both the Hubble and Webb telescopes' Deep Field findings have taken the iconic phrase from the book *2001: A Space Odyssey* "It's full of stars!" (Clarke, 1968/1993, p. 202) and expanded it to "It's full of galaxies!" In 2016, *Science Daily* reported that the Hubble telescope had provided data leading to the conclusion that the "[o]bservable universe contains two trillion galaxies, ten times more than previously thought."[4] Thus, the human view of space has developed from the primitive views of the sky as a set of fixed structures—a tent or set of crystalline spheres—to an expanding *place*, amplifying the conjuring of potential extraterrestrial inhabitants into an active *Zeitgeist*. It is therefore not unusual that narratives of encounters with UFOs and alien presences can be viewed as a psychological phenomenon that derives naturally from expanding cosmological knowledge and technological advances. The first contact *Zeitgeist* is a prominent psychological and cultural theme of our late modern era. As Ramos (2021) notes in an article on first contact, "[i]n the American public imagination, flying saucers are both the ultimate symbol of the alien—of everything unfamiliar and inaccessible—and also a reassuring symbol of human possibility—a portent of our possible intergalactic destiny."

When *Mysterium* and Technology Merge

As sightings of UFOs proliferate, media and science fiction incorporate their images and advance their themes, including the concept of interstellar travel. Although the Pew poll found only 7% of respondents consider the possibility of "unfriendly" aliens, it also suggested that a large segment of the population is more likely to expect an "alien Other" to resemble that portrayed in the movie *Independence Day* (Emmerich, 1996) than in *E.T. the Extra-Terrestrial* (Spielberg, 1982). Jacques Vallee noted decades ago that:

> This third aspect is the social belief system which has been generated in all the nations represented on this committee by the expectation of space visitors. This belief has been nurtured by the lack of serious attention given to genuine reports of UFOs, and it is creating new religious, cultural, and political concepts of which social science has taken little notice.
>
> (1978, p. 2)

Fear also takes the forms given to it by Rudolf Otto (1917/1923). His *mysterium tremendum et fascinans* (mystery both fearful and compelling) highlights that a *mysterium* is a presence which is "wholly other," and *tremendum* implies a paralysis of wonder. In psychological terms, such an experience triggers the third sympathetic autonomic nervous system response to massive stress: neither flight nor fight, but freeze. These categories present a straightforward way to describe a specific kind of report. The more naturalistic UAPs engage *fascinans*, while the reports of alleged alien contact generate a profound and sometimes paralytic fear as *mysterium tremendum*.

Based on the fears inherent in reported alien encounters, Scribner (2003) undertook an intensive study of prominent public "abductee" narratives. The alien fears study focused on published AAN texts, criticized the use of hypnosis for "recovered memories" data, and proposed a phenomenological-narrative approach as a more objective method. The acknowledged AAN "common denominator"—the presence of fear—required an appropriate fear model. After consideration of several available methods, Scribner selected a phenomenological framework developed by Robert Sardello, whose "geography of fear" (1999) describes nine realms of presence, which are also found in modern literature, cinema, and television. Scribner (2003) applied this framework to five original publications of the most prominent AAN narratives placed into the public domain before 1995. The full literature review, methodology, data, and findings can be accessed online.

The evolution of the cosmological picture over time also suggests a growing transfer of the sources of wonder from beatific manifestations—Guadalupe, Mary, angels, and so on—also seen as coming "from above" to new representations of cosmic wonder, as elaborated in sociocultural manifestations by McAvan in 2012 and elsewhere in this volume.

UFOs and AANs: A Field of Dreams?

Differences in attitudes and temperament may help explain the wide variety of beliefs within different explanatory contexts. Many *UFO believers* accept the existence of UFOs and aliens as physical realities (Friedman, 1996). Other believers assert their reality while conceptualizing UFOs or aliens as non-physical (Strieber, 1987). Members of this latter group may hold to some spiritual explanation—part of the religio-spiritual hypothesis (RSH) described later—or prefer the more secular paranormal hypothesis (PNH). Believers in non-physical UFOs tend to be philosophical dualists. Some propose that UFOs and alien abductions constitute a bridge between matter and spirit (Thompson, 1990).

UFO agnostics—skeptics—believe that UFO sightings—and, by implication, alien abductions—are probably the result of misperception, confusion, delusion, or mental illness (Sagan, 1995). They profess a belief in the possibility of alien life elsewhere in the universe, but they do not believe that UFOs visit Earth. UFO skeptics include all those who offer rational explanations of UFOs or AANs without prejudice, but with the clear implication that they are chimerical occurrences. Skeptics differ on the question of their cultural importance. Some believe that UFOs and AANs have major sociological significance. This group includes anthropologists who observe the UFO beliefs of others with empathy for the psychological—but not physical—reality of the phenomena.

Moving further on the continuum to incredulity, *UFO atheists*—debunkers—believe that UFOs and alien beings do not come to Earth, and they also believe that UFO reports and AANs are pernicious to society, or at least threaten the mental health of the individuals who become involved with them (Klass, 1989). Debunkers "know" that alien abductions are not real—if they were, they would be investigated as kidnappings by the FBI. Thus, they believe that the dissemination of UFO stories constitutes a potentially dangerous irrational trend, if not outright deception or fraud. Debunkers tend to be philosophical materialists. Many debunkers also tend to discount reports of paranormal events and disdain religious claims. Ironically, some conservative Christians also practice UFO debunking based on their theological mandate that supernatural events ended in New Testament times.

Debunking—the primary stance of the dominant scientific worldview—has proven ineffective in discouraging the proliferation of UFO reports and AANs, or even in slowing claims for the transforming effects of such "experiences." As in the history of religious disputes—or twentieth-century attempts to eradicate belief in communist countries—confrontational approaches may tend to strengthen believers' resolve. Belief systems growing out of UFOs and AANs can also produce powerful defensive protections—fundamentalist and even cultic—to ward off criticism.

Amid their disputes, many believers and debunkers alike impose implicit materialist interpretations on the same phenomenological gestalt. Both sides hold their ground as champions of common sense, whether about flying saucers or swamp gas. However, each side focuses its energies on some specialized forensic and scientific method or theoretical framework, which narrows their attention away from the totality of the human experience. In other words, all sides can become hypnotized by their methods.

Some researchers are loathe to hear psychosocial interpretations of UFOs and AANs (Jacobs & Shermer, 1998). The reluctance to approach the phenomena with a psychosocial lens can be seen on both sides of the debate. If UFOs and AANs are a type of psychological phenomenon—subject to theories of cognitive and emotional development—they might lose their appeal as either "real" physical science or "true" spiritual revelation. Despite professional psychology's over-a-century-long quest for acceptance, its explanations are still perceived to hold a lower credibility than those of the physical sciences. However, these narratives tap deep psychological roots, and current psychological tools may not be adequate to investigate their underlying spiritual implications. It is important to consider personal identity and social development when seeking to understand their enduring power. For example, self-worth can be enhanced through identification with superior beings—alien or otherwise. The belief that "I've been selected since childhood" implies specialness and provides a cosmic context for a unique individual life.

Intense debate occurs among those who believe claims of alien contact but who differ about the intentions of the "visitors." One faction fears imminent invasion or human–alien conspiracies or both—represented by Budd Hopkins, Jacques Vallee, and David Jacobs; another camp appears to welcome alien "salvation"—Leo Sprinkle, Edith Fiore, Richard Boylan, and perhaps John Mack (1929–2004); and a third group remains neutral about alien intentions—Raymond Fowler (1979) and Whitley Strieber (1987). These differences may presage a form of UFO denominationalism. Such religious issues have been discussed at length in *The Gods Have Landed* (Lewis, 1995).

Since Scribner's 2003 study, we have expanded the proposed schematic model for analyzing such narratives, taking into consideration their complex media sources and subsequent elaboration, public presentation, and commodification, while reserving judgment on the ontological status of any alleged "event." Toward this goal, we offer a proposed social transmission model for any strange narrative at the end of this chapter.

The following sections sample the proliferation of offered explanations for UFOs and AANs. Each type of explanation constitutes a worldview in its own right; each imposes assumptions on the data and sets rules for what is real.

"What Is Happening?": UFO Explanations and AAN Beliefs

As explained in earlier text, qualitative differences exist between modern UFO sighting reports and alien abduction stories. The former focus primarily on explanatory questions, such as "What is happening?" "What is causing this?" while the latter bring to the fore questions of meaning and response such as, "What does this mean to us?" "What must be done about it?" These interrelated themes become more visible as UFOs and AANs become part of the fabric of American culture. While the early UFO sightings stirred wide general interest, most responses originated from the military and private hobbyists. It took the increased prominence of AANs to reflect a level of fear comparable to the UFO panic caused by Orson Welles's aforementioned *War of the Worlds* broadcast on the eve of World War II.

These different but interrelated perspectives highlight the distinction between (1) a phenomenon "out there" that both reflects and impacts our continuously evolving views of the universe and (2) human events "down here" that simultaneously mirror and influence our way of life. As noted earlier, Wheeler (2000) identified this distinction as the difference between *Weltbild* (world picture) and *Weltanschauung* (worldview), respectively, which interact to form a dynamic cosmological perspective.

Forensic and Natural Science Explanations

The *Weltbild* perspective is exemplified by the predominant American belief about UFOs: they are a physical phenomenon that will yield eventually to scientific study. Possible physical explanations include spaceships, military aircraft, weather phenomena, or other naturalistic events.

Extraterrestrial Hypothesis (ETH)

This perspective can be summarized as: UFOs come from other star systems, may have visited Earth many times in the past, and may be abducting human beings now. The ETH is the most familiar theory of UFOs and AANs, and the one that most closely fits the modern scientific worldview in its popular form. This hypothesis proposes that visitors from other physical places in the universe come to Earth in spaceships. They may have visited throughout history and might have created the human race through genetic engineering. They abduct humans for their own purposes, much like humans capture animals for study. The main problem with this theory is that it does violence to our current understanding of physics. The distances to Earth from other star systems are so great that the amount of technological effort and fuel required seem insurmountable to us and hardly justifiable for zoology. A range of attitudes prevails within the ETH, from skeptical but curious, such as Drake and Sobel (1992) and Sullivan (1960), to believers, like Hynek (1972) and Friedman (1996).

Terrestrial Hypothesis (TH)

This thesis shifts the proposed origin of the vehicle: UFOs originate somewhere on or inside the Earth. A terrestrial origin for UFOs would not violate our current physical assumptions about travel to distant worlds. These craft may be vehicles piloted by strange—but earthly—beings, or they may even be UFO-shaped biological creatures (Brookesmith & Truzzi, 1992). The vehicles may fly from hidden bases, from under the oceans (Sanderson, 1970), or even from inside a hollow Earth (Bernard, 1969).

In the skeptical version of the TH, there are no alien beings but instead top-secret vehicles flown in Earth's skies by human military forces. These groups may be kidnapping human beings, who may remember alien images because they were drugged or hypnotized to do so.

Naturalistic Theories

Various naturalistic theories exist but are joined by the conviction that UFOs are natural phenomena, and aliens are hallucinations caused by natural phenomena. Some skeptical theories seek to explain UFO sightings as naturalistic events, such as electromagnetic phenomena (Rutkowski, 1988). Similarly, alien abduction experiences have been attributed to seismic movements within the Earth that create electrical fields, leading to strange experiences, or other microwave or ionizing radiation that have similar effects (Burt, 1970; Budden, 1995).

Neuropsychological Models

Shifting the etiology of the phenomena, neuropsychological models assert that UFOs and alleged aliens are hallucinations caused by internal neurochemical or electrical disturbances. Neuropsychologists view all human awareness as anchored in organic structures and processes. Neurophysiological explanations of AANs are exemplified by the work of Michael Persinger (1992), who found that identifiable deformations of perception occurred in cases of deliberate disruption of cortical function, particularly in the temporal lobe.

AANs as Psychosocial Phenomena

Rather than focusing on neurostructural or neurochemical explanations, psychosocial theorists state that UFO sightings and AANs are, in fact, reports of complex false memories or waking dreams. AANs can occur when a person's need to feel special is met by membership in a shared belief system. The psychosocial hypothesis (PSH) includes all attempts to understand AANs in terms of social science. For example, it considers the limitations of the hypnotic regression method and the possibility of cogent alternative psychological explanations (Newman & Baumeister, 1996). This view demonstrates why regression hypnosis and abduction reports are far from convincing evidence of alien contact when seen from the perspective of conventional research psychology.

Deception Explanations

Leaving aside any claim to an actual experience, the stance favored by most debunkers is that UFOs and AANs are all hoaxes or frauds. This non-belief position views UFO reports and AANs as hoaxes or criminal activities. Examples include controversial cases, such as Gulf Breeze and Travis Walton (Klass, 1989; Gordon, 1995). Debunkers believe that narrators are either hoaxers or dupes spreading stories for financial gain or publicity. Examples of such deceptions include the Philadelphia Experiment (Moore & Berlitz, 1979) and the "men in black" (Barker, 1956).

Psychosocial Explanations

The line between the forensic and natural science explanations of the preceding section and the psychological explanations can be subtle, especially with regard to the neuropsychological and psychosocial explanations. Nevertheless, the following explanations place the origins of UFOs and AANs within the human psyche rather than neurology or the cultural context of the individual.

Experimental Psychology

The late Nicholas Spanos (1942–1994), an experimental psychologist, proposed that AANs are complex false memories arising from the interaction of human needs and our specific cultural period when technology seems so dominant over all of life (see Spanos, 1996; Spanos et al., 1993, 1994). McNally (Clancy et al., 2002; McNally et al., 2004; McNally & Clancy, 2005; McNally, 2012) has been involved in a series of studies which have attempted to address the emotional distress of abductees. These studies found, among other results, that people who believed they had been abducted by aliens had the same physiological responses as persons who had experienced verified traumas. Because such studies assume that alien abductions are imaginary, their findings are not likely to end the controversy.

Although he is not a developmental psychologist, Alvin Lawson's (1929–2010) birth trauma imagery studies (1984, 1989) also fall into this category. Lawson hypothesized that AAN images originate in the experience of one's own birth or other traumas in early life.

Social Psychology

These researchers interpret human behaviors in terms of—or as influenced or imposed by—social interactions. This category includes the work of Roy Baumeister (1989) and Daniel O'Keefe (1982). Socially based theories include the study of rumor and urban legends (Allport & Postman, 1947). The creation of unusual stories can originate from different motives—psychological disturbance, entertainment, boredom, anomie, power, financial gain. Strange stories can also result when people are affected by technological changes (Kipness, 1997). Conspiracy theories can arise from the conjunction of personality styles and social trends. Persons and groups with political and religious motives add more ingredients, and so on. Some social movements set up self-referential peer groups who iteratively reinforce a shared worldview—the "agreement to agree." Examples of such groups include Budd Hopkins's Intruder Foundation, Whitley Strieber's Communion Foundation, and John Mack's PEER organization.

Consciousness Research

Tart (1969), Lilly (1972), McKenna and McKenna (1975), and Strassman (2001) represent this field. Researchers investigate anomalies of awareness, even to the extent of creating them through meditation, drugs, or sleep deprivation. However, consciousness research raises significant questions about how our critical faculties might be compromised by either the states of consciousness or the methods that these researchers propose. The dangers of falling down an epistemological rabbit hole are distinct. If we alter or modify the very instrument that makes our understanding of reality possible (i.e., the mind), how can we have confidence that any finding has validity or meaning? AANs appear to include perceptions of realities that are dramatically different from normal awareness.

Sociocultural Models

Sociologists consider AANs as a form of social contagion under some model of explanation, such as the theory of memes, which posits a genetic model of social ideas that propagate, compete, and survive as genes do in the biological realm (Lynch, 1996; Showalter, 1997). Some sociologists (J. Lewis, personal communication, 1997) see AANs as a subset of a peculiarly American narrative construct, the kidnap narrative, such as portrayed in the John Wayne movie *The Searchers* (Ford, 1956).

Social anthropologists see AANs as examples of what Caughey (1984) labels *imaginary social relationships*, such as occur in non-Western cultures with ancestors and spirits. In American society as elsewhere, imaginary relationships— sometimes labeled "parasocial interaction"—can be formed with celebrities, television and film actors, and fictional characters. Such relationships can have significant emotional consequences. Caughey's approach is promising because (1) it is cross-cultural, (2) it helps explain disagreements on the reality status of strange stories, and (3) it proposes the global media culture as a channel for imaginary social relationships.

Cultural anthropologists view AANs as primitive spiritual phenomena in the tradition of shamanic initiation rites (cf. Eliade, 1951/1964; Harner, 1980; McKenna & McKenna, 1975). This viewpoint sees AANs as modern shamanic journeys arising from deep structures developed in man's past but now exposed to technological change and urban conditions.

Religious anthropologists have studied the contactee movement extensively and see AANs as the narrative basis for new religions. The anthology *The Gods Have Landed* (Lewis, 1995) characterized the UFO myth as millenarian, that is, concerned with the "end of time" both as historical movement and perceptual dynamic. Carl Jung (1958) proposed that UFO stories form the basis of a new mythology that is developing in our highly technological age. One of the most influential examples of the "new myth" position is described in the book *Angels and Aliens* (Thompson, 1990). Thompson proposed that aliens originate in an "imaginal realm" that mediates between the "worlds" of matter and spirit. One problem with this concept is that if the dualistic conception of reality is incorrect—possibly the production of our own misperceptions—then an imaginal realm introduces a third factor that may prove to be a kind of double unreality. Another weakness of the neo-Jungian position is its reduced emphasis on the social dimension. For example, Thompson's discussion makes almost no mention of the potentially negative consequences of UFO mythology in a world armed with nuclear weapons.

Other Cultural Interpretations

AAN cultural interpretation also has taken the form of literary criticism. Combining social criticism and politics, the book *Aliens in America* (Dean, 1998) interpreted AANs as the expressions of dispossessed political groups who use the narrative form to dissent from modern bureaucratic institutions and an impersonal "big science." In ethnic studies, the essay "Alien Abductions and the End of White People" (Newitz, 1993) proposed that the "gray" alien imagery bespoke white fears of losing their racial identity—their "whiteness"—in an integrated and intermarried culture. In the field of literary criticism, Kelley (1999) studied the forms of rhetoric used in alien abduction stories. Using a narrative-mythic analysis that examined relationships between form and function of the narratives, she found them to be highly significant—a "living myth"—to those who told them.

Religious and Spiritual Explanations

The *religio-spiritual hypothesis (RSH)* suggests that UFO reports and AANs are modern religious texts. They describe visits by the same heavenly beings that have interacted with humans throughout history. They may or may not be from other physical places in the cosmos. This hypothesis is based on similarities between AANs and traditional religious narratives, such as the Christian Gospels (Downing, 1968). Even within evangelical Christianity, leading spokesperson Billy Graham proposed that UFOs are angelic vehicles sent by God in his 1975 book *Angels*.

Hindu religious traditions contain many tales of beings from the heavens (Thompson, 1990, 1993). Traditional Buddhism cautions about encounters with "*skandha* demons" from the heavens (Hua, 1996). Some religious interpretations concentrate on one theological view of anecdotal material. For example, Richard Thompson's Hindu perspective in *Alien Identities* (1993) asserted a single orthodox religious meaning for AANs. Such apologetical approaches neither confirm nor invalidate strange narratives, because they only "work" if one is open to the chosen belief context—in Thompson's case, Hinduism.

In *The Imagination of Pentecost* (1994), Richard Leviton expands on Rudolf Steiner's ideas about forces or "beings" from the future that are introducing images and ideas to humanity "before we are ready." Leviton holds that UFO reports and AANs indicate that our human future interpenetrates the present time but appears to us as advanced beings or higher consciousness.

In some metaphysical conspiracy theories, UFOs and alien abduction are plots carried out by cabals of the military, secret societies, fugitive Nazis with Atlantean technology, and so on (Kanon, 1997). Such theories tend to violate a key conclusion of Descartes's *evil genius* argument (Eaton, 1927). In effect, Descartes argues that even if we believe that a Demiurge or the Devil—or some all-powerful conspiracy—can deceive us totally and completely, we should still think and act rationally. But for some conspiracy theorists, the idea that the "absence of evidence is evidence of a conspiracy" can lead to a cycle of self-reinforcing paranoia. The conspiracy theorists' convictions give them license for what seem like distinctly irrational lived worlds.

AANs can share with religion a similar narrative status when viewed from the perspective of secular science and ordinary common sense. When someone talks about visions or other highly subjective experiences which have led them to a religious conversion—an activity called witnessing—their testimony constitutes personal knowledge based on perceived events that are real to them. Nevertheless, AANs differ from traditional religious witnessing in that they assume a modern technological worldview capable of acknowledging UFOs, but they are similar in bypassing the normal verification requirements of scientific or social consensus. If the physical reality of UFO abduction claims cannot be corroborated after the fact—even the New Testament Gospels are comparable stories in this sense—the different sides cannot agree on what "really" happened and might not agree even if they all had been present. This also applies to so-called past life regression and other types of hypnotically obtained recollections, which are just as vulnerable to aggressive scientific critique.

UFOs and AANs as Reflections of Social Conditions

Along with the many explanatory—science-oriented—models for UFOs and AANs, there are medical, social, and spiritual approaches that emphasize amelioration of anxiety and life problems. Each model sees AANs as symptoms of social or health problems. In this sense, they illustrate the worldview-oriented approach: "how should we live?"

Psychiatry applies the medical model to psychological issues and emphasizes the chemical management of behavior. Psychiatrists try to rule out identifiable disruptions of consciousness due to sub-ictal seizures, drug and alcohol use, sleep disorders, transient psychoticism, and other causes. Within a traditional psychiatric framework, a clinician would consider AANs as hallucinations and delusions rooted in some form of psychopathology. Similarly, conspiracy theories could, in the extreme, be examples of pathological ideas of reference. These symptoms may be manageable with medication. There may be life in outer space, but it is not visiting our patients.

Psychoanalysts have active ideas about alien abduction accounts. AANs reflect intrapsychic conflicts rooted in the nervous system. They are a new kind of dream. These theories include object relations theories (e.g., infantile longing for a "mother ship") or the problem of fear and paranoia as initial alienating conditions resulting from identity confusion, health problems, abuse, failure of adaptation, or a sense of threat. Or as Elizabeth Slater (1983) concludes, storytellers are hypersensitive "watchers" whose inner images derive from paranoid ideation. Some attribute the experience to dissociation.

Clinical psychologists may consider AANs to be screen memories of actual abuse, such as child sexual abuse. Individual psychotherapists emphasize treatment of AAN-related distress, symptoms, and emotional problems—that is, until their professional license is suspended, as happened to Richard Boylan in 1995 and Edith Fiore in 1997. Psychotherapists who endured in their practice include the late psychiatrist John Mack (viz., 1992, 1994, 1999) and social worker John Carpenter (viz., 1991, 1994). However, their conclusions about the absence of psychopathology on standard psychological tests overlook the weakness of such measures for detecting many conditions, such as dissociative identity disorder, borderline personality, sociopathic personality, and other conditions that are not easily measurable. In the view of many psychotherapists who work with abductees, AANs are expressions of trauma. Therefore, these therapists conclude that it is better to empathize with storytellers than to "argue about reality" (J. Mack, personal communication, 2002). In such an approach, the reality status of aliens appears to be set aside without judgment, but over the course of many therapeutic interactions, belief in their existence is likely to become implicit. Some researchers, like John Mack, claim objectivity or neutrality, but their activities—such as attending Native American rituals and New Age conferences—indicate movement toward the UFO believer camp.

Archetypal psychologists examine current cultural phenomena as often representing crises of the individual and world soul. James Hillman (1926–2011), in works such as *Pan and the nightmare* (1972) and *The dream and the underworld* (1979), and Robert Sardello, in *Freeing the soul from fear* (1999), address the role of fear in the modern psyche. Within this framework, AANs can be symbolic dreams or spiritual visions that reflect the spiritual crisis of modernity: humankind alone, cut off from Nature and, therefore, the true self, sees forms and images which reflect and enact this crisis. This model is promising because it employs the phenomenological method, which recognizes that the total human experience must not be set aside in the service of any specific interpretive framework.

Conclusion

Research on UFOs and AANs has always been controversial. Some assert that ufology—the study of unidentified flying objects and related phenomena—has failed as a science (viz., Sturrock, 1999; Jacobs & Shermer, 1998). The field has become so polemical that promising investigators are discouraged or even driven out. As Wheeler observed in 2000, when academic scientists say that UFO data would be better when it is "scientifically collected," their implicit message was that the previous 50 years of study had produced little of value. There still is no agreement on what constitutes a legitimate first contact science (Ballesteros-Olmos & Heiden, 2023).

Some of the issues raised by AANs are also encountered in areas identified by sociologists as "wild psychotherapies" (O'Keefe, 1982). These include near-death experiences (NDEs) (Ring, 1992), out-of-body experiences (OOBEs) (Monroe, 1973), reincarnation and so-called past life regression (Fiore, 1989; Weiss, 1992), satanic ritual abuse (SRA) (Bottoms et al., 1996), and dissociative identity disorder (DID), formerly known as multiple personality disorder (Friesen, 1997).

As a social science, ufology is still on the margins along with research on past life regression and satanic ritual abuse. Marginalized fields issue scientific disclaimers when they say, "Look at the evidence and decide for yourself." Such a presentation can cloak an in-group agreement to agree instead of promoting critical scrutiny because what constitutes "evidence" can become determined by the social context. Sociologist James Lewis (personal communication, 1997) asserts that intragroup behavior is shaped through "conversations." To the in-group, the "evidence" is what new arrivals are supposed to accept by initiation into the group agreement.

As can be seen earlier, the methodological problem is not that there are too few models but too many, and most of them are nonfalsifiable. The elusive nature of UFO research derives from approaching the phenomenon from a predefined set of assumptions: materialist, psychosocial, paranormal, or religious. After 75 years of UFO research, these wide-ranging approaches have not produced more clarity. Even with the risks of hoax and deception, continued interest in the phenomenon does not abate. We must consider UFOs and AANs in terms of what can be agreed about them, rather than shifting from one theoretical context to another—ground much treaded by others without resolution. A reliable approach should be based on what can be known objectively: human behaviors, human values, and the narrative acts themselves, considered as transmittable and influential social facts.

Any worldview or belief system can become a matter of ultimate concern, resulting in clashes with contradictory worldviews in its environment. Failure to understand and properly respond to the powerful influence of mythic narratives as social forces has led to numerous catastrophes: from Hitler's National Socialism to the Branch Davidian cult activities culminating in the siege outside Waco Texas in 1993, to the Aum Shinrikyo (Japanese: Om Supreme Truth) cult implicated in the Tokyo nerve gas attacks in 1994 and 1995, and to the terroristic "Islamism" of al-Qaeda and Daesh (Lifton, 1999). We need better understandings of worldviews and worldview conflict to develop proper strategies and responses. We need to take seriously our virtual habitation within a pervasive media environment where the boundaries between our personal identities and those of what Caughey (1984) presciently labels imaginary social relationships are more permeable than we might wish to admit.

The psychological state of an observer experiencing "high strangeness" evokes perceptual filters influenced by their past experiences and presuppositions. These conditions can result in quite different stories about what was witnessed and lead to different conclusions, depending on the observer. Taking into consideration the interactions of reality testing, fantasy imagery (e.g., imagination, hypnagogia, dreaming), and media influences, the difficulty of determining witness reliability can be profound, as summarized by Ioan Culianu (2001, p. 5):

> The outside world could not exist without the mental universe that perceives it, and this mental universe in turn borrows its images from perceptions. . . . Thus, the world outside us and the world inside us are not truly parallel, for not only do they interfere with each other in many ways, but we cannot even be sure where one of them ceases to be and the other commences.

Addendum: A Proposed Social Transmission Model for Any "Strange" Narrative

Widespread publication of UFO reports and AANs has disseminated their words and imagery throughout global media and culture. Despite the extensive attention paid to their alleged sources, content, and interpretations, the complex layering process that leads to their formation has been neglected. The development of any strange narrative follows a discernable process:

1. An individual or group of individuals is motivated to distinguish, identify, and describe a "strange" event or experience. These narratives can have different degrees of strangeness; the strangeness of a disclosure is defined by its social context. We do not have to analyze or discern the human motivations for the disclosure—or its epistemological status—to appreciate the story as a new object in the world. The storyteller's disclosure typically places their story into a local (i.e., *emic*, or folk) setting. The implied stimuli or triggers for such a disclosure—whether presented as an event or experience—are *always in the past*. This is a social necessity because an anomalous event reported *as if in real time* would be disconcerting to any witnesses who were not perceiving the same events. In a secular culture, witnesses might attribute the disclosure to confusion or mental instability. In a more religious setting, the disclosure could be interpreted as spiritual election, seership, or blasphemy.

2. A private conversation ensues within a local social circle, where the story develops further. For example, in the alleged Linda Cortile case (Hopkins, 1996), the inner circle was initially the Cortile family, but the outer circle quickly became Budd Hopkins's alien abduction support group. A story becomes more detailed and refined as the individual and the local social group look for understanding and other forms of resolution. This development may produce transcriptions or other records.

3. For reasons relating to the story's strangeness and its impact on the storyteller's well-being, professional contacts may be made outside the immediate social circle. There can be multiple contacts (e.g., police, medical, journalistic). In some cases, hypnosis may be employed to recover more memories.

4. At a certain point, the story can be considered significant enough to require a *narrator* role. A narrator creates an intentional project to organize "the evidence" into a form of communication which becomes "etic"—public and subject to out-group examination and consensus. There can be various motivations for a narrator to do this, including intellectual curiosity, psychological need, publicity, or economic gain. The narrator could be the original storyteller (e.g., Whitley Strieber), a journalist (John Fuller), a private researcher (Raymond Fowler, Budd Hopkins), or some prestigious professional figure (Harvard psychiatrist John Mack).

5. The narrative is released to the public—undergoes publication—in the form of a media product. This may occur in easily accessible forms initially (e.g., local press, magazine serialization, the internet), unless the narrator already has access to wider media and copyright control of the material. In the latter case, the communication's release can be both more refined and controlled (e.g., major book publication).

6. As public media impact increases, the narrative may be reformulated into a television production or motion picture.

As an allegedly "true" account, any strange story can be mapped and explored as the following iterative chronological sequence:

$$\sum E_x <\text{-} [(S) \text{->} L \text{->} P \text{->} N] \text{->} [M \text{->} C] \text{->} E_{n \, (\text{so many} \ldots)}$$

where multiple "inputs" E_x represent the storyteller's unique cognitive assembly of perceptual sets—including media stimuli—that its originator considers "the event" or "the experience." Subscript x acknowledges that their origins may be unknowable, undiscoverable, or nonfalsifiable. In the "outputs" E_n, subscript n indicates the vast potential spread of new perceptual sets as social memes. Brackets indicate that elements can occur together or in different order.

- Storytelling—creation of an original account.
- Localization—discussions within and among local social circles (-> changes).
- Professionalization—involvement of specialized personnel (-> changes).
- Narration—packaging of an "official" story (-> changes).
- Mediatization—distribution as tweets, posts, books, films (-> exponential changes).
- Commodification—monetization, marketing, and sale of products.

S is the **storytelling** by a person or group who, through verbal reports, writings, meetings, and other behaviors, introduces a new story into the world. The storyteller's motivations may vary, but the story itself typically involves some category of strangeness or anomaly; otherwise, it would not be remarkable enough to be noticed. This principle is the basis of carnival sideshows, which display not mundane but outlandish "attractions."

L is the **localization** of the account through contacts near the local social circle of the storyteller, such as family members and friends. Their participation further shapes the story's development through the dynamics of their reception and responses.

P are any **professional** contacts beyond the local social circle of the storyteller and, more specifically, any specialized professionals who are called on for assistance. They supply additional contexts that can affect the story dramatically.

N is the **narrator**—a person with some combination of communication skills, social prestige, and media contacts—who casts the story into a form to be presented to the wider world, outside previous private and professional social contacts. "Narrator" is the term here for an author-researcher who has chosen to assemble and disseminate alien abduction stories. In this sense, the narrator adds a point of view—often as explicit narration—alongside the storyteller accounts. The distinction between storyteller and narrator is significant. Many layers of meaning can be added between the original testimony—with its own complex aspects, including psychological experiences and retrospective memories of events, through the interviewing process, to the publication—in its double sense of being *public* and *published*, and in some cases, leading to the release of a television dramatization or motion picture. The special relationship between storyteller and narrator is reflected in the very existence of the AAN. The narrator can become one of the most important influences in a storyteller's life, essentially witnessing the significance of that life for all others. A narrator is the main vehicle through which a storyteller is selected, and their particular story told. In Christianity, the writers of the four canonical New Testament Gospels are narrators in this sense, although other ancient writers, such as Tacitus and Josephus, also corroborated some historical details.

M marks the **mediatization** of the narrative, as packaged by a narrator and issued through media channels, including books, television, films, and internet posts. Such publication may also include specifically selected images which can play a critical role in the story's impact and salience, as exemplified by the striking book cover of Whitley Strieber's *Communion* (1987).

C marks the **commodification**—and monetization—of the established narrative into more widely available packages. Each dissemination of words and images forms more events and experiences in the lives of all who encounter them.

The transmission of strange narratives within and through culture is iterative. Because this is the case, what happens to the "evidence" of a story's original "truth," its "pure" initial "event" or "experience"? The proliferation of quotation marks in the preceding sentence should telegraph an answer: a search for such evidence can become increasingly elusive. The social reality behind a story becomes embedded in its evolving form and transmission. The many layers of McLuhan's "the medium is the message" (McLuhan, 1964) permeate this discourse, because for researchers of such phenomena, the messages are embedded in the media, and in its proliferation from storytelling through mediatization and commodification, the medium also effects the "massaging" of the messages (McLuhan & Fiore, 1967). Although a story's "truth" may not be located in any one layer of the discourse, the story's perceptual and media constituents, and the processes of their assembly, might be discovered and deduced through careful analysis and comparison of original storyteller testimony with occurrences of pre-existing texts and public media images. Artificial intelligence can provide additional tools to prospect text and image databases for story antecedents, enabling more precise research in this field.

The added consideration of the implicit predecessor conditions, triggers, and motivations demonstrates that at each stage in its development, a story always looks *backward in time*. This fact is clear even if little about these conditions, triggers, or motivations is known. In the previous diagram, $\sum E_x$ represents the retrospective events or experiences implicit in the story—x denotes their unknown aspects. With most events in the past, many details are not subject to objective verification. A search for the *causes* of any experience may be fruitless, yet such searches are the focus of most UFO and AAN research, which employ either forensic and scientific techniques or hypnosis.

E_n stands for the potential for an unspecified number (n) of new encounters of the narrative's words and images by other witnesses within the potentially vast range of the mediatized and commodified AAN. These new encounters feed back into the evolving social matrix, further affecting interpretations of alleged events and also changing basic understandings of the events themselves. This flexible model meets the requirement for a more objective specification of unusual narratives than one typically finds in current literature. Theoretically, any single element of the narrative's chronological development—except E_x, S, and E_n—is optional or can be combined with others. These structures inhabit periods and streams—not single points—in time and memories. Metaphorically, these structures constitute linguistic neurons within the cultural nervous system, which continuously propagates words and images—the elements of magic—throughout the social world. These types of structures are to *memes* what DNA is to *genes*: potentially discoverable media structures of the informational or linguistic reality.

Notes

1 www.loc.gov/resource/rbctos.2017gen33968/?sp=15&r=-0.606,0.016,2.211,1.413,0.
2 Prelimary-Assessment-UAP-20210625.pdf (dni.gov).
3 Most Americans believe life on other planets exists | Pew Research Center: www.pewresearch.org/fact-tank/2021/06/30/most-americans-believe-in-intelligent-life-beyond-earth-few-see-ufos-as-a-major-national-security-threat/.
4 www.sciencedaily.com/releases/2016/10/161013111709.htm.

References

Allport, G., & Postman, L. (1947). *The psychology of rumor*. Henry Holt.
Ballesteros, V. J., & Heiden, R. W. (Eds.). (2023). *The reliability of UFO witness testimony*. UPIAR.
Barker, G. (1956). *They knew too much about flying saucers*. University Press.
Baumeister, R. (1989). *Masochism and the self*. Lawrence Erlbaum Associates.
Bernard, R. (1969). *The hollow earth: The greatest geographical discovery in history made by Admiral Richard E. Byrd in the mysterious land beyond the poles—the true origin of the flying saucers*. Lyle Stuart.
Bottoms, B. L., Shaver, P. R., & Goodman, G. S. (1996). An analysis of ritualistic and religion-related child sex abuse allegations. *Law and Human Behavior, 20*(1), 1–34.
Brookesmith, P., & Truzzi, M. (1992). *UFO encounters: Sightings, visitations, and investigations*. Publications International.
Budden, A. (1995). *UFOs—psychic close encounters: The electromagnetic indictment*. Blandford.
Bullard, T. E. (1982). *Mysteries in the eye of the beholder: UFOs and their correlates as a folkloric theme past and present* [Unpublished doctoral dissertation, Indiana University, Bloomington].
Bullard, T. E. (1991). The folkloric dimension of the UFO phenomenon. *Journal of UFO Research, 3*, 1–57.
Burt, E. (1970). *UFOs and diamagnetism: Correlations of UFO and scientific observations*. Exposition Press.
Carpenter, J. (1991). *Multiple participant abductions*. Paper presented at the UFO Research Conference, Seattle, WA.
Carpenter, J. (1994). Resolution of phobias from recall of abductions. In A. Pritchard, D. E. Pritchard, J. E. Mack, P. Kasey & C. Yapp (Eds.), *Alien discussions: Proceedings of the abduction study conference held at M.I.T.* (pp. 367–368). North Cambridge Press.
Caughey, J. (1984). *Imaginary social worlds: A cultural approach*. University of Nebraska Press.

Clancy, S. A., McNally, R. J., Schacter, D. L., Lenzenweger, M. F., & Pitman, R. K. (2002). Memory distortion in people reporting abduction by aliens. *Journal of Abnormal Psychology*, *111*(3), 455–461.

Clarke, A. C. (1993). *2001: A space odyssey*. Penguin Books (Original work published 1968).

Copernicus, N. (1952). On the revolutions of the heavenly spheres. In R. M. Hutchins (Ed.), *Great books of the western world: Ptolemy. Copernicus. Kepler*. W. Benton (Original work published 1543).

Crowe, M. J. (Ed.). (2008). *The extraterrestrial life debate, Antiquity to 1915*. University of Notre Dame Press.

Culianu, I. (2001). *Out of this world: Otherworldly journeys from Gilgamesh to Albert Einstein*. Shambala Publications.

Danielson, D. R. (Ed.). (2000). *The book of the cosmos*. Perseus Publishing.

Dean, J. (1998). *Aliens in America*. Cornell University Press.

Downing, B. (1968). *The Bible and flying saucers*. Harper & Row.

Drake, F., & Sobel, D. (1992). *Is anyone out there?* Delacorte Press.

Drezner, D. W. (2019, May 28). UFOs exist and everyone needs to adjust to that fact. *Washington Post*.

Eaton, R. M. (Ed.). (1927). *Descartes selections* (E. S. Haldane & G. R. T. Ross, Trans.). Charles Scribner's Sons.

Eliade, M. (1964). *Shamanism: Archaic techniques of ecstasy* (W. R. Trask, Trans.). Princeton University Press (Original work published 1951).

Emmerich, R. (director, writer), Devlin, D. (producer, writer) (1996). *Independence day*. Centropolis Entertainment.

Falk, S. (2020). *The light ages: The surprising story of medieval science*. W. W. Norton & Company.

Fiore, E. (1989). *Encounters. A psychologist reveals case studies of abductions by extraterrestrials*. Doubleday.

Ford, J. (director), Nugent, F. S. (screenplay writer) (1956). *The Searchers*. C. V. Whitney Pictures.

Fowler, R. (1979). *The Andreasson affair: The documented investigation of a woman's abduction aboard a UFO*. Prentice-Hall.

Friedman, S. (1996). *Top secret/Majic*. Marlowe.

Friesen, J. (1997). *Uncovering the mystery of MPD*. Thomas Nelson.

Gordon, S. (1995). *The book of hoaxes: An A-Z of famous fakes, frauds, and cons*. Headline Book Publishing.

Graham, W. (1975). *Angels: God's secret agents*. Word Publishing.

Grant, E. (1993). Medieval cosmology. In N. S. Hetherington (Ed.), *Cosmology: Historical, literary, philosophical, religious and scientific perspectives* (pp. 181–200). Garland Publishing.

Haldane, J. B. S. (1927). *Possible worlds and other essays*. Chatto and Windus.

Harner, M. (1980). *The way of the shaman*. Harper & Row.

Hillman, J. (1972). *Pan and the nightmare*. Spring Audio & Journal.

Hillman, J. (1979). *The dream and the underworld*. HarperCollins.

Hirschfelder, A., & Molin, P. (1992). *The encyclopedia of native American religions*. MJF Books.

Hopkins, B. (1996). *Witnessed: The true story of the Brooklyn Bridge UFO abductions*. Pocket Books.

Hopkins, B., Jacobs, D. M., & Westrum, R. (1992). *Unusual personal experiences: An analysis of data from three national surveys conducted by the Roper Organization*. Bigelow Holding Corporation.

Hua, H. (1996). *The fifty skandha-demon states* (*The Shurangama sutra*, Volume 8) (Buddhist Text Translation Society, Trans.). Buddhist Text Translation Society.

Hynek, J. A. (1972). *The UFO experience: A scientific inquiry.* Henry Regnery.

Jacobs, D. M., & Shermer, M. (1998, January 14). KPCC-FM radio interview.

Jung, C. G. (1958). *Flying saucers: A modern myth of things seen in the skies* (R. F. C. Hull, Trans.). New American Library (Signet).

Kanon, G. (1997). *The great UFO hoax: The final solution to the UFO mystery.* Galde Press.

Kelley, S. (1999). *The rhetoric of alien abduction* [Unpublished doctoral dissertation, University of Kansas].

Kinnard, R. (n.d.). *Flash Gordon.* Retrieved February 3, 2024, from www.loc.gov/static/programs/national-film-preservation-board/documents/flash_gordon.pdf

Kipness, D. (1997). Ghosts, taxonomies, and social psychology. *American Psychologist, 52*(3), 205–211.

Klass, P. (1989). *UFO abductions: A dangerous game.* Prometheus Books.

Lawson, A. H. (1984). Perinatal imagery in UFO abduction reports. *Journal of Psychohistory, 12*(2), 211–239.

Lawson, A. H. (1989). The birth memory hypothesis: A testable theory for UFO abduction reports. In D. Stillings (Ed.), *Cyber-biological studies of the imaginal component in the UFO contact experience.* Archaeus Project.

Leviton, R. (1994). *The imagination of Pentecost: Rudolf Steiner and contemporary spirituality.* Anthroposophic Press.

Lewis, J. R. (Ed.). (1995). *The gods have landed: New religions from outer space.* SUNY Press.

Lifton, R. (1999). *Destroying the world to save it: Aum Shinrikyo, apocalyptic violence, and the new global terrorism.* Henry Holt.

Lilly, J. C. (1972). *The center of the cyclone.* Ronin Publishing.

Lindsey, H. (1983). *The rapture: Truth or consequences.* Bantam.

Lynch, A. (1996). *Thought contagion: How beliefs spread through society.* Basic Books.

Mack, J. E. (1992). Other realities: The alien abduction phenomenon. *Noetic Sciences Review, 23,* 5–11.

Mack, J. E. (1994). *Abduction: Human encounters with aliens.* Scribner.

Mack, J. E. (1999). *Passport to the cosmos: Human transformation and alien encounters.* Ballantine Books.

Mastrogiovanni, A. M. (2023). Exoheliotrope: Metaphor in the texts of astrobiology and deconstruction. *The Oxford Literary Review, 45*(2), 208–228.

Matthews, D. (2021, July 3) What if the truth isn't out there? The wishful thinking behind the search for alien life. *Vox.* www.vox.com/future-perfect/22556083/ufo-uap-report-fermi-paradox-aliens

McAvan, E. (2012). *The postmodern sacred: Popular culture spirituality in the science fiction, fantasy and urban fantasy genres.* McFarland & Company.

McKenna, D. J., & McKenna, T. K. (1975). *The invisible landscape: Minds, hallucinogens, and the I ching.* Seabury Press.

McLuhan, M. (1964). *Understanding media: The extensions of man.* McGraw Hill.

McLuhan, M., & Fiore, Q. (1967). *The medium is the massage.* Penguin Books.

McNally, R. J. (2012). Explaining "memories" of space alien abduction and past lives: An experimental psychopathology approach. *Journal of Experimental Psychopathology, 3*(1), 2–16.

McNally, R. J., & Clancy, S. A. (2005). Sleep paralysis, sexual abuse, and space alien abduction. *Transcultural Psychiatry, 42*(1), 113–122.

McNally, R. J., Lasko, N. B., Clancy, S. A., Macklin, M. L., Pitman, R. K., & Orr, S. P. (2004). Psychophysiological responding during script-driven imagery in people reporting abduction by space aliens. *Psychological Science, 15*(7), 493–497.

Mendoza, R. G. (1995). *The acentric labyrinth: Giordano Bruno's prelude to contemporary cosmology.* Element.

Monroe, R. A. (1973). *Journeys out of the body*. St. Martin's Press.

Moore, W., & Berlitz, C. (1979). *The Philadelphia experiment: Project invisibility*. Fawcett Crest.

Newitz, A. (1993, May). Alien abductions and the end of white people. In *Bad subjects: Political education for everyday life, 5*. Retrieved August 16, 2003, from http://eserver.org/BS/06/Newitz.html

Newman, L. S., & Baumeister, R. F. (1996). Toward an explanation of the UFO abduction phenomenon: Hypnotic elaboration, extraterrestrial sadomasochism, and spurious memories. *Psychological Inquiry, 7*(2), 99–126.

O'Keefe, D. (1982). *Stolen lightning: The social theory of magic*. Random House.

Otto, R. (1923). *The idea of the holy* (J. W. Harvey, Trans.). Oxford University Press (Original work published 1917).

Persinger, M. A. (1992). Neurological profiles of adults who report "sudden remembering" of early childhood memories: Implications for claims of sex abuse and alien visitation/abduction experiences. *Perceptual and Motor Skills, 75*, 259–266.

Ramos, S. (2021, October 16). First contact: Extraterrestrial encounters and human possibility. *Commonweal*. www.commonwealmagazine.org/first-contact

Ring, K. (1992). *The Omega project: Near-death experiences, UFO encounters and mind at large*. William Morrow.

Rutkowski, K. W. (1988). The terrestrial hypothesis: Geophysical alternatives. In J. Spencer & H. Evans (Eds.), *Phenomenon: Forty years of flying saucers* (pp. 301–307). Avon.

Sagan, C. (1995, March). The first new planet. *Astronomy Magazine*.

Sanderson, I. (1970). *Invisible residents: A disquisition upon certain matters maritime and the possibility of intelligent life under the waters of this Earth*. Avon.

Sardello, R. (1999). *Freeing the soul from fear*. School of Spiritual Psychology.

Scribner, S. (1999). Alien abduction narratives. In J. Lewis (Ed.), *Encyclopedia of UFOs and popular culture*. ABC-CLIO.

Scribner, S. (2003). *Alien fears: Toward a psychology of UFO abduction beliefs* [Unpublished doctoral dissertation]. www.academia.edu/30207679/TOWARD_A_PSYCHOLOGY_OF_UFO_ABDUCTION_BELIEFS

Scribner, S., & Wheeler, G. (2003). Cosmic intelligences and their terrestrial channel: A field report on the Aetherius Society. In J. Lewis (Ed.), *Encyclopedic sourcebook of UFO religions*. Prometheus Books.

Showalter, E. (1997). *Hystories: Hysterical epidemics and modern culture*. Columbia University Press.

Slater, E. (1983). *The final report on the psychological testing of UFO abductees*. Fund for UFO Research.

Spanos, N. P. (1996). *Multiple identities and false memories*. American Psychological Association.

Spanos, N. P., Burgess, C. A., & Burgess, M. (1994). Past-life identities, UFO abductions, and satanic ritual abuse: The social construction of memories. *International Journal of Clinical and Experimental Hypnosis, 42*(4), 433–446.

Spanos, N. P., Cross, P. A., Dickson, K., & DuBreuil, S. C. (1993). Close encounters: An examination of UFO experiences. *Journal of Abnormal Psychology, 102*(4), 624–632.

Spielberg, S. (director, producer), Mathison, M. (writer), Kennedy, K. (producer). (1982). *E. T. the extra-terrestrial*. Amblin Entertainment.

Strassman, R. (2001). *DMT—The spirit molecule: A doctor's revolutionary research into the biology of near-death and mystical experiences*. Inner Traditions.

Strieber, W. (1987). *Communion*. Beech Tree Books.

Sturrock, P. (1999). *The UFO enigma: A new review of the physical evidence*. Warner Books.

Sullivan, W. (1960). *We are not alone*. McGraw-Hill.

Sutter, P. (2021, December 10). Why are we still searching for intelligent alien life? *Space. com*. www.space.com/why-humans-search-intelligent-alien-life-SETI

Tart, C. T. (1969). *Altered states of consciousness*. John Wiley.

Thompson, K. (1990). *Angels and aliens: UFOs and the mythic imagination*. Ballantine Books.

Thompson, R. (1993). *Alien identities: Ancient insights into modern UFO phenomena*. Govardian Hill Publishing.

Vallee, J. (1969). *Passport to Magonia: From folklore to flying saucers*. Henry Regnery.

Vallee, J. (1978, November 27). *Statement on the UFO Phenomenon*. Prepared for delivery before the Special Political Committee of the United Nations Organization, New York. www.jacquesvallee.net/research/#research

Weiss, B. L. (1992). *Through time into healing*. Simon & Schuster.

Wells, H. G. (1898). *War of the worlds*. Harper & Bros.

Wheeler, G. J. (2000). Cosmology. In J. Lewis (Ed.), *UFOs and popular culture: An encyclopedia of contemporary myth*. ABC-CLIO.

Chapter 4

The Human and the Smart House

Speculative Psychology and Systems of Attachment

Anna Bugajska

Emma Baranowski, Kaitlyn Guay, and Mckenna Dahlen provided copyediting for this chapter as part of the Northeastern University Psychological Humanities Workgroup.

Residential spaces, be they considered on macro- or microscale, constitute an important element of individual psyche and are expressive and formative of one's personality. Attachment to territory and environment contributes to the formation of community bonds and directly impacts one's psychological makeup and physical shape. With the atomization of societies in first-world countries, more and more immersive technology, and the access to customized gadgets enhancing the user experience, the natural attachments between people weaken, replaced with attachments to objects. A good example of such an attachment, and especially relevant in the context of this chapter, is a well-known instance of bonding with cars, turning them into a domestic space, which, in turn, leads to the privatization of experience and the consequent separation of individuals (Graves-Brown, 2000). However, this attachment grows out of the anthropocentric stance and the position of a user: for all the emotional investment in the things that surround us, the experienced bond is frequently not based on defamiliarization of objects and spaces, and they are seen mostly as extensions of self and not acknowledged as agents able to co-create us. The advances in smart technology, augmented reality, ambient computing, etc., as well as on the Internet of Things, enabling ever-deepening surveillance technologies, seem to be the response to this social isolation and individual yearning for relations. Children can talk to Hello Barbie; adults choose, for example, Siri or Alexa; and as Poupyrev notes in a 2019 TEDTalk, we learn to make the language of plants audible to our ears. The residential spaces become "alive" and make researchers ask questions about the development of complex systems of attachment on the part of the human, extending oneself toward multiple smart agents, but also about the ties which do develop between smart objects and a user, or multiple users, leading further to the questions of "dehumanization" in relations with objects, the transformations of psychological makeup, and the object-oriented perspective.

Long before the problems of these systems of attachment were readily observable, an Argentinian writer, Mujica Láinez, in his novel *La Casa* (1954), tried to

DOI: 10.4324/9781003519102-4

assume the perspective of a house to describe the relationship it had with people. From the description emerges a complex entity, not only an architecturally structured edifice, but also a community of objects that "inhabit" it, together with humans. At the beginning of the novel, the house complains that it—or, rather, "they," a complex subject—belongs to the sphere of techne, which consigns them to the role of the enslaved, with their telos indelibly branded on them, denying them voice and agency. The source for that would be anthropocentric pride—expressed in Spanish as both *dignidad* and *orgullo*—which would be challenged by attuning oneself to objects. The house even perceives the consequences on the humans of this anthropocentrism as a weakness, depriving people of "valuable insights" and "best friendships" of objects incessantly gathering data about human activity. As a result, the world is filled with powerful loneliness, while the remedy would be to open oneself and use the natural human sensibility. Such a diagnosis is even more pertinent today when the gathering of data and the communication between objects are a fact, and fits in well in the speculative realism developed, among others, by philosophers Timothy Morton (2013) and Steven Shaviro (2014).

Following Mujica Láinez's (1954) cue and multiple questions sparked by the increasingly digitalized environment, one could ask, How could the contemporary human interact with objects and obtain the benefits and valuable insights? How can we understand the invitation to the dialogue coming from the objects? How might we hone our sensibilities to attune ourselves to the language of the non-human Other and discover "the best friendships"? The challenges posed here are much greater than simply the questions of the bonds people develop with Gatebox's waifus, with Siri or Alexa, or with their household plants. Mujica Láinez's house is a compound subject, a consciousness uniting within itself a cupboard, an inkwell, a basin, and a host of subordinate Others existing, as it were, in a mode of an assemblage, or a system, quite independent from the human user. One can indeed read the narrative of the Argentinian novelist in terms of a metaphor, a personification, and a literary animization in the tradition of magical realism; nevertheless, this magical realism corresponds to the contemporary animization of objects, described by Asma (2020) as "hijacking our social emotions by non-agents or jabbering objects" in a way that we actually enjoy and appreciate.

Thus, to more fully understand this technological complexity that opens our understanding to ontological plurality, at least for the sake of the discussion, we should accept the variety of modes of being, as explained by Bruno Latour (2013). Asma (2020) focuses on the "irrationality" of human–smart object experience and seems to subscribe to the view that our readings of materiality can only be mediated by psychology because the animization arises in our minds. Latour (2013), to the contrary, acknowledges the existence of both invisible and visible parts of being, and he asks, "How have the Moderns managed to miss the strangeness, the ubiquity, and yes, the spirituality of technology? How could they have missed its sumptuous opacity?" (p. 210). Various commentators have underlined the bonds between humans and technological artifacts, and it seems that the general agreement is that one cannot think of human beings in separation from objects. Verbeek

(2000) has written on technologically mediated experience of reality, where our relation with, for example, road bumps has the potential to influence our morality. Graves-Brown (2000, p. 160), in relation to the art of tattooing, writes even that "it is the technical, including the body technical, which sets people apart, which raises them above mere animality by becoming artefacts in their own right." To be human, then, one would need to understand one's nature as an artifact, and the connections with other artifacts.

As can be seen, both the everyday experience of the people living in the contemporary digitalized societies and the sociological and philosophical discussion reveal the need to observe the nature of human–object and object–object relations more closely, especially in the face of the crisis of the basic notions—like "human," "person," and "death"—in highly technological societies. Metaphorism, suggested by Bogost (2012), can be one of the ways of approaching the subject, especially that fiction abounds in examples of "alive" residential spaces. Worth noticing, it is often the type of fiction more typical of a Gothic or a fairy-tale genre which has important implications for how the objects or compound objects would be conceptualized and how metaphorism would work. A relevant example from science fiction that has a clearly Gothic flavor is "The Veldt" (1950/1951), a story by Ray Bradbury, in which emotions of fear and lack of control dominate the narrative space and the psychology of characters. In the present chapter, examples will be sourced from a differently flavored fiction which intends to provide insights into the complex speculative psychology of a smart house, especially in relation to its human creators and owners.

The aim of this chapter is primarily to look at the systems of attachments between humans and objects in a twofold manner. First, I investigate the theory of attachment in relation to attachment to objects and the formation of systems and networks of relations, with the acknowledgment of various modes of existence. In the second part of the chapter, I move on to the insights from Scott Westerfeld's space opera series *Succession*, made up of *The Killing of Worlds* (2003b) and *The Risen Empire* (2003a), as an example of what Bogost, in his work *Alien Phenomenology* (2012), calls "metaphorism" and relating to the approach in speculative realism using fiction to reconstruct the internal life of things.

Attachments and Modes of Existence

Attachment theory has long been known to psychology and psychiatry and relates to the existence of affective bonds, especially between humans. Its beginnings date to the fifties of the past century and the work of John Bowlby (1907–1990), who observed the reaction of children to the separation from their mothers. Together with his colleague Mary Ainsworth (1913–1999), they developed the classification of attachment styles, with more patterns appearing in subsequent research. Bowlby and Ainsworth offer a strong summary of their method and results in a 1991 article.

However, in the theory of materiality, one finds reference to the importance of the bonds we form with our possessions. Rephrasing Descartes's "je pense donc je suis," we can say that "we are what we are attached to," as Muecke (2012) notes in a review of Latour. That is, we are what we are attached to both in terms of objects and of the values they represent. Thus, another theory of attachment appeared concerning the attachment to objects. On the one hand, we can speak about creating intimate connections with the things around us as they naturally arise in psychological development of an individual, as noticed by Asma (2020), a professor of philosophy at the Columbia College Chicago, and Rose (2014), an entrepreneur and a lecturer at MIT Media Lab. Building upon his experience in object design, Rose also enumerates the features of enchantment with objects, and apart from obvious affordability and usability, he mentions lovability. The key idea behind distinguishing these "abilities," as he calls them, is their unique character, thanks to which they make "enchanted" objects different from mere prosthetics or robots. The lovability mentioned earlier reposes on the psychological reaction to politeness and subtlety of objects, and to their unobtrusive design and patterns of behavior. Rose predicts the future of interconnected systems with which people have to learn to live—and for it to be successful, they have to develop certain patterns of interaction based on emotional connection. On the other hand, there are visions quite different from the peaceful coexistence of humans and increasingly more autonomous objects than the one of Rose. In usually monstruous imaginations, we see ourselves as appropriated by objects. One can see a graphic example in one of Quino's (1932–2020) *Mafalda* comic strips cited by Latour in his paper "Factures/Fractures: From the Concept of Network to the Concept of Attachment" (1999), where Mafalda's father is supposedly being smoked by a cigarette (Quino, 1986). However, departing from such horrifying images, Latour (1999) affirms that the attachment between people and things is not about control, and it is a mistake to position the relationship between them in a spectrum between liberty and alienation, mastery and emancipation—just like the house in Mujica Láinez's (1954) novel complained. In the 1999 article, Latour writes, "The question to be addressed is not whether we should be free or bound but whether we are well or poorly bound" (p. 22). For Latour, it is impossible to remove the attachment altogether: it can only be substituted with another. The point, then, is not to state if we are attached to objects and whether this is pathology or not (Hoffman & Novak, 2018) but to consider the quality of this attachment and how it impacts the participants in the relation.

It is especially true about residential spaces, with which we come into complex relations. On the one hand, we are the owners and users, the designers and inhabitants; on the other hand, these spaces serve as extensions of ourselves. As frequently cited, Karen Lollar states:

> My house is not "just a thing." The house is not merely possession or a structure of unfeeling walls. It is an extension of my physical body and my sense of self that reflects who I was, am, and want to be.
>
> (Lollar, 2010, p. 262)

This self-extension becomes problematized when we talk about the smart environment. Smart homes have been considered as consumer–object assemblages

(Hoffman & Novak, 2018), in which smart devices are personified and possess different functions, such as a student, a data gatherer, or a market researcher. Thus, the extension of the human self encounters an increasingly autonomous agent, with whom we can enter in close personal relationships—in the literature of the subject appearing under different guises, ranging from intimacy to emotional attachment. As the authors of the article "My Roomba Is Rambo" (Sung et al., 2007) report, it can be considered that "objects have an affective quality if they cause changes in a person's mood, emotions, and/or feelings" (p. 146). The authors also note that research supports that machines can be endowed by their users with such qualities as politeness, gender, or ethnicity, and that the owners of Roomba ascribe personality traits to them.

What is more, with the advent of smart technology, the systems of attachments we can form with various objects become functional systems, as they are understood by David Roden (2015): sets of elements, including humans, connected by non-necessary relations, however forming a coherent whole usually united around a dominating presence. In this sense, he speaks of a toothbrush as a human: belonging to a system with humans at the center. These relations may be built of affordances and functionalities; however, an increasing body of research suggests the existence of affective bonds that should be taken into account while studying contemporary technologies. The pre-programmed electronic emotions or affective stickiness already on the level of human-inscribed telos position many emerging technologies as primarily imposing a kind of relation on their users (see Berriman & Mascheroni, 2019; Vincent, 2015). While electronic toys, such as Tamagotchi, elicit emotions from their users, mobile phones provide communication as well as such values as identity or dignity, thus fundamental human values.

Further, following Roden (2015), one might assume the existence of functional autonomous systems apart from humans, centered on another conscious agent, which may produce emotional demands via a set of independently crafted interactions (see Mascheroni & Vincent, 2016; Vincent, 2015). This leads Zwart (2017) to believe that human users can also become objects "used" by gadgets, making the phrase "human resources" acquire a different shade. As he comments:

> We no longer feel at ease in man-made technological environments, but rather experience chronic discontent as we ourselves become increasingly targeted by an enframing force (*Gestell*) turning us into a standing reserve of human resources, the raw material of a global technological system currently unfolding. We are inescapably thrown out of our familiar dwelling into hypermodern existence, as vulnerable and fragile beings, saved by, but also irrevocably infected by technology.
>
> (p. 32)

This potential for what humans necessarily view as the reversal of roles makes one especially wary about what kind of impact objects can have on the human part of the assemblage and about human users becoming objects of play on the part of their technological companions—or their creators.

Examples can be multiplied. Worth noting, for instance, are the experiments of designers Anthony Dunne and Fiona Raby, described on their website Dunneandraby.co.uk, together with the theories of design presented in their book *Speculative Everything* from 2013. They assumed that, in the future, parts of our domestic environment will become "technological cohabitants." That is, they will form with us emotional bonds—they do not speak about legal bonds; however, attempts to legalize certain forms of bonds between humans and software are being made, for example, Shibuya Mirai bot granted Tokyo residency in 2017 (Cuthbertson, 2017). Authors develop this vision in much contemporary fiction, among others, in *QualityLand* (2017), a satirical novel written by a German author, Marc-Uwe Kling, in which people bond with their highly interactive environment—kissing the smartphone, having a virtual friend, etc. And while Kling's humorous, exaggerated imagination of the world-to-come serves mostly as criticism of excessive and pathological digitalization today, the increasing presence of autonomous artificial agents in our lives also sparks more serious reflection, leading to speculative psychology.

What Is It Like to Be a Smart House?

In 1974, Thomas Nagel wrote a famous essay, "What Is It Like to Be a Bat?" claiming that it is largely impossible to answer this question. Similarly, it is impossible to understand what it is like to be a smart house. However, here we can speak of a certain advantage, as it is likely that the human emotional system will model the network one and, thus, result in a psychological continuity, at least to some extent. In a 2003 essay reviewing the history, status, and prospects of the smart house, Aldrich offers a working definition:

> a residence equipped with computing and information technology, which anticipates and responds to the needs of the occupants, working to promote their comfort, convenience, security and entertainment through the management of technology within the home and connections to the world beyond.
>
> (p. 17)

However, this definition does not approach the nature of the connections between the objects themselves and between the objects and humans, while currently, speculative philosophers, psychologists, and designers talk widely about reversing the focus from the human user to the non-human participant in the relation.

While contemporary ostensibly nonfictional speculations relating to the interaction with limited artificial intelligence cannot be taken to have any real domain (i.e., there is no actual internal life of an object that we can be said to be able to experience and describe), the attempts to break into the speculative psychology of objects have been numerous on the part of science fiction. Gwyneth Jones's *The Universe of Things* (2011) example has gained a broader audience with the discussion provided by Steven Shaviro (2014). This kind of cognitive exercise would correspond to what Bogost called "metaphorism" in his aforementioned *Alien Phenomenology* (2012) and would constitute one of the available tools to answer the question of what it is like to be an object.

Nagel's (1974) essay also provides inspiration to Bogost (2012) to build upon his own "alien phenomenology." Bogost claims that because of the inaccessibility of the alien experience to the human observer, it can only be understood by analogy. Building on the object-oriented ontology of Graham Harman (as later summarized in 2018), Bogost (2012) claims that "we never understand the alien experience, we only ever reach for it metaphorically" (p. 66). In the bat case, the example he gives is "bat operates like submarine" (p. 64); still, it only brings us down to the mechanics of the alien experience and not so much to its psychology. Bogost asserts the inevitability of anthropomorphizing as the closest approximation to what we can do within our subjective perception of things, and this seems to be what happens in the attempts at speculative psychology. First, the analogy "object is like a human being" is implicitly established, and only later does this analogy become problematized, given the alien materiality. For instance, if a smart house would be like a human being, it would probably be like one with many eyes, but instead of eyes, a host of other sensors humans do not have or do not have attuned to such an extent. If a smart house were truly like a human being, given its creation by a person, we could give it the role of a child—or a host of people, in which case the theories of the extended family apply. The list of anthropomorphic options could go on.

For this chapter, I have chosen the relation between a smart house and its owners featured in Scott Westerfeld's space opera *Succession*, which consists of two volumes: *The Risen Empire* (2003b) and *The Killing of Worlds* (2003a). The duology of the American writer portrays the world of a distant future in which humanity has conquered death, mastered interstellar travel, and formed an empire of diversified forms of humanity and non-humanity. Westerfeld seems to be more interested in the non-human actors with their minds and ways of developing relations than he is in the human ones, with the best example being the relationship between a non-human Rixwoman H_rd and her human captive, Rana Harter. The Rix are cyborgs that seem not to have individuality but to be always connected and dispersed. For example, H_rd has a screw in place of her heart, filters in place of her lungs, and her ovaries have been removed and put in cold storage. She exists as "the Rix commando," which means that she does not have an individuality and identity of her own. In this way, one may profitably parallel her compound nature, also physically, to the alien nature of the smart house. However, through her relationship with Rana, H_rd discovers what it means to love and be afraid, what it means to wish for life, and to suffer and miss someone.

In the *Succession* novels, Westerfeld explores Otherness in relation to various aspects of what we currently take to be fundamental limits of the human condition, asking, How will our ability to function together, love, and form bonds be different were we to become immortal, were we to become cyborgs, or were our bodies surgically modified? This leads him to ask questions about the speculative psychology of such entities as compound artificial intelligences or smart objects, wherein consciousness and identity were not programmed but developed in time and through interaction.

In the case of the smart house Westerfeld (2003b) describes, it has an additional feature of combining high-level smart systems and the technology similar to the one used today in "living bricks": self-repairing and partly made of natural, living components. The author frequently draws attention to the extension of the house's "self" into multiple objects that are either bionic or at least shaped like living beings (e.g., butterflies), thus collapsing the boundary between the bios and techne. This blurring or collapsing of boundaries complicates technological selfhood—or personhood—with the addition of the biological element that possesses its telos. In fact, Westerfeld, a trained philosopher, makes use of an image familiar from Aristotle's *Physics*: the seed, with its purpose ingrained in it and not inscribed in it externally by human architects. This plays well with his vision of an autonomous mind hosted by and uniting the dispersed technological devices.

Seeded on a lonely planet as an investment by an anonymous owner who never actually cares or visits, Westerfeld (2003b) describes that the house is allowed to make decisions by itself as far as its development. When the first owner puts himself into a deep, cold sleep—a common practice in the immortal society—the house passes to a new owner, one of the protagonists of the novels, Senator Nara Oxham, an opponent of the immortality policy. She visits, bringing more life to the place, which allows the house to learn her habits and preferences.

Westerfeld (2003b) describes the house from the omniscient narrator's point of view and situates the house firmly in the linguistic domain used for objects—using the pronoun "it" (cf., the affectionate gendering of Roomba or Alexa by their owners)—and alternates between the nouns "house" and "mind" to speak about it. Thus, on the level of the vocabulary choice, the author signals that he intends to retain the Otherness of the object in relation to its human owner. Westerfeld uses the word "mind" in his book for the general artificial intelligences and usually to describe self-learning compound systems, which corresponds to the image of the house as an assemblage. The "house" signifies the set of objects and the material construction that host the mind. Thus, from the very start, we know that the house exists in a network of attachments to other objects and other humans, be they only hypothetical in its mind. One of them would be the first owner, and others would be unnamed project engineers, builders, masons, etc., similar to examples for networks in Latour's *Modes of Existence* (2013, p. 223): invisible "technicians, engineers, inspectors, surveyors, intervention teams, repairmen, regulators, *around* and *in addition* to material objects," admittedly, forming only a part of the bigger picture.

Through non-interference into its existence, the human participants in the system described by Westerfeld (2003b) generated the rise of a psychological makeup in the house based on abandonment, loneliness, and neglect. Also, Westerfeld suggests that there existed a barrier in communication between the house and the managers, maybe because of the faulty language interpreters or other technical reasons, which resulted in the independent development of the house. The remark about the language interpreters is ironic here because, as Hoffman and Novak (2018) state, the bulk of the communication between the user and the smart object is ambient, that is, going on in the background rather than through direct communication. This echoes Latour's sentiment that technology "likes to hide" (2013).

In Westerfeld's (2003b) universe, this communication was severely lacking, as the architects seemed to think that the house could only be managed through commands and neglected the attention to its psychological side. The house felt "alone" and started communicating its loneliness, not so much through verbalization, but through its creative architectonic choices, demonstrating its need for warmth, for example, by creating a fireplace. Westerfeld tempts the reader to see if there appear any patterns known from the psychology of attachment, perhaps a withdrawal from further relations, shallow bonding, or hostility; however, the author does not develop this thread. Rather, Westerfeld presents the house's reaction in ways suggesting typical features of grief. When the house realized that the first owner would not come home/back, it "brooded." It lived what we might call a mild depressive episode, lasting two decades—a lot, in comparison with the duration of the psychological response in humans, but not so in the radically different timelines of the house. A further consequence was the development of greater independence and expansion in search of changes and new bonds.

Although anger is not visible in the pattern described by Westerfeld, denial and bargaining appear in the moment when one would think the house achieved independence from psychological reliance on the owner. Thus, it can be seen as a pattern of chronic, complicated grief. The appearance of Senator Nara Oxham in the house's life fills it with excitement; however, "[t]hat first absentee landlord still weighed on its mind like a stillborn child; the house kept his special coffee hidden in a subterranean storage room" (Westerfeld, 2003b, p. 131). The fact that the author mentions a stillborn child leads the reader to see the house as not only a child that lost a parent but also a parent that lost a child before its birth. The house keeping the specialty coffee in a subterranean room suggests removing the memory of the past bond to the subconscious—or unconscious?—which could theoretically impact every new process of bonding. Also, despite the house being happy to acquire a new owner, it is not quite the person it originally expected. Thus, it must not only confront an actual person rather than expectations but also face the fact that there are many differences between what was originally planned for and the actual needs and personality of the new owner.

In time, however, Westerfeld (2003b) narrates that the house creates a bond with Nara. Perhaps the relationship is facilitated by the senator's natural closeness to objects: she is a powerful empath, which makes it difficult for her to interact with humans, who tend to project many strong emotions. With her psyche attuned to the environment and the high capacity for adjusting to the inner voices of others, such a person seems to be the perfect respondent to the Otherness of smart objects. She restores the damaged self-esteem of the house and makes it feel valued. Still, the relationship she later develops with General Laurent Zai throws the house into confusion. Whereas it seems to be aware of how human relationships function, it experiences many difficulties figuring itself into this relationship, especially that Zai does not approve of "talking machines." It intends to give the couple privacy; however, this is not entirely possible because of its dependency on various sensors and smaller assemblages. Retiring the surveillance mechanisms would signify losing the ties with Nara Oxham. The house fills with the sensation of "inadequacy and self-doubt": these feelings do not relate to the emotional incapability but to the technical organization of space for two people instead of one over a period of time. However, it needs to be noticed that the author, in the second volume (Westerfeld, 2003a), starts treating the house as a comic relief of some sort, ascribing to it preoccupation with food supplies and etiquette over the actual well-being of the couple, which creates a humorous contrast with the overall serious themes of the duology.

Although Westerfeld's addition of the voice of the house to the polyphonic posthuman narrative seems promising, in the end, he falls back on familiar literary tropes, inscribing the relationship between Nara and the house in the pattern of the "mistress and the butler" story. As the relationship between Nara and Laurent develops, the connection with the smart system falls to the background, rather in tacit accordance with the conviction that the connection with objects for humans is a substitute for the connection with another human being. It is certainly the first volume that is more revealing as far as the speculative psychology of objects is concerned. The relationship with the first owner shows the house suffers from prolonged grief, refusing to let go of the things that reminds it about the man. In these terms, Westerfeld's house can be described as a "collapsed act," per the terminology proposed by George Herbert Mead (1863–1931) already in 1934, or perhaps more so, "a network of collapsed acts," marked by the entanglement with the lives of human owners and inhabitants. Still, it is more than that. From the beginning, Westerfeld describes the house as possessing its own consciousness and mind, and its own affective system. Rather than underlining emotional dryness that is frequently associated with technological objects, Westerfeld purposefully foregrounds the aliveness in the physical sense and its affective capability. As the story progresses, the house can let go of the hurtful memories and does it through the management of other objects: the reintroduction of the coffee that was the first owner's favorite brand now serves to foster the relationship between Nara and Laurent.

Through Westerfeld's narratives, we can see that the pattern of communication and working through the house's emotional issues comes mediated via its connection with other objects in the first place. In an interesting dynamic between an Alife—part biological, part technological—and simple technological devices, the speculative psychology of the smart house finds its expression in the relations that it forms with other objects. This mediated communication could be another way to access the psychological language of the functional autonomous systems once they arise. It suggests that the meeting place between the smart house and the human would be through mutual relation to objects.

Conclusions

Concluding, one should come back to the initial question sparked by Mujica Láin-ez's (1954) novel. What would be the nature of the attachment to residential spaces transformed through smart technology and the Internet of Things? The interaction of Nara and the smart house in Westerfeld's novels suggests, on the one hand, very simple projection techniques on the part of human agents: they should give the creative machines freedom and autonomy to act, treat them well, and project on them emotions humans would like their smart companions to develop—that is, employ the ethics of care signaled by Latour (2012) and Floridi in La Porte and Narbona (2021). On the other hand, Westerfeld's novels suggest the need for transformation of the human agent to suit this type of communication, not to become parasitized by the affective stickiness or electronic emotions. One way is to acknowledge and appreciate one's Otherness and extend one's mode of being to participate in possibly broad connectivity, akin to the one the Internet of Things enjoys. The attachments should also be viewed in a systemic way: not a stable and focused attachment, but an attachment rich in its plurality, protean in nature. For that, though, as follows from the science-fictional example, the human capacity for empathy probably should be enhanced, like in the case of Nara. This is not to make a case for human enhancement practices or ideologies but to signal the limitedness of the possible human response to the attachment of objects.

For all the challenges, it seems worthwhile to work in the development of the bonds with objects. What Latour (2013) says about the beings of metamorphosis may well be carried on to speak about the objects constituting our more and more technologically alive space and our attachment to them:

> What would we do without them? We would be always and forever the same. They trace throughout the multiverse—to speak like James—paths of alteration that are at once terrifying (since they transform us), *hesitant* (since we can deceive them), and *inventive* (since we can allow ourselves to be transformed by them). As soon as we begin to recognize them, consequently, we simultaneously measure the gulf into which they pull us, the means of pulling out, and the formidable energy that would be available to us if we only knew "how to go about it." It is only if we are afraid of them that they start deceiving us cruelly. This is why the word "metamorphosis" designates at one and the same time what happens to these beings, what happens to the humans who turn out to be attached to them, and what happens during the therapies that allow us to spot them and sometimes to install them.
>
> (p. 175)

Thus, there is no need to be afraid, like Mafalda's father in the cartoon, that the objects will possess the owners, because the relationship goes beyond ownership or mastery and emancipation. The connection between Nara and the smart house in Westerfeld's second volume (2003a) becomes rather one-sided, and it falls back on the patterns known from preceding fiction. It is telling that Westerfeld—although he does come back to his non-human character in the second volume—shifts away from psychological depth, prioritizing the more human connections over "artificial" bonds. However, what he does write about in the first part allows us to speculate that investigating human–object relations is crucial for existence in a digitalized, hyperconnected world, and he suggests interesting features of the possible internal life of objects. Some of them would be modelling artificial emotional systems on human systems and the length of psychological response. For a house to work through some of its traumas could take decades, even if it learns new skills and acquires information in the blink of an eye. This metaphorization, as Bogost (2012) would say, must be taken precisely as a kind of approximation and evaluated critically not to be confused with reality. The connection humans form with smart objects can go well beyond today's most common attachments and beyond hopes and fears painted by science fiction. Following the words of Steven Pinker from 2011 about the benefits of reading, fiction can become the meeting space to develop empathy for emerging technologies, which can help orient oneself in the world to come and in designing it to the benefit of all.

References

Ainsworth, M., & Bowlby, J. (1991). An ethological approach to personality development. *American Psychologist*, *46*(4), 331–341. http://doi.org/10.1037/0003-066X.46.4.333

Aldrich, F. K. (2003). Smart homes: Past, present and future. In R. Harper (Ed.), *Inside the smart home* (pp. 17–40). Springer.

Asma, S. T. (2020, February 25). Ancient animistic beliefs live on in our intimacy with tech. *Aeon*. https://aeon.co/ideas/ancient-animistic-beliefs-live-on-in-our-intimacy-with-tech

Berriman, L., & Mascheroni, G. (2019). Exploring the affordances of smart toys and connected play in practice. *New Media & Society*, *21*(4), 797–814.

Bogost, I. (2012). *Alien phenomenology, or what it's like to be a thing*. University of Minnesota Press.

Bradbury, R. (1951). The veldt. In *The illustrated man* (pp. 7–18). Doubleday & Company (Original story appeared in 1950 as "The World the Children Made.").

Cuthbertson, A. (2017, November 6). Tokyo: Artificial intelligence "boy" becomes world's first AI Bot to be granted residency. *Newsweek*. www.newsweek.com/tokyo-residency-artificial-intelligence-boy-shibuya-mirai-702382

Dunne, A., & Raby, F. (2013). *Speculative everything: Design, fiction, and social dreaming*. The MIT Press.

Graves-Brown, P. (2000). Always crashing in the same car. In P. Graves-Brown (Ed.), *Matter, materiality and modern culture* (pp. 155–165). Routledge.

Harman, G. (2018). *Object oriented ontology: A new theory of everything*. Pelican.

Hoffman, D. L., & Novak, T. P. (2018). Consumer and object experience in the internet of things: An assemblage theory approach. *Journal of Consumer Research*, *44*(6), 1178–1204.

Jones, G. (2011). *The universe of things*. Aqueduct Press.

Kling, M.-U. (2017). *QualityLand*. Ullstein Verlag.

La Porte, J. M., & Narbona, J. (2021). Colloquy with Luciano Floridi on the anthropological effects of the digital revolution. *Church, Communication and Culture*, *6*(1), 119–138. https://doi.org/10.1080/23753234.2021.1885984

Latour, B. (1999). Factures/Fractures: From the concept of network to the concept of attachment. *Res: Anthropology and Aesthetics*, *36*(1), 20–31.

Latour, B. (2012). The Berlin Key or how to do words with things. In P. M. Graves-Brown (Ed.), *Matter, materiality, and modern culture* (pp. 10–21). Routledge.

Latour, B. (2013). *An inquiry in the modes of existence: An anthropology of the moderns*. Harvard University Press.

Lollar, K. (2010). The liminal experience: Loss of extended self after the fire. *Qualitative Inquiry*, *16*(4), 262–270. https://doi.org/10.1177/1077800409354066

Mascheroni, G., & Vincent, J. (2016). Perpetual contact as a communicative affordance: Opportunities, constraints and emotions. *Mobile Media and Communication*, *4*(3), 310–326. https://doi.org/10.1177/2050157916639347

Mead, G. H. (1934). *Mind, self, and society from the standpoint of a social behaviorist*. University of Chicago Press.

Morton, T. (2013). *Realist magic: Objects, ontology, causality*. Open Humanities Press.

Muecke, S. (2012). "I am what I am attached to": On Bruno Latour's "Inquiry into the Modes of Existence". [Review of the book *An Inquiry in the Modes of Existence: An Anthropology of the Moderns* by B. Latour]. *Los Angeles Review of Books*. https://lareviewofbooks.org/article/i-am-what-i-am-attached-to-on-bruno-latours-inquiry-into-the-modes-of-existence/

Mujica Láinez, M. (1954). *La Casa*. Sudamericana.

Nagel, T. (1974). What is it like to be a bat? *Philosophical Review*, *LXXXIII*(4), 435–450.

Pinker, S. (2011). *The better angels of our nature: Why violence has declined*. Viking Books.

Poupyrev, I. (2019). *Everything around you can become a computer* [video]. TED Conferences. www.ted.com/talks/ivan_poupyrev_everything_around_you_can_become_a_computer?language=en

Quino. (1986). *Le Club de Mafalda* (10), 22. Editions Clénat.

Roden, D. (2015). *Posthuman life: Philosophy at the edge of human*. Routledge.

Rose, D. (2014). *Enchanted objects: Design, human desire, and the internet of things*. Scribner.

Shaviro, S. (2014). *The universe of things: On speculative realism*. University of Minnesota Press.

Sung, J.-Y., Guo, L., Grinter, R. E., & Christensen, H. I. (2007). "My Roomba is Rambo": Intimate home appliances. In Krumm et al. (Eds.), *International conference on ubiquitous computing* (pp. 145–162). www.cc.gatech.edu/~hic/hic-papers/Roomba-Ubicomp.pdf

Verbeek, P.-P. (2000). *What things do: Philosophical reflections on technology, agency and design*. Pennsylvania State University Press.

Vincent, J. (2015). The mobile phone: An emotionalised social robot. In J. Vincent, S. Taipale, B. Sapio, G. Lugano & L. Fortunati (Eds.), *Social robots from a human perspective* (pp. 105–116). Springer.

Westerfeld, S. (2003a). *The killing of worlds*. Tor.

Westerfeld, S. (2003b). *The Risen empire*. Tor.

Zwart, H. (2017). "Extimate" technologies and techno-cultural ciscontent: A Lacanian analysis of pervasive gadgets. *Techné: Research in Philosophy and Technology*, *21*(1), 24–55.

Chapter 5

Repetition and Return in Mervyn Peake's *Gormenghast* Trilogy

Dorothy Chang

Rose-Maëlle Florestal, Emma Baranowski, and Sammie L. Keenan provided copyediting for this chapter as part of the Northeastern University Psychological Humanities Workgroup.

In Mervyn Peake's (1911–1968) *Gormenghast* series—*Titus Groan* (1946/2011), *Gormenghast* (1950/2011), *Boy in Darkness* (1956/2011), and *Titus Alone* (1959/2011)—readers are struck by vivid images of death, decay, and stuckness. In fact, from the castle to the characters themselves, one of the major motifs appears to be moral, psychological, and physical stuckness, as Alice Mills states in her book *Stuckness in the Fiction of Mervyn Peake* (2006). While these images of death and decay are major themes in these texts, they are often accompanied by images of rebirth and regeneration, seemingly providing a hopeful high note for the characters. Despite this, the characters are never truly reborn, and all the characters remain stuck. In this chapter, I endeavor to show the cycle of truncated rebirth in the *Gormenghast* series.

The *Gormenghast* series documents Titus's encounter with the completely Other and alludes to the tensions this newness brings. More than once, Titus confronts the alien in his world: Steerpike, the main antagonist of the first two novels, and the Thing, his foster sister. Titus faces the tension between the change and repetition that accompanies these encounters. It is with this in mind that I seek to discuss the images of birth and rebirth in the narrative of the story. In the series, Peake brings up references to the womb and the underworld, and he constantly alludes both to mythic and Christian imagery. Using Mircea Eliade's (1907–1986) work about the mythic cycle of birth and rebirth as a starting point to help us understand the narrative of the series, I will begin by describing the castle as a maternal, mythic body before delving into Peake's various allusions to Titus's birth, such as his descent into the Lamb's lair and the Underworld. I suggest that, ultimately, while Titus continues to escape and is "reborn" time and again, Titus remains stuck within Gormenghast and her maternal waters.

Rebirth and Myth

Pierre François, in his 2004 work on Mervyn Peake's novels, argues that even more than Christian imagery, the central guiding structure of Peake's novels is

DOI: 10.4324/9781003519102-5

mythopoeic. Elsewhere, François (2013) notes the resonances between the character Keda and the Great Mother from mythology. Yet the Christian imagery occupies François's (2004) attention more deeply: Sepulcrave and the Fisher King, and Gormenghast Castle as a recreation of the Sacred Mountain motif which, as François points out, is described as a " 'hierophany,' a manifestation of the sacred to the human beings inhabiting the place" (p. 9). Given this, it is possible to read a mythic cycle of rebirth into the novels.

To help us understand the cycle of birth and rebirth, I turn briefly now to Mircea Eliade's 1958 study on puberty rituals within pagan religions as a helpful heuristic device to guide this chapter. In Eliade's study on these initiation ceremonies, there is always an act of rebirth. Eliade notes that, in these rituals, the novices are separated from their mothers, stating that the separation constitutes "a break, sometimes quite a violent break, with the world of childhood—which is at once the maternal and female world and the child's state of irresponsibility and happiness, of ignorance and asexuality" (p. 8). Through the repetition of the traditional rites, the entire community is regenerated (p. 4). What emerges after these rituals is the symbolic death and rebirth of the individual as well as the community and the cosmos. Similarly, as Nietzsche writes in *The Birth of Tragedy*, the "tremendous historical need of unsatisfied modern culture" suggests "the loss of myth, the loss of the mythical home [Heimat], the mythical maternal womb" (1872/2009, p. 136). For the novice that is about to be initiated into adulthood, this move is a transition from the profane to the sacred, passing through death before returning to a temporal and spatial beginning.

The Castle as Mother and Ritual Space

There is a similar logic in Titus's own journey from childhood to adulthood, and I would like to explore these themes of death and rebirth in the series itself. As is the case in these initiation rituals in the religious traditions studied by Eliade, Titus must also "die" or otherwise enter and exit the "womb" in order to be reborn into the world of adulthood. In fact, the impetus for most of Titus's actions throughout the narrative of the series is his attempted flights from women or, more specifically, flights from surrogate mothers, such as Gertrude, Juno, and Cheeta. However, in his effort to find his freedom by doing so, he fails to fully escape from the mother, only succeeding in running from womb to womb and returning to Gormenghast either literally or in his mind. As Titus's mother, Gertrude, warns him at the end of the second novel: "There is nowhere else. . . . You will only tread a circle, Titus Groan. There's not a road, not a track, but it will lead you home. For everything comes to Gormenghast" (Peake, *Gormenghast*, 1950/2011, p. 943).

Within this narrative logic, Gormenghast functions as a kind of mother in Titus's life. The castle itself is portrayed as a post-natal womb whose placental waters and expansiveness keep Titus and the rest of its inhabitants stuck within its walls. Peake offers images of a large and billowing space, painting a portrait of the castle's life-like characteristics. Yet the castle is as much a rigid prison for the inhabitants as it is a living, breathing organism that houses them. In one passage, Peake describes the breath of the castle, its sighs and groans, as its structure mimics a body. He writes, "The crumbling castle, looming among the mists, exhaled the season, and every cold stone breathed it out" (*Titus Groan*, 1946/2011, p. 190).

Aside from the massiveness and breath of the castle, Peake also links Gormenghast with floodwaters. For example, in the second book, *Gormenghast* (1950/2011), a devastating flood threatens to engulf all life in the castle, slowly filling it up with floodwaters. But even so, the floodwaters wipe the castle clean, restoring balance after Steerpike is cornered by Titus and the rising waters. Early in his chronology, during the Earling ceremony of the toddler Titus, he is brought on his mare to be crowned the 77th Earl of Gormenghast. This is after his father, Sepulcrave, dies. Peake plays with the imagery of shadow and water to juxtapose the tension between potential regeneration and stuckness. Nevertheless, the hope that a new earl would lead to the rejuvenation of life in the castle is quickly drowned in the watery grave of the castle's shadows. Peake writes:

> The terrain about them was as though freshly painted, or rather, as though like an old landscape that had grown dead and dull it had been varnished and now shone out anew, each fragment of the enormous canvas, pristine, the whole, a glory.
>
> (*Titus Groan*, 1946/2011, p. 364)

The inhabitants are faced with a moment of optimism, but it is not as simple as it seems. As 2-year-old Titus and his family make their way to the lake for the ceremony, the sinister shadows of the castle threaten to drown them. Peake writes:

> The leading mare with Titus on her back, still fast asleep in the wickerwork saddle, was by now approaching that vaster shadow, cast by the Castle itself out prodigiously, like a lake of morose water from the base of the stone walls. . . . [O]ne by one the tiny figures lost their toy-like brilliance and were swallowed. . . . One by one, the bright shapes moved into the shadows and were drowned.
>
> (*Titus Groan*, 1946/2011, p. 364–365)

As noted earlier, the castle represents both comfort and horror for Titus. It seemingly swallows or drowns all passions or individuality of its children and inhabitants. As Lesly Glen Marx observes in *The Dark Circus*, "[t]he smothering control of the Castle is apparent. These lives are only meaningful insofar as they fulfil the needs of the Castle" (1983, p. 103).

The castle asserts its control on Titus and the other inhabitants not only through its sheer size and the depths of the waters but also through the ritual laws and the keeping of sacred time. Much of the strangeness of the series centers on ritual and the different laws that surround these rituals. To the various characters, Gormenghast is unchangeable—in a realm where the most heinous and heretical act of the kingdom is change. The characters muse time and again about their uneasiness with change, sometimes going as far as to label change "evil." In one passage, the character Irma reflects, "It was that the House of Groan was different. Different. Yet, how could it be different? 'Impossible! I said Impossible!' she repeated to herself through a lather of fragrant suds, but she could not convince herself" (Peake, *Titus Groan*, 1946/2011, p. 294). She continues by asserting that the other inhabitants of the castle could feel the oppressiveness of this change, that "at the back of their personal troubles, hopes and fears, this less immediate trepidation grew, this intangible suggestion of change, that most unforgivable of all heresies" (Peake, *Titus Groan*, 1946/2011, p. 294).

Peake explains in no uncertain terms that the castle's esoteric rituals are the life-blood of the inhabitants that must be protected from the intrusion of outsiders and outside worlds. During the Earling ceremony, Barquentine, the Master of Ritual, declares that it will be the young earl's duty to defend the castle of his fathers "in every way against the incursions of alien worlds" (Peake, *Titus Groan*, 1946/2011, p. 357). Peake's castle is effectively a self-sustaining, hermetically sealed world that is unaware of and hostile to anything beyond its walls.

In addition to this resistance against change, Peake takes great pains to highlight the seasons and times of these rituals. The characters of the story are focused on ritual and cycles, and time is kept meticulously by the inhabitants. We are told that these practices and rituals are ancient and significant, but none of the characters are able to properly articulate the importance of these rituals. All that the inhabitants of the castle know is that there is nothing outside of Gormenghast. The readers are given the impression that the castle is timeless and that the seasons come and go with a repetitive inevitability. Peake writes, "Drear ritual turned its wheel. The ferment of the heart, within these walls, was mocked by every length of sleeping shadow. The passions, no greater than candle flames, flickered in Time's yawn, for Gormenghast, huge and adumbrate, out-crumbles all" (*Titus Groan*, 1946/2011, p. 297). In another passage, Peake further illuminates this, saying, "Autumn returned to Gormenghast like a dark spirit re-entering its stronghold. Its breath could be felt in forgotten corridors—Gormenghast had itself become autumn. Even the denizens of this fastness were its shadows" (Peake, *Titus Groan*, 1946/2011, p. 139). The main impression from the text, as noted by Marx, is that the castle is an "impregnable, unchanging centre of the world, as timeless and inevitable as the natural cycle, which contains change within the rhythm of repetition," and in this way, the castle offers "comforting stasis and security," while "ensuring communal harmony and a sense of meaningful identity" (1983, pp. 84–86). Growing up in the castle that always threatens to smother him, Titus longs to escape the confines of the castle walls and the stultifying rituals of the place. Yet while he eventually leaves the castle, Titus remains stuck.

Titus's Underworldly Journeys

Gormenghast Castle is a combination of mother, graveyard, and sacred space. Peake draws out the tension in the spatiality of the castle and suggests that Gormenghast is a liminal space between its mythic past and a modernity. In order to reach adulthood, Titus must escape from the castle-mother and leave his home to encounter alien worlds. On two separate occasions, Peake depicts Titus escaping the walls of Gormenghast to enter otherworldly spaces. Both scenarios entail a descent into a subterranean world and an eventual return. The first description of the underworld is from the novella *Boy in Darkness* (1956/2011), which takes place during the events of *Gormenghast* (1950/2011) on Titus's 14th birthday; the second is depicted in the third book of the series, *Titus Alone* (1959/2011). These episodes of rebirth show that while the story follows the logic of mythic eternal return and rebirth, that birth does not entail a return to a primordial beginning or a renewed life.

The narrative of *Boy in Darkness* (1956/2011) begins simply enough. Titus, though never explicitly named in the text, is sick of his life in the castle. Throwing caution to the wind, he leaves one night, wiggling through tunnels and descending the castle through a cord until he reaches a sluggish waterway surrounded by Cerberus-like hounds from "out of somewhere else" (p. 35) that lead him across this murky river into the lair of the Lamb, the Goat, and the Hyena. As if he were traversing the River Styx or the Lethe of the underworld, the hounds guide him through the river until he reaches a dusty, barren wasteland. The Lamb is the king of this land and is the epitome of evil, a parodic inversion of the Christian symbol of the lamb as Christ. Unlike the Christian symbol, however, the Lamb here does not represent resurrection or life—only death. Whereas Christ's body was sacrificed for the sins of humankind, the Lamb demands human sacrifices to satisfy his bloodlust. He cannot give or sustain life; he can only pervert. This wasteland is an inversion of Gormenghast, Titus's home. This inverted land reminds the reader of war-torn Europe with its structures of metal. Peake writes:

> There had been a time when these deserted solitudes were alive with hope, excitement and conjecture on how the world was to be changed. All that was left was a shipwreck. A shipwreck of metal. It spiralled; it took great arcs; it rose tier upon tier; it overhung vast wells of darkness; it formed gigantic stairs which came from nowhere and led nowhere. It led on and on; vistas of forgotten metal; moribund, stiff in a thousand attitudes of mortality; with not a rat, not a mouse; not a bat, not a spider.
>
> (*Boy in Darkness*, 1956/2011, p. 21)

There is only death everywhere as Titus turns in this wasteland of broken metal and machinery. It is clear that Titus has now entered into this womb-like underground, albeit a dried-up womb. Here Titus confronts death and evil. After killing the Lamb, Titus finds his way back to the river, and the dogs bring him back to Gormenghast. However, while I read this as a kind of underworldly journey into the womb of the earth, nothing has actually changed for Titus. No new revelation is gained, and there is no triumphant return. This encounter is nowhere alluded to or mentioned again in the events of *Gormenghast* (1950/2011), the second novel, and there is no heroic resolution with the castle-as-mother. Therefore, in the narrative of rebirth, there is a return to his primordial home, but there is no conversion or newness. At the end, he is carried back into the castle, returning to that womb.

We see this underworldly journey occur once again in *Titus Alone* (1959/2011), the third book. Titus once again escapes the maternal waters that had threatened to consume him and encounters a new "alien" city via a quasi-mythical river. This is a city not unlike a modern British city, full of cars, death rays, helicopters, and skyscrapers. However, this new alien world of fluorescent lights and flying cars is unlike any Titus has ever seen, and the inhabitants of this new world have never heard of or seen Gormenghast. As Hindle notes in a commentary describing these and other landscapes in Peake's works, like "the Styx, which bore the dead to Hades, and the Lethe, its twin, in whose waters all memories of life were carried away" (1996, p. 14). Once Titus traverses the river into this city, his memories of his ancestral home begin to fade. The narrative is symmetrical, beginning with Titus's emergence from the river leading him into the city and ending with an ascent up Gormenghast mountain. In the very middle of the story is his descent to the underbelly of the city, the Under-River. If we read his entrance into the city as his entrance into the Hades, the Under-River might be seen as the very heart of the underworld, full of darkness and "relics of another age" (Peake, *Titus Alone*, 1959/2011, p. 831). As Titus traverses this subterranean world, he once again encounters the embodiment of evil in a man named Veil. When he sees Veil, Titus feels as though he is being confronted with death itself. As Titus confronts death itself and his waning memories of his past and his home, he is forced to fully confront the threat of alienation and what Marx describes as a "fractured identity" (1983, p. 192). In this disjunction, Titus becomes birthed as a fully modern subject, once again confronting the "reality of modern existence" (Marx, 1983, p. 9).

Despite these events, Titus once again finds himself captured by the villainous Cheeta and her father, the Scientist, in *Titus Alone* (1959/2011). Refusing to become a surrogate mother to Titus, Cheeta attempts to torture him by creating a parodic pageant of the people he knew from the castle. Mills notes that Cheeta "does her best to infantilize Titus, first by rendering him helpless, bound and blindfolded," taunting him with his "toys" (2006, p. 201). At the end of *Titus Alone* (1959/2011), being rescued by helicopter from Cheeta and her death factory, Titus yearns for his childhood home and his mother in the same breath. He exclaims:

> Have we no destination? We are moving, that is all; from one sky to the next. Is that what you think? Or am I mad? I have drowned my birthplace with rant until its name stinks to heaven. Gormenghast! O Gormenghast! How can I prove you?
>
> (Peake, *Titus Alone*, 1959/2011, p. 940)

He is reduced to a childlike state, unable to reach his potential as a "man" and a "modern subject." And once again, he wails, "Mother . . . mother . . . mother . . . mother . . . where are you? Where . . . are . . . you? Where . . . are . . . you?" (Peake, *Titus Alone*, 1959/2011, p. 941).

Titus is dropped "unharmed, like a child in a cradle" (Peake, *Titus Alone*, 1959/2011, p. 941), to the mountains outside of Gormenghast, finally affirming to himself that his home and his memory are all real. However, after spending the entirety of *Titus Alone* searching for the castle, he does not return and instead realizes that he "had no longer any need for home, for he has carried his Gormenghast within him. All that he sought was jostling within himself" (p. 943). At the end of his journey, Titus recognizes the inescapability of his home, the maternal womb from which he came. Gormenghast now resides within him. In one sense, this could be read as Peake's optimistic attempt at showing that Titus has matured, having internalized his mother's voice. He no longer has the need for Gormenghast as a mother, because he is able to fully integrate her into himself, and what is left for him to do is to chart a new path for himself. However, in light of this cycle of stunted rebirths and returns, this reading of the ending feels unsatisfying. For Titus, as Mills notes, it is clear that any escape results in a "different kind of tyranny" (2006, p. 203). Perhaps in this situation, too, Gormenghast and its smothering are inescapable.

Conclusion

Unfortunately, because of Peake's mental degeneration and early death, we will never hear the continuation of Titus's journey, let alone the conclusion. If he does not return home, where does he go after all this? What role will Gormenghast play for him after this realization that his home is always within him? Does this integration of the maternal within himself allow him to change, or is he doomed to repetition? Given the trajectory of Titus's journey, it is not a stretch to say that the route will always end in a repetitive circle. Unlike the circle of birth and rebirth that had been outlined by Eliade, Titus remains stuck in an unending cycle that never amounts to any regeneration or return to any primordial beginning. He is forever stuck within Gormenghast.

References

Eliade, M. (1958). *Birth and rebirth: The religious meanings of initiation in human culture.* Harper & Brothers.

François, P. (2004). Godless religion and maimed earldom in "Titus Groan". *Peake Studies*, *9*(1), 5–34. www.jstor.org/stable/24776655

François, P. (2013). The Keda mystery. In G. P. Winnington (Ed.), *Miracle enough: Papers on the works of Mervyn Peake* (pp. 33–47). Cambridge Scholars Publishing.

Hindle, R. (1996). Elysian fields, Hadean glooms: Titus Groan's mythical quest. *Peake Studies*, *4*(4), 7–20. www.jstor.org/stable/24776056

Marx, L. G. (1983). *The dark circus: An examination of the work of Mervyn Peake, with reference to selected prose and verse* [Unpublished master's thesis, University of Cape Town].

Mills, A. (2006). *Stuckness in the fiction of Mervyn Peake*. Rodopi.

Nietzsche, F. (2009). The birth of tragedy. In W. Kaufmann (Trans.), *Basic writings of Nietzsche*. Modern Library (Original work published 1872).

Peake, M. (2011). *Boy in darkness and other stories* (S. Peake, Ed.). Peter Owen Publishers (Original work published 1956).

Peake, M. (2011). *The illustrated Gormenghast trilogy*. Vintage (Original Works: *Titus Groan*, 1946; *Gormenghast*, 1950; *Titus Alone*, 1959).

Chapter 6

Alienation, Obsession, and Enthrallment in Thomas Ligotti's "The Small People," "Nethescurial," and Other Weird Fiction

Jason Marc Harris

Emma Baranowski, Gracie Vogel, and Amelia Maybrun provided copyediting for this chapter as part of the Northeastern University Psychological Humanities Workgroup.

Julia Kristeva's (1980/1982) notion of the abject addresses an unconsciously rooted repulsion that causes people to avoid others and to feel self-loathing. Although, drawing on Georges Bataille (1897–1962), Imogen Tyler has expanded the abject to socio-political contexts, this chapter focuses on private psychological encounters with the dissolving barrier between *self* and *Other.* In some Weird fiction, characters experience an erosion of borders between who they think they are and what they fear or detest, leading to alienation, which weakens subjective distinctions between the pure self and the detestable abject. Although Kristeva (1980/1982) points to rather-specific developmental ambivalence toward one's mother as a source of the abject, the abject tension between what she refers to as the "unapproachable and the intimate" (p. 6) helps capture the dynamic of immanent Weirdness that characterizes the subversion of human identity in texts of Weird horror. These crumbling modules of identity manifest a disturbing disclosure: we have met the alien monster—whether friend or foe—and it is us, or at least we are perversely determined that it be so, perhaps because we hope we can see more clearly in the dark if we embrace that darkness.

In Thomas Ligotti's "The Small People" (2014), the beings referred to in the title are an uncanny unknown group, perhaps interdimensional sentient simulacra, and the artifice and chaos of these small people become an existential threat to the narrator's identity. This alienation expressed in terms of xenophobic existential fear extends to other weird fiction of the twentieth to the twenty-first century. This alienation often includes enthrallment with the Other, whether sexual, bestial, or even vegetative mutation. In Luigi Ugolini's (1891–1980) story "The Vegetable Man" (1917/2012), a plant transforms a human host into a member of the green tribe. In Hanns Heinz Ewer's (1871–1943) "The Spider" (1915/2012), a young man is hypnotized into suicide by a mysterious female hotel occupant. In Abraham Merritt's (1884–1943) story "The People of the Pit" (1918/2013), the narrator fears

DOI: 10.4324/9781003519102-6

psychic domination by an invisible race. Jon Padgett's "Origami Dreams" (2016) offers readers entrance into the narrator's physical world, which seems subverted by his mental existence, when reading notes about lucid dreaming alters his waking life. In Michael Cisco's story "The Water Machine" (2021), a psychic state transfers from a patient to a psychiatrist. In my own novella, *Master of Rods and Strings* (2021), the protagonist's obsessive ambition to become a master puppeteer and exact vengeance leads him to identify with a puppet, alienating himself from family and humanity. Whether emerging from xenophobia, romanticism, surreal encounters, scientific fascination, or ambitious obsession, contagious alienation with or from the Other distinguishes Weird fiction, which tests borders of identity. Alienation in Weird tales combines surreal horror and psychological fascination and the consequent derangement—and sometimes monstrous reconfiguration—of the individual whose identity is cut loose from a coherent and stable human community.

Preceding Weird horror, gothic modes of literature also include alienating surreality. Consider Kate Chopin's Southern Gothic novella *The Awakening*: "It is like a night in a dream. The people about me are like some uncanny, half-human beings. There must be spirits abroad to-night" (1899/1993, p. 17). Although there is whimsy in the character Edna's intimation of spirits and uncanny people surrounding her, Edna's disassociation from her community manifests as both anhedonic and solipsistic alienation:

> Edna looked straight before her with a self-absorbed expression upon her face. She felt no interest in anything about her. The street, the children, the fruit vender, the flowers growing there under her eyes, were all part and parcel of an alien world which had suddenly become antagonistic.
>
> (Chopin, 1899/1993, p. 32)

Her identity drifts away from communal conventions, and her despair and apartness result in suicide.

The dislocation that follows from alienation is surreally highlighted in the aforementioned Weird tale "Origami Dreams" (2016) by Jon Padgett. The story concerns a narrator who discovers a dream narrative written in an origami structure by a prior resident of his home. The found narrative reveals an encounter between the origami's creator and a strange entity known as Daddy Long Legs—an unraveling of reality follows. Although the origamist believes he is engaging in lucid dreaming when he attempts to exorcise this entity by altering the form of the dream house, the origamist's entire world slips away from and with him, house by house and street by street. Even his wife and children disappear, and his daily life becomes an unwilling dream in the role of the exorcist, whose identity he'd thought he had created for lucid dreaming adventures. Moreover, as the layers of the story, dreams, and frame narrative shift and overlap, the line between the origamist's identity and the narrator of the frame story blurs too; readers are left contemplating a surreal nexus of people-as-nesting-dolls. The narrator's periodic checking of his fingers as a means of discerning whether he is truly awake culminates in the implication that he is actually the mysterious Daddy Long Legs. Like the titular "Origami Dreams," the story's structure folds fiction, memory, and dream into a new metamorphic structure where human identity subordinates to a power that operates more as a chaotic art than science—a metaphysics guided by terrifying aesthetics of amoral malleability.

Alienation in Padgett's (2016) story leads to transformative erasure, whereby the narrator himself becomes an Other, eliminating borders between waking and dreaming states. This subversion of any stable individualism—communicated through reading as a contagious conjuration—is reminiscent of the epistemological metaphysics of Thomas Ligotti's "Nethescurial" (1991/2015a). The narrator in "Nethescurial" has a gradual gnosis of alienating Otherness, which is not limited to a reconfiguration of his own body, mind, and regional surroundings, as it is largely with Padgett's (2016) story. Instead, Ligotti (1991/2015a) offers the visionary awakening to the underlying corruption of the entire cosmos. "Nethescurial" is also a serviceable example of the so-called "New Weird." Most essentially, Ann and Jeff Vandemeer define the New Weird in terms of "choosing realistic, complex real-world models as the jumping off point for creation of settings that may combine elements of both science fiction and fantasy" and often offers "elements of surreal or transgressive horror" (Vandemeer & Vandermeer, 2008, p. xvi). Relying upon the definition presented by Ann and Jeff Vandemeer, Atene Mendylyte contrasts the New Weird with the Old Weird in terms of the impossibility of circumscribing the Weirdness: "While in the weird of old one can localize the source of the weird/horror, in the new weird that source is omnipresent, and seeps through every fibre of reality" (2019, p. 106). This retreat from marginality with the New Weird is exemplified in the essential omnipresence of the Weird in Ligotti's "Nethescurial" (1991/2015a), which is underscored by the compelling chant of the cult the narrator presents: "Amid the rooms of our houses—across moonlit skies—throughout all souls and spirits—behind the faces of the living and the dead" (p. 332). This chant blurs the distinction between "living and the dead" with the disquieting connective tissue of the pantheistic entity Nethescurial. The narrator is left struggling with denials of the visions he continues to see that suggest the omnipresence of malign evil. In his apophatic attempts to protest, the chant's diction and syntax invade his thoughts and writing:

> That shape is not drawing something out of me and putting something else in its place, something that seems to be bleeding into the words as I write. . . . [N]o shadows fall across the moon, no churning chaos of smoke that chokes the frail order of the earth. . . . [N]ot the cancerous totality of all creatures, not the oozing ichor that flows within all things. *Nethescurial is not the secret name of the creation.* It is not amid the rooms of our houses . . . behind the faces of the living and the dead.
>
> (Ligotti, 1991/2015a, p. 333)

Ligotti concludes an interview with *The New Yorker* explaining, "The only interest I've taken in psychological aberrancy in fiction . . . has been as a vehicle of perceiving the derangement of creation" (Berbegal, 2015). "Nethescurial" (1991/2015a) embodies that derangement. The narrator's alienation is a consequence of his dawning perception that his very sense of self is dissolving. However, it should also be noted that although Ligotti is himself anthologized in the Vandemeers' "New Weird," he does not subscribe to their ethos stressing realistic settings that they claim characterize much of the New Weird. Ligotti expands upon this theme in his interview with Berbegal, who emphasizes that "his stories exist in 'enclosed environments' that have more in common with dreamscapes than any real-life locations" (Berbegal, 2015).

The ethos of Weird horror that operates in Ligotti's fiction is part of a gnawing alienation—a constant undermining of complacency where there is no definite position of realistic stability. Brad Baumgartner, in *Weird Mysticism* (2021), argues that "[h]orror tends to subvert and interrogate the foundational binaries of culture and language, problematizing the relations between self and other, animate and inanimate, and being and thinking" (p. 46). Ligotti's "Nethescurial" (1991/2015a) is exactly such a story, where the knowing of self is intermixed with reading the document of an encounter with Nethescurial, which is simultaneously a revelation that all of existence necessitates encounters with Nethescurial, whether "animate" or "inanimate" (Baumgartner, 2021, p. 44). Also, noting Ligotti's work, Baumgartner emphasizes the use of rhetorical negation—apophaticism—as a tool adopted from earlier mystical thinkers in which mystics and authors alike apply a "logic of negation . . . in relation to the horror of reality—a horror effectuated by our alienation from absolute unreality, horror's analog to the medieval mystic's God" (p. 5).

The alienation of the narrator, who is a literary scholar, is aptly called "self-abnegation" by Alijandro Omidsalar (2018) and reveals a "flagging sense of individuality" (p. 718) which fails to preserve the self from the assimilating, reductive, and essential wrongness of the universe. Omidsalar also identifies Ligotti's "Nethescurial" (1991/2015a) as an example of a story that shows how Ligotti refuses "to maintain cosmic horror's normally sacrosanct separation between ontologically befuddled humans and godlike monsters" (Omidsalar, 2018, pp. 717–718). In this respect, Omidsalar argues that Ligotti has obliterated the rules of cosmic horror established by H. P. Lovecraft, where "entities operate on geological or even cosmological scales of time that are narratively framed as incomprehensible to humans" (Omidsalar, 2018, p. 717).

I would agree with Omidsalar (2018) that Ligotti has fundamentally shifted the discourse and frame. Ligotti's horror allows readers to find the alienating ubiquitous cosmic horror within the quotidian space that encloses us once we are acquainted with the singular vision of essential corruption that his stories offer. Steven Mariconda (2013) explores another dimension Ligotti utilizes which Lovecraft helped initiate: "Lovecraft's exploration of nonrational perception—visions, dreams, and madness—which Ligotti has most especially picked up on and expanded" (Mariconda, 2013, p. 172). However, I would add that "madness" in Lovecraft is often a result of encountering unfathomable knowledge beyond human capacity.

In Ligotti, the role of madness is far more nuanced and speaks to a recognition that to be human is to live in an inherently alienating state. Ligotti's narrators may not even need some outside influence to perceive the fit of the puzzle pieces that offer visionary shape to the immanent horror of the universe. Such madness does not rely upon encountering a Great Old One, as in Lovecraft, but only demands looking too closely at key details at hand or gaining access to the tools for unfolding those layers of uncanny significance.

It is useful to build on Omidsalar's (2018) claims by adding Baumgartner's (2021) assertion that part of Ligotti's portrayal of horror is that "horrors we cannot yet comprehend are rooted within us" (p. 4). In this sense, then, humanity becomes a microscopic lens for macroscopic cosmic horror. We are the concentrated—though still disturbingly opaque—image of what we fear to know and perhaps can never know. Also, it is intriguing to consider how the move from the massive scale of divine monstrosities in Lovecraft's Cthulhu Mythos to the humanoid puppets, mannequins, clowns, and Small People of Ligotti's stories is a diminishment in scale of the sublimity of cosmic horror but not at all a diminishment in the power of the disconcertion. In these respects of stressing alienating subversions of human identity and authority, Ligotti's "Nethescurial" (1991/2015a)—with its reduction of the forms of the universe down to the malign essence of a pantheistic evil which can infect the mind of a single reader—serves as an underlying model for understanding Ligotti's "The Small People" (2014).

The diminutive figures in Ligotti's "The Small People" (2014) are not dwarves or fairies of legend; they are ahistorical doppelgängers of humanity and all the chaotic horror whose potential feels alien within the human psyche. When the narrator and his friend are confronted by the Small People after the boys have intruded upon one of their new settlements, the narrator notes that the Smalls are "unwrinkled, unworn by time and somehow immortal. . . . [A] mirror of us—of what we wanted for ourselves" (Ligotti, 2014, p. 45). And the touch of the Smalls as they bump against the boys is repulsively and unexpectedly "soft."

> Their shapes felt as if they were giving way as they lightly pressed themselves against us. But they were also swivel-headed dummy-things—freakish unrealities like their town and maybe everything having to do with small country. . . .
> What were these things that seemed to be all appearance and no substance?
> (Ligotti, 2014, p. 46)

The refrain of "one of us" from Tod Browning's 1932 film *Freaks* feels implied by the grotesque intimacy of how the Small People "lightly press themselves against us" and the explicitly "freakish unrealities" stated as associated with their culture (Ligotti, 2014, p. 46). The young narrator of the story grows increasingly troubled not only by abject revulsion from the Small People but also the absence of any information about them, including why they spoil their surroundings with rubbish. They are forces of subversive entropy that infect the narrator's own perspective,

though it is ambiguous whether he is paranoid about the failings of human civilization or he is objectively apprehending portentous flaws:

> When I looked closely at the city hall, for instance, I could see it was wob-
> bly. . . . Or take the post office. If my mother had ordered me in her most calmly
> intimidating voice to go buy her some stamps, I wouldn't do it. Not one foot
> would I set inside, because its bricks were set together all wrong. One of them
> could slide a little, I gauged, and the walls might come crashing down in a flash
> and bury me alive as I was standing in line to buy some rotten stamps which had
> images on them that were so faded and cock-eyed I couldn't tell anymore what
> they were supposed to represent.
>
> (Ligotti, 2014, p. 52)

The narrator's distrust of the Smalls, and particularly the Half-Smalls, evolves into
an unsettling fear of the stability of the everyday. The reliance that the narrator used
to have for the foundations of his society is shaken—not merely by the intimations
of shoddy architecture but by his alienation from human civilization, expressed in
the unreliable designs for important buildings and the degradation of iconic communication in stamps.

Compounding the narrator's disconcertion is his intuition that there exist
Half-Smalls, hybridizations or artificial imitations of humans passing as normal.
These Half-Smalls are tying together humans and Smalls via a psychic or rather
"spectral link":

> With its small people, this world just seemed a preposterous mess to me, and
> now it was revealed to be even worse than I knew. . . . [T]he existence of the
> half-smalls . . . inspired in me a crawling fear. . . . I've mentioned having this
> sensation in dreams, along with a hatred of them for having what I thought was
> a weakness connecting them in some spectral manner with the small people. At
> least the latter were something of a phenomenally known quantity to my mind,
> however little I understood about them. But the halfers were something else—
> interlopers in a world where they didn't belong.
>
> (Ligotti, 2014, p. 51)

This sense of being invaded by "interlopers in a world where they didn't belong"
is heightened because the narrator dreads that he might even be a Half-Small, born
from parents who "belonged to that weird species" (Ligotti, 2014, p. 55). This obsession with Half-Smalls is a notable example of how a writer of horror like Ligotti
can invisibly transcend the *Uncanny Valley* by offering intuitive rather than material
leaps of alienation: it is no longer the unsettling artifice of the humanoid features
of the Smalls that is troubling the narrator but the very lack of distinct features of
wrongness in the Half-Smalls. He only has this impression of a "spectral link" that
connects Smalls with Half-Smalls. Before losing himself in doubt over the question
of his own human purity, the narrator becomes convinced that as a human boy, he

was viewed by his parents as merely a "prop, something to aid them in not being found out for what they were" (Ligotti, 2014, p. 55). Acting upon his hunch that his parents are Half-Smalls, the narrator murders his parents—or adopted parents—and is incarcerated. The epistemology of the hatred of the Half-Smalls is taken to the fatality of its logic, and the surety of the abject disgust of the difference the narrator perceives in the Smalls is undercut by the more tentative nature of the Half-Smalls. The murder of his parents reveals the intensity of that hatred, though whether his parents were indeed Half-Smalls or not remains unknown, and perhaps beside the point. The obsession of the narrator with the intolerably corrupt world around him is what is most pervasive. Doubting his own purity coalesces his uncanny doubts and abject revulsion, though the result is the dissolution of his identity—or perhaps the revelation that he was essentially always akin to a Half-Small since there is no escaping the inextricable spectral link with the flawed cosmos.

A notable connecting text for "The Small People" (2014) and "Nethescurial" (1991/2015a) is Ligotti's "The Night School" (1991/2015b), which also emphasizes the notion of a flawed cosmos and dissolves any hope of coherent knowledge in such an inherently corrupt matrix. To have cosmic knowledge is presented as a fool's doomed desire, an unsolvable riddle, and a state of being that is implicitly heinous and destructive to the ideal of human cognition and illusion of identity; in fact, the desire of knowledge is gradually suggested to be something that should be purged from one's being:

> My desire to know something that was real about my existence, something that could help me in my existence before it was my time to die and be put into the earth to rot, or perhaps have my cremated remains drift out of a chimney stack and sully the sky—that would never be fulfilled. I had learned nothing, and I was nothing. Yet instead of disappointment at my failure to fulfill my most intense desire, I felt a tremendous relief. The urge to know the fundament of things was now emptied from me, and I was more than content to be rid of it.
>
> (Ligotti, 1991/2015b, p. 402)

The word "fundament" is not mere wordplay here; the story's imagery consistently presents knowledge as execrable rather than the basis of enlightened civilization and postulates that existence itself is a cesspool. Better not to know what the cosmos really is, since approaching any "knowing" will not help but likely be all the more annihilating.

"The Small People" (Ligotti, 2014) ends with another form of negation and disruption—not of the useless impossibility of knowledge, but the alienating anguish of being deprived of an anchor of identity. The narrator's anguished entreaty of psychological and existential despair to the psychiatrist punctuates the story with a more than rhetorical question of identity: "For the love of all that is real—Who am I? What am I?" (p. 59). Readers, too, must wonder by what spectral links they connect to illusions and more sinister components behind the execrable and uncanny alienating cosmic puppetry that surrounds and compels them. The conclusion of "The Small People" erodes the sense of the narrator's self by its anti-egoism, and at the end of the story, readers may struggle with a similarly unsettling alienation as the protagonist, whose true nature cannot be reliably determined. We are used to binary categorizations—rational and irrational, living and dead, known and unknown, and sane and insane; but Ligotti's fiction wears away polarized barriers as merely rhetorical rather than reliable, such as between the aberrant and the normal, the alien and the familiar.

Like Ligotti's "The Small People" (2014), Michael Cisco's "The Water Machine" (2021) offers an anti-egoistic model of identity in a non-anthropocentric cosmos where the narrator is changed in his interactions with what appears to be an aberrant form of identity: a female patient obsessed with a semi-divine alien totality she refers to as "the water machine." The psychiatrist believes he communicates with this schizophrenic patient, even after her death, by using mathematics and cryptic syntax. The psychiatrist's own diction and syntax come to emulate his dead patient, as though his consciousness has been replaced or infected by whatever moderated her communication. But rather than suggesting an underlying connection to a unified consciousness that transcends death, he comes to believe that there is no meaningful conjunction between component "vectors"—seemingly living things—scattered haphazardly about in a malign cosmos. Indeed, his final words emphasize fatalistic negation without consolation of even a mechanistic deism and stress the absence of personality by their very insistent impersonal repetition: "No one escapes. There is no water machine. There is no water machine. There is no water machine" (p. 140).

Subtle and sinister connections and communications that produce alienation appear in other Weird horror, such as Hanns Heinz Ewers's "The Spider" (1915/2012), where the protagonist realizes he has become manipulated by a mysterious woman who can compel his limbs to move like a suicidal marionette. Although he believes they are engaging in amorous "telepathy or thought transference" (p. 83), he is terrified and yet ecstatically enthralled by this dissociation from his own body and the subordination to his possessor: "a compulsion of an unheard nature and power, yet so subtly sensual in its inescapable ferocity" (p. 88). The narrator's encounter with the unknown woman at the window appears to combine the fascination of the death drive along with an inextricable Eros—caught in the spider's web, to be sure.

My own novella *Master of Rods and Strings* (Harris, 2021) involves a symbiotic psychic interaction between the narrator, Elias, and his favorite puppet, Virgil. Elias develops an emotional and communicative link with Virgil that helps foster their mutual ambitions toward potent ascendancy in the competitive sphere of occult puppetry:

> In Virgil dwelt something beyond words and memory that had existed long before humanity squatted in dirty huts. I had given him clothes and drawn close to give ear to his voice. I could not take credit for his wisdom and strength.

Our union transcended physical puppetry, a spiritual symbiosis beyond religious dogma, deluded mysticism, or bloodless aestheticism.

(Harris, 2021, p. 43)

However, the progress of this ambitious development is focused on vengeance, and there is consequent alienation from the protagonist's more humane qualities, particularly his attachment to his sister. He participates in necromantic incest to absorb her powers and strengthen his bonds of occult puppeteering:

Virgil guided me to do that which I alone could not have had the strength. I felt then how Virgil completed me and my sister. Together we had formed a triumvirate that destiny had summoned to wreak justice upon a fallen world. To the uninitiated we were the vilest of sinners, but in the glory of what we would achieve, we were the most courageous and enlightened puppets dancing in wondrous communion with the Supreme Will unseen behind the stars.

(Harris, 2021, p. 70)

In his identification with his puppet Virgil, Elias transgresses more and more grievously until he is closer to the Outside in communion with otherworldly forces pulling the strings of uncanny puppets than in fellowship with other humans. Like stories by Cisco, Padgett, and Ligotti, *Master of Rods and Strings* explores the role of alienation as perhaps a metamorphic stage in evolving, degrading, or unmasking from the human to something Other lurking beyond the egoistic threshold—disconcerting in its uncanny apartness but with its own potent claims for a weird and esoteric existence not discernible, accessible, or reconcilable to anthropocentric "civilized" modes of knowledge.

Thus, I will end this chapter with a return to where it began with Kristeva (1980/1982). Kristeva's emphasis on the abject plumbs the depth of the revulsion toward material-that-is-not-ourselves. The abject echoes from early childhood primal relationships and forms closely to our developmentally human selves—particularly with regard to the ambivalence with the role of maternal influence. Weird horror portrays the Other as typically inhuman and disruptive, whether extrinsic or intrinsic to the self. Weird horror's Other is often actively infecting dangerously curious protagonists. These characters' ambivalence toward the Other—fascinated revulsion, fear, or a tenuous admixture of these affects—allows for avenues of intrusion or activation of nascent chaos that subverts the integrity of their sense of self. Each story includes characters that come to identify with that which they would—or even should—reject—on the grounds of physical revulsion, but also for the sake of any remaining shreds of psychological integrity. The mechanics of the gradual identification with the alien in Weird horror via obsession, possession, and derangement serves to erode human complacency of rationality and a sense of a stable real self. The Other comes to subsume and dissolve human identities into a disorder where the barrier between the self and the alien becomes as absurd as the pretension that we can see any more clearly in the dark than we can in the light.

References

Baumgartner, B. (2021). *Weird mysticism: Philosophical horror and the mystical text.* Lehigh University Press.

Berbegal, P. (2015, October 29). The horror of the unreal. *The New Yorker* [online publication]. www.newyorker.com/books/page-turner/the-horror-of-the-unreal

Browning, T. (director & producer), Goldbeck, W., & Gordon, L. (screenplay) (1932). *Freaks.* Metro-Goldwyn-Mayer.

Chopin, K. (1993). *The awakening.* Dover Publications (Original work published 1899).

Cisco, M. (2021). Water machine. In *Antisocieties* (pp. 123–142). Grimscribe Press.

Ewers, H. H. (2012). The spider. In A. Vandermeer & J. Vandemeer (Eds.), *The weird* (pp. 77–89). Tor Books (Original story published 1915).

Harris, J. M. (2021). *Master of rods and strings.* Vernacular Press. (This novella is now available in a 2024 edition from Crystal Lake Publishing.)

Kristeva, J. (1982). *Powers of horror: An essay on abjection* (L. S. Roudiez, Trans.). Columbia University Press (Original work published 1980).

Ligotti, T. (2014). The small people. In *The spectral link* (pp. 45–94). Subterranean.

Ligotti, T. (2015a). Nethscurial. In *Songs of a dead dreamer and grimscribe* (pp. 319–333). Penguin (Original work published 1991).

Ligotti, T. (2015b). The night school. In *Songs of a dead dreamer and grimscribe* (pp. 391–402). Penguin (Original work published 1991).

Mariconda, S. J. (2013). Chapter fourteen: Easy as falling off logic—A consideration of Lovecraft and Ligotti as "weird realists". In R. Waugh (Ed.), *Lovecraft and influence: His predecessors and successors* (pp. 165–169). Scarecrow Press.

Mendylyte, A. (2019). Thomas Ligotti's bungalow universe and the transversal aesthetics of the weird. *Horror Studies, 10*(1), 105–122.

Merritt, A. (2013). People of the pit. In A. Vandemeer & J. Vandemeer (Eds.), *The weird* (pp. 101–109). Tor Books (Original work published 1918).

Omidsalar, A. (2018). Posthumanism and un-endings: How Ligotti deranges Lovecraft's cosmic horror. *The Journal of Popular Culture, 51*(3), 716–734.

Padgett, J. (2016). Origami dreams. In *The secrets of ventriloquism* (pp. 35–56). Dunhams Manor Press.

Ugolini, L. (2012). The vegetable man. In A. Vandemeer & J. Vandemeer (Eds.), *The weird* (pp. 97–104). Tor Books (Original story published 1917).

Vandemeer, A., & Vandemeer, J. (Eds.). (2008). *The new weird.* Tachyon.

Chapter 7

The Alien Inside

Jean Laplanche's Internal Other in the Fiction of Brian Evenson and the Case of Ana

Michael Waldon

Emma Baranowski, Amelia Maybrun, and Sarah Breckner provided copyediting for this chapter as part of the Northeastern University Psychological Humanities Workgroup.

Psychoanalysis and Weird fiction share a mutual fascination with the alien. Whether it is the reader's encounter with interstellar beings or the patient's transference relationship to the analyst, both disciplines rely on the unknowability of the alien other to provoke the reader, or the analysand, into contact with their own internal strangeness. Something uncanny happens in these encounters with what Daniels has called the "inscrutably alien": as the reader, or the patient, engages with an external other, the exchange activates an awareness of what we might call the *internal other*. Harris makes a related proposal that, in reading Weird fiction, "we have met the alien monster . . . and it is us."

The psychoanalyst Jean Laplanche (1924–2012), whose ideas I will explore in what follows, would tend to agree that the perception of strangeness outside is always underwritten by the strangeness inside. In a 1992 paper on the phenomenon of transference in psychoanalysis, he doubles Harris's assertion, writing that "[t]he other is other than me because they are other than themselves. External otherness relates back to internal otherness" (1992/2020b, p. 523). Laplanche is saying here that the experience of a real external other is so provocative because that external other is also other to themselves, meaning that they too have an unknowable alien core at the center of their subjectivity. The decentered self of the psychoanalytic subject, who is "not master in its own house" (Freud, 1917/1955, p. 141), and thus never fully known to itself, inheres in both the analyst and the analysand, likewise in the author and the reader.

So what is important about this strange recursive quality at the center of human subjectivity, and what can it tell us about reading Weird fiction or practicing psychoanalysis? In the same essay, Laplanche quotes André Green (1927–2012), a fellow French analyst known for his literary and cultural criticism: "In applied psychoanalysis, the analyst is the analysand of the text" (1992/2020b, p. 526). The quote is pithy, and Laplanche does little to unpack it.

Green himself can help. When asked in an interview (Raymond & Rosbrow-Reich, 1997), to reflect on his meaning, Green explains that the "power of the

DOI: 10.4324/9781003519102-7

text" is to "trigger a process of elaboration" (p. 98) in the mind of the reader. By these means, the reader gives a specific psychic life to the words and intentions of the author, creating a tighter correspondence between the consumption and the production of the work of art, and yet "always preserving a gap, which can never be filled" (p. 98).

Both psychoanalysis and Weird fiction invite us to peer deeply into that gap and explore the possibilities that lie within. It is this immeasurable distance between the mind of the reader/patient and the intention of the author/analyst—configured here as the objective "meaning" of a text—that propels the subject forward through creative engagement with a piece of fiction or the experience of psychoanalytic psychotherapy.

In Laplanche's theory, this is the work of a process that he calls translation, and it is the limitless territory of his uniquely envisioned unconscious— an inexhaustible unconscious that could be aligned with Daniels's formulation of Miéville's "abcanny" as "beyond meaning-ness." With Laplanche's process of translation, we encounter not the "known unknown" of a repressed to be revealed and exorcised but an *unknowable* unconscious that nonetheless agi- tates and presses upon the subject, demanding to be formulated. As we will see, translation is how the subject takes up this "demand for work" (Freud, 1926/1989) and, ideally, channels it toward creative forms of expression and self-understanding.

It is also an unconscious indelibly linked to the alien other. For Laplanche, this encounter with the other always lies at the origins of the unconscious, which he memorably describes as "an alien inside me, and even put inside me by an alien" (Laplanche, 1992/2020a, p. 18). As we will see, the connection between the origins of the unconscious and later encounters with "alien others" is critical to understanding the peculiar qualities of both.

In the following chapter, I offer an anonymized case study from my own practice alongside excerpts from a piece of short fiction. Read together with Laplanche's theory, they can, it is my hope, elaborate some of the connections I have tried to describe. For the lover of Weird fiction, for the subject of psychoanalysis, or even for the reader of this chapter, I suggest that these connections may yield themselves more fully through the experience of the encounter itself than through any exposi- tory understanding I can provide here.

"Windeye" (Evenson, 2012)[1]

They lived, when he was growing up, in a simple house, an old bungalow with a converted attic and sides covered in cedar shake. In the back, where an oak thrust its branches over the roof, the shake was light brown, almost honey. In the front, where the sun struck it full, it had weathered to a pale gray, like a dirty bone. There, the shingles were brittle, thinned by sun and rain, and if you were careful you could slip your fingers up behind some of them. Or at least his sister could. He was older and his fingers were thicker, so he could not.

Looking back on it, many years later, he often thought it had started with that, with her carefully working her fingers up under a shingle as he waited and watched to see if it would crack. That was one of his earliest memories of his sister, if not the earliest.

His sister would turn around and smile, her hand gone to knuckles, and say, "I feel something. What am I feeling?" And then he would ask questions. *Is it smooth?* he might ask. *Does it feel rough? Scaly? Is it cold-blooded or warm-blooded? Does it feel red? Does it feel like its claws are in or out? Can you feel its eye move?* He would keep on, watching the expression on her face change as she tried to make his words into a living, breathing thing, until it started to feel too real for her and, half giggling, half screaming, she whipped her hand free.

(Evenson, 2012, p. 1)

This brief excerpt opens the short story "Windeye" by the American writer Brian Evenson. Evenson is the author of numerous collections of very short fiction, sometimes called "epistemological horror," because his stories tend to place characters in situations where knowledge of the world around them is unstable and unsettling. He writes his best works the way an old-time detective dusts for fingerprints: deliberate and precise strokes reveal traces of an unseen presence, a past other, who has left a disturbing effect on the subject of the scene.

This quality makes it well-suited to read through the psychoanalytic theory of Jean Laplanche.

Translation and the Laplanchean Unconscious

Unique among analytic theorists, Laplanche proposed that the child is born without an unconscious and forms one later, through early interactions with adult caregivers. This is because the adult *does* have an unconscious, one that is riddled with inhibited sexual and sadistic conflicts that affect the child.

Throughout their exchanges, the child will perceive the effect of the adult's unconscious but will be unable to make sense of it. In part, this is because children lack the necessary cultural knowledge to interpret what they encounter. Importantly, it is also because clear knowledge of the unconscious is foreclosed to the adult. Laplanche says we can never know this part of ourselves. It is like an alien inside us.

In communicating with the child, adults inevitably express unconscious desire and excitation beyond their intended meanings. This transmits as an "enigmatic charge" from the adult's unconscious, compromising the normal everyday verbal and nonverbal messages addressed to the child. If the messages—the things the adult says and does—are chains of signifiers that can be made into meaningful communications, then the enigmatic charge is "an element of noise" mixed in with the signal (Laplanche, 2003/2011, p. 175; see also Fletcher, 2007, p. 1251). It is a "hollow" signifier, "stripped of meaning," that refers back to an unknowable signified (Laplanche, 1997/2015, p. 241). Encountering the influence of the adult's unconscious—what Laplanche calls the "enigma" of the parent—is both exciting and confounding for the new human. It activates in the child a meaning-making process that Laplanche calls "translation."

Translation describes the child's attempt to make sense of the enigmatic adult messages addressed to the child. It is a creative, narrativizing act—it is also, inevitably, at least a partial failure. The hollow signifier always resists meaning, such that this part of the message that is "parasitized" by the parental enigma (Fletcher, 2007, p. 1251) can never be adequately translated (Laplanche, 1987/2016, p. 148).

Nonetheless, the child must try. They will do so by drawing on the two sources of translational codes available to them: a developing knowledge of the surrounding culture and the experience of their own embodiment. What the child successfully translates will become the ego. What they fail to translate will be repressed, forming the unconscious as a storehouse of enigmatic signifiers stripped of their capacity to refer back to any original signified. This is the alien inside the child, the nascent unconscious, and it has been installed by the alien outside.

For Laplanche, this is how the animal *Homo sapiens* is made human (Laplanche, 1992/2020b, p. 527). Culture and the unique experience of embodiment, mediated by fantasy (Scarfone, 2016), begin to fill the gaps between ourselves and the world, gaps first created by early attachments to an ever-elusive object. The process inaugurates the infant's subjectivity, which the infant will continue to build through self-theorization and endless translation across the lifespan.

In "Windeye" (2012), Evenson's narrator and his sister are a good allegory for the strange circumstance of the Laplanchean subject in formation. The children are presented with a structure, something pre-existing them, built by adult human hands, exceeding their understanding, and yet seemingly addressed to them. It is the building where they live. They explore it piece by piece, as though parsing semantic units. Using their bodies and culturally mediated fantasies, the children translate what they encounter.

It is thrilling in a way that is both enlivening and profoundly disturbing.

Ana

Ana was referred to me by a friend. The friend was worried and frustrated with her. Worried because Ana was isolating, and her drinking seemed self-destructive. Frustrated because Ana was neglecting shared commitments. Ana explained this pattern in our intake, telling me "everything becomes overwhelming," causing her to "shut down" and "seclude" herself. She floats in a dissociated state for as long as possible, "depending on when [her] next commitment is."

By her own account, she has come here to address trauma. She tells me that memories have started coming back to her, "a few things related to sexual assault . . . a bad relationship . . . and some bulimic episodes."

Ana takes a handful of naproxen sodium pills with wine between our first and second sessions. Then she starts taking Benadryl. She passes out and wakes up feeling awful. Ana tells me it wasn't a suicide attempt; she just wanted to be unconscious for a while. We make some agreements about safety and plan to meet twice weekly.

At first, we don't talk about the sexual assault. Later, she will tell me she appreciates that I don't pressure her to move too quickly. We start by discussing some of the men in her life, beginning with a recent ex-boyfriend who became verbally and then physically abusive. She had shared with him some of the things that happened to her. When they fought, in fits of rage, he would shout these things back at her, hurling them like stones. During one outburst, the boyfriend grabs Ana by the arm, hard enough that it hurts and leaves marks.

Months into our work together, Ana argues with her father on a family trip. She is stunned when he grabs her in the same place, on the same arm. The uncanny resonance of these two moments begins to elaborate a central metaphor in Ana's experience of the world: *men take control of my body.*

A few words about Ana's father: he can be difficult and domineering. He is overinvested in her career; it's one of the few things that they can talk about. Ana wants to be a director in the theater. Her father is a successful funder and investor in productions. Ana's parents were teenagers when she was born. They come from high-class status in their home country, so this early pregnancy was unusual amongst their peers. Her parents sometimes went abroad in her adolescence, to pursue studies or employment. Ana usually came along, and since her parents' friends didn't have kids yet, she spent much of her childhood in a world of adults.

She recalls when she began to write. She was maybe 12 years old. Her parents took her to the events around Paris Fashion Week. At a runway show, someone gifted Ana a souvenir notepad. Since then, she has never been without one. She writes and draws constantly. When she was alone amongst the adults, the notebook became a way both to escape and to engage on her own terms. She would sit quietly at the table, surrounded by conversation that she couldn't understand, and she would write or draw whatever came to mind. Eventually, someone would ask what she was writing, and she would have something to talk about.

To apply Laplanche's term, we could say that Ana's writing is a translational effort. Saturated with the overwhelming, enigmatic presence of the adults around her, Ana used the privacy of her notebooks to formulate the world and her place in it. Her use of this strategy is crystallized in a scene described by Ana, on the cusp of puberty, watching a runway show in Paris, overstimulated, wondering, What is she meant to see in the display of these women's bodies?

"Windeye": Translation and the Mythosymbolic

Back to our story (Evenson, 2012).

Something about the house troubles the narrator. He discovers that there is a window they can see outside the house but not on the inside. A kind of "half-window," they call it.

For a time, it felt like he had brought the problem to life himself by stating it, that if he hadn't said anything the half-window wouldn't be there. Was that possible? He didn't think so, that wasn't the way the world worked. But even later, once he was grown, he still found himself wondering sometimes if it was his fault, if it was something he had done. Or rather, said.

Staring up at the half-window, he remembered a story his grandmother had told him. . . . Where she came from, his grandmother said, they used to be called not windows but something else. He couldn't remember the word, but remembered that it started with a *v*. She had said the word and then had asked, *Do you know what this means*? He shook his head. She repeated the word, slower this time.

"This first part," she had said, "it means 'wind.' This second part, it means 'eye.'" She looked at him with her own pale, steady eye. "It is important to know that a window can be instead a *windeye*."

So he and his sister called it that, *windeye*. It was, he told her, how the wind looked into the house and so was not a window at all.

(Evenson, 2012, pp. 3–4)

In Laplanche's theory, translation doesn't stop in childhood. Translation continues throughout the lifespan. Enigmatic signifiers incorporate into the subject's unconscious through the inevitable failures of translation and remain there, unresolved. They are activated again and again through further encounters with unknowable others, stimulating new attempts at translation.

Laplanche says that the analytic situation is modeled on the template of the early encounter between parent and child, in order to reinvoke its provocative asymmetry: a controlled environment locates the analyst in the position of the unknowable adult other, while the analysand assumes the position of the child, grappling after meaning (Laplanche, 1992/2020b, p. 530; Laplanche, 1987/2016, pp. 175–188). Avgi Saketopoulou's (see 2019) work suggests that psychoanalysis can hypercharge the effects of that scenario, leading the patient to a state of "overwhelm," which shatters pre-existing translations and makes space for new ones to form.

Culture plays an important role here. The parent and the attachment relationship supply what Laplanche calls the "mythosymbolic order" (see 1997/2015). Simply put, culture provides the available set of concepts that we draw on to make sense of what we cannot fully know. We use the building blocks of the mythosymbolic and our lived experience to compose our translations. After the translations are deconstructed in analysis, we rebuild them (Saketopoulou, 2019, p. 161). At this point, ideally, new blocks have become available to us through new experiences. They can be used to remake the foundation, stronger and more adaptive. In Laplanche's theory, this is due to the peculiar operation of the *après-coup* (Laplanche, 1989/2020). The *après-coup*—lit. "afterwards"— is a uniquely human temporal structure that both carries the effects of enigma forward in time and also invites the subject to retroactively alter their meaning through new translations.

Ana: The Scene of Address

Gender and sexuality are powerful sites for translational activity, and they are also highly subject to cultural encoding. In Ana's case, this is visible in her experience of her gender, her sexuality, and her sexual assault. Our work together, and her creative work outside of sessions, will help her compose new translations that allow her to experience these things differently.

Ana decides that she's ready to address the incident. As we approach it, she has numerous dissociative episodes. She comes late or doesn't show. She speaks in vague and halting sentences that trickle off into panic.

Finally, we talk about it.

I don't need to tell you the details; the story would be familiar. It was on the last night of a summer educational program abroad. They were drinking. It was confusing when it happened, but Ana tells me she knows now that she was raped. She wouldn't, and couldn't, have said this at that time. When Ana's parents arrived the next day to pick her up, she gushed about the program. She needed to be okay for them, and probably for herself. On the flight home, she wrote in her notebook about the assault, but she didn't write about it the way that I'm telling it now. Instead, she recast it as something she enjoyed, a love scene that she delighted in. This became the story she told.

Back in her home country, in her final years of high school, things somehow changed for Ana. She developed a reputation as promiscuous. She drank heavily and dissociated uncontrollably. There were other assaults. Photos of her were passed around the school. She was mostly numb. She locked herself in a dark bathroom to vomit when she felt overwhelmed.

In our sessions, Ana makes a new connection about the darkened bathroom. For a time, in her middle teens, while Ana's parents were in another country, she came home to live with her grandmother. This was a strange time for Ana. Her grandmother seemed afraid, vulnerable, and resentful. She followed Ana through the city, concerned about her safety. Ana would go out for an exercise class around the corner, and her grandmother would show up at the back of the class. She would watch Ana, then forcibly walk her home. One day, Ana returns to find the lights out in the apartment. Down the hall, the bathroom door is open. It's dark inside. Her grandmother is there, crying, and vomiting.

Not all messages are verbal, but they all involve a scene of address. There is a place and time where the message is transmitted, and a receiver to whom it is delivered. Often, the circumstances of the scene become a part of how the receiver translates its meaning (Fletcher, 2013, pp. 269–275). This can be true even though, by its very nature, the receiver does not know what the message signifies—only that it signifies *to* the receiver (Laplanche, 1987/2016, pp. 52–53).

When Ana saw her grandmother in the bathroom that day, a mysterious potency charged the scene. There is a sense in which it seemed to be meant for her. Overwhelmed by the inability to explain herself in session, she told me:

Since I was born . . . the things . . . all the things that have happened to me . . . not just the rape, but things before. I know that the rape wasn't my fault but . . . all of the things that have happened . . . the only common thing is me.

Ana felt that what happened to her was addressed to her. Like Evenson's (2012) narrator, she imagined that she was somehow responsible for "the problem." And like Evenson's narrator, who discovers that the windeye is for the wind to look into the house, Ana is porous, buffeted by the winds of enigmatic others around her. The internal other, the alien inside, responds to this wind, harmonizing in increasing agitation.

"Windeye": Implantations and Intromissions

In Evenson's story (2012), the grandmother's concept of a windeye provides a theory for what's happening. The siblings get a closer look. They determine which of the other windows is closest to the windeye and open it from the inside. If they lean far enough out of this window, they can see the windeye. It is "small and round, probably only a foot and a half in diameter"; the glass is "dark and wavery" (p. 4). The sister leans out of the window, stretching, while the narrator holds her legs. He starts to say something to stop her, but she presses on. He is about to pull her back inside when she leans harder. Her finger just touches the windeye, and she dissolves into smoke, seemingly sucked in. She is gone.

The boy panics. He runs home to tell his mother.

> He tried to explain it best he could. *Who?* She asked at first and then said *Slow down and tell it again*, and then, *But who do you mean?* And then, once he'd explained again, with an odd smile:
>
> "But you don't have a sister."
>
> (p. 4)

He protests.

> "No," she said firmly. "You don't have a sister. You never had one. Stop pretending. What's this really about?"
> Which made him feel that he should hold himself very still, that he should be very careful about what he said, that if he breathed wrong more parts of the world would disappear.
>
> (pp. 4–5)

He tries to get his mother to come outside and look at the windeye.

> "Window you mean," she said, her voice rising.
> When they go outside together, the windeye is gone.
>
> (p. 5)

And for the narrator, we are told, "that was when the trouble really started" (p. 5).

Translation is a normal and inevitable part of being human. What's important is that we have enough freedom to translate in our own way, to make adaptive meaning from the unknowable world around us. The trouble comes when a person's ability to translate is radically restricted. One way this can happen is when a caregiver has a powerful, unformulated need that is forced upon the child.

Laplanche distinguished between two kinds of enigmatic transmissions: implantations and intromissions. *Implantations* are "common, everyday, normal, or neurotic," allowing the individual to "take things up actively, at once translating and repressing" (Laplanche, 1999, p. 136). By contrast, *intromissions* are their "violent variant," involving "a process that blocks that activity . . . and puts inside an element that resists all metabolization" (Laplanche, 1990/2020, p. 447). This is to say that the subject can digest and make adaptive changes to an implantation as it occurs. *Intromissions*, on the other hand, are swallowed whole and cannot be modified.

Ana: New Translations

Around the same time as the incident with her grandmother, Ana witnesses a fight between her aunt and a male lover. She doesn't tell anyone about this. She doesn't know how. In my office, she tells me that she's never even written about it. It exists only in her head. When I ask about this, she says:

> It's like if I couldn't name a feeling. Or if there was no one around to allow me to share it or allow me to notice. If no one tells you what cold is and it's cold, you'd never know. You'd live your whole life being cold without knowing what cold is.

These experiences from Ana's childhood register in her psyche as carriers of inchoate meaning, traces of excitation or agitation beyond language and "outside representation" (Saketopoulou, 2019, pp. 155–156) that nonetheless relentlessly insist she find ways to narrativize them. As her therapist, I find it tempting to address Ana's case by trying to unveil the hidden meaning behind her symptoms and her memories. We could do this. To understand Ana's story, we could talk about her relationship to her father: the intense identifications passing between them, and the way that her traumatic encounters with male peers replicate his impositions on her. We could also talk about a different kind of identification: with the grandmother, a female elder whose experience of womanhood has left her, in Ana's eyes, fearful, guarded, vulnerable, and overwhelmed. We could talk about the significance of Ana adopting this woman's coping strategies.

But this isn't a story about those things; it's a story about what Ana does with them. About how the unknowable feelings that Ana had been alone with for so long begin to take new shape when she brings them into language, when she says for the first time: "cold." The feeling is cold.

Ana writes a script. The story is about a transwoman and her male lover. It's written in overlapping flashbacks to their relationship during her illness with AIDS and present-day scenes following her death. Her wealthy, powerful father claims the body— "takes control of the body," we could say—and insists that she is buried as a man.

Ana interviews players and casts a young Black transwoman from the city. They spend time together off-set. After a rehearsal, Ana goes out with her. They attend a vigil for another transwoman killed by police. Over the course of the evening, Ana sees these women cry and shout, weeping and furious, vulnerable and defiant. After the vigil, they go out for drinks. She sees them laugh and hug one another. Recounting this in session, she is tearful, amazed by their ability to hold and express so many conflicting emotions.

As Ana's story concludes, the lover fails to convince the father. He drives home to the city with the dress his partner wanted to be buried in. Their favorite song comes on the radio. He pulls onto the shoulder, reduced to tears. A sudden wind whips the dress out of the car. He chases it, catches it, pulls it close. Beside the road, he dances with the dress, a specter of his deceased lover.

The story represents a new kind of translation for Ana, trading on the themes that are important in her own history and using new ideas that she's learned from new experiences. Like her protagonist, she is not in control of what has happened to her or what will happen next. But she improvises, doing her best to dance gracefully with the windblown artifacts of her psychic life.

Ana is not "cured," but she is happier. In a Laplanchean framework, that's okay. The alien core at the center of the subject never fully retreats, though successive translations can, at least temporarily, reduce its excitatory potential (Laplanche, 1987/2016, p. 165). Ana still struggles with avoidant tendencies, but she dissociates less. She has a new language for what happens to her now and a new story about what happened in the past. It is a small step toward taking back control of her body—a journey that can never be complete, since parts of the self are never fully known.

Conclusion

The intrusion of the alien outside and its resonance with the alien inside are like the wind in Evenson's story. Wind can fill your sails, and it can break your mast. Daniels's "inscrutably alien" other, whose "alterity can never be fully grasped" (McAvan, 2012), transmits the potential for inspiration and the potential for enduring trauma.

Through Laplanche's lens, Ana's story shows the deeply human function of translation. She shows how retranslation can make adaptive change to the relationship with the internal outsider, the alien inside.

Evenson's narrator is not so successful. His sister, real or imagined, represents his internal effort to understand what he encounters in the world outside. His mother's injunction against the sister—that he never had one—has frozen his capacity to translate, to make adaptive meaning. In the end, he lives to an old age, ever more uncertain of what really happened, ever more plagued by symptoms that betray his inability to reconcile or theorize the gap between himself and the outside world. Long after the death of his mother, he still imagines his lost sister returning to him, unchanged by time, young, with her small fingers exploring the cracks of the house.

"What is it?" he would say in a hoarse voice, leaning on his cane.

"I feel something," she would say. "What am I feeling?"

And he would set about describing it. *Does it feel red? Does it feel warm-blooded or cold? Is it round? Is it smooth like glass?* All the while, he knew, he would be thinking not about what he was saying but about the wind at his back. If he turned around, he would be wondering, would he find the wind's strange, baleful eye staring at him?

(Evenson, 2012, p. 6)

Note

1   All excerpts from "Windeye" (2012) used with the kind permission of the author, Brian Evenson. The entire story is available to read at https://pen.org/windeye/, where the story has an original posting date in 2009, preceding its collection into the author's 2012 volume.

References

Evenson, B. (2012). Windeye. In *Windeye: Stories* (pp. 1–6). Coffee House Press.

Fletcher, J. (2007). Seduction and the vicissitudes of translation: The work of Jean Laplanche. *Psychoanalytic Quarterly*, *76*(4), 1241–1291.

Fletcher, J. (2013). *Freud and the scene of trauma*. Fordham University Press.

Freud, S. (1955). A difficulty in the path of psycho-analysis. In *The standard edition of the complete psychological works of Sigmund Freud (1917–1919): "An infantile neurosis" and other works XVII* (pp. 135–144). The Hogarth Press and The Institute of Psycho-Analysis (Original work published 1917).

Freud, S. (1989). *Inhibitions, symptoms, and anxiety* (J. Stachey, Ed.; A. Strachey, Trans.). W. W. Norton & Company (Original work published 1926).

Laplanche, J. (1999). *Essays on otherness*. Routledge.

Laplanche, J. (2011). Gender, sex and the sexual. In J. Fletcher (Ed.), *Freud and the sexual* (pp. 159–202). The Unconscious in Translation (Original work published 2003).

Laplanche, J. (2015). Psychoanalysis: Myths and theory (J. Mehlman, Trans.). In J. House (Ed.), *Between seduction and inspiration: Man* (pp. 219–244). The Unconscious in Translation (Original work published 1997).

Laplanche, J. (2016). *New foundations for psychoanalysis* (J. House, Trans.). The Unconscious in Translation (Original work published 1987).

Laplanche, J. (2020). Implantation, intromission (L. Thurston, Trans.). In J. House (Ed.), *The unfinished copernican revolution: Selected works 1967–1992* (pp. 443–448). The Unconscious in Translation (Original work published 1990).

Laplanche, J. (2020). Temporality and translation: Toward making the philosophy of time work again (L. Thurston, Trans.). In J. House (Ed.), *The unfinished copernican revolution: Selected works 1967–1992* (pp. 423–442). The Unconscious in Translation (Original work published 1989).

Laplanche, J. (2020a). The unfinished Copernican revolution (L. Thurston, Trans.). In J. House (Ed.), *The unfinished copernican revolution: Selected works 1967–1992* (pp. 3–40). The Unconscious in Translation (Original work published 1992).

Laplanche, J. (2020b). Transference: Its provocation by the analyst (L. Thurston, Trans.). In J. House (Ed.), *The unfinished copernican revolution: Selected works 1967–1992* (pp. 515–540). The Unconscious in Translation (Original work published 1992).

McAvan, E. (2012). *The postmodern sacred: Popular culture spirituality in the science fiction, fantasy and urban fantasy genres*. McFarland & Company.

Raymond, L., & Rosbrow-Reich, S. (1997). *The inward eye: Psychoanalysts reflect on their lives and work*. Taylor & Francis.

Saketopoulou, A. (2019). The draw to overwhelm: Consent, risk, and the retranslation of enigma. *Journal of the American Psychoanalytic Association, 67*(1), 133–167.

Scarfone, D. (2016). Fantasme et processus de fantasmatisation. *Revue Francaise de Psychosomatique, 2*(50), 47–68.

Index

For Product Safety Concerns and Information please contact our EU
representative GPSR@taylorandfrancis.com
Taylor & Francis Verlag GmbH, Kaufingerstraße 24, 80331 München, Germany

www.ingramcontent.com/pod-product-compliance
Lightning Source LLC
Chambersburg PA
CBHW070344270326
41926CB00017B/3974